The Accountability State

STUDIES IN GOVERNMENT
AND PUBLIC POLICY

The Accountability State

US Federal Inspectors General

and the Pursuit of Democratic Integrity

NADIA HILLIARD

UNIVERSITY PRESS OF KANSAS

Published by the University Press of Kansas (Lawrence, Kansas 66045), which was organized by the Kansas Board of Regents and is operated and funded by Emporia State University, Fort Hays State University, Kansas State University, Pittsburg State University, the University of Kansas, and Wichita State University

© 2017 by the University Press of Kansas

Library of Congress Cataloging-in-Publication Data
Library of Congress Control Number: 2016051180
ISBN 978-0-7006-2397-6 (cloth)
ISBN 978-0-7006-2398-3 (paperback)
ISBN 978-0-7006-2399-0 (ebook)
British Library Cataloguing-in-Publication Data is available.

Printed in the United States of America
10 9 8 7 6 5 4 3 2 1

The paper used in this publication is recycled and contains 30 percent postconsumer waste. It is acid free and meets the minimum requirements of the American National Standard for Permanence of Paper for Printed Library Materials Z39.48–1992.

For Aouicha, Raymond, and Jeremy Hilliard,
with love and gratitude

CONTENTS

PART III: THE DEMOCRATIC PERSPECTIVE

ACKNOWLEDGMENTS

In writing this book, I found myself in debt to numerous generous individuals, and I now express appreciation for their support: my doctoral supervisor, Desmond King, for making opportunities available, for excellent intellectual guidance and endless patience, and for years of encouragement and friendship; the Rothermere American Institute, a great source of intellectual, social, and academic support, and in particular Nigel Bowles, for his kindness, pastoral care, and steady support; George Frederickson and Mel Dubnick for scholarly motivation; Marc Stears and Gary Gerstle for probing examination and encouragement; Robert Holtom for patient writing advice; Lisa L. Miller for academic advice (delivered with much humor and warmth) and friendship; Gary Schmitt and Harold Relyea for introducing me to the IGs; Glenn Fine for thorough and thoughtful commentary; Steven J. Ackerman for his eager support and resourcefulness; my hardy Mortimer Drive family—Doireann Lalor, Marlene Bovenmars, Imogen Davies, Julian Cottee, and Charlie Fisher—for years of good cooking, good music, daily camaraderie, community, the collective navigation of many a housing disaster narrowly averted, and friendship; Philip Stewart for years of tender friendship, and to Philip and Lucile Stewart for welcoming me to the "Writing Up Hermitage"; the animals and plants of Boars Hill, Oxford, for providing me with social stimulation in the final months before completing my doctoral studies; Chuck Myers, an astute and supportive editor; Larisa Martin, Karen Hellekson, and Matt Steele for eagle-eyed editing; David Daniel for his probing intellectual criticism, patient daily encouragement, and more than a decade of friendship; Neil Armstrong for the future; and my parents for so much.

LIST OF ABBREVIATIONS USED IN TEXT

ACLU	American Civil Liberties Union
ATF	Bureau of Alcohol, Tobacco, Firearms, and Explosives
BOP	Bureau of Prisons
CA	Consular Affairs
CIA	Central Intelligence Agency
CIGIE	Council of Inspectors General on Integrity and Efficiency
DEA	Drug Enforcement Administration
DFE	designated federal entity
DHS	Department of Homeland Security
DOD	Department of Defense
DOJ	Department of Justice
ECIE	Executive Council on Integrity and Efficiency
ECPA	Electronic Communication Privacy Act
EMU	Emergency Management Unit
FBI	Federal Bureau of Investigation
FEMA	Federal Emergency Management Agency
FISA	Foreign Intelligence Surveillance Act
FOIA	Freedom of Information Act
FSO	Foreign Service Officer
GAO	Government Accounting Office
IC	independent counsel
IG	inspector general
INS	Immigration and Naturalization Service
IT	information technology
MERO	Middle East Regional Office
NASA	National Aeronautics and Space Administration
NPM	New Public Management
NPR	National Performance Review
NSA	National Security Agency
NSLs	National Security Letters
O&R	Office of Oversight and Review
OIG	office of the inspector general
OLC	Office of Legal Counsel
OPR	Office of Professional Responsibility
P-A	principal–agent

PCIE   President's Council on Integrity and Efficiency
PIERS   Passport Electronic Records System
POGO   Project on Government Oversight
S/IG   Inspector General of Foreign Service
SIGAR   Special Inspector General for Afghanistan
SIGIR   Special Inspector General for Iraq Reconstruction
SIRU   Special Investigations and Review Unit
TSA   Transportation Security Administration

PART I

INSPECTING THE TERRAIN

CHAPTER ONE

INTRODUCTION

Quis Custodiet Ipsos Custodies?

The Administrative-Democratic Paradox

In the early 1950s, Dwight Waldo sparked a debate with public administration theorist Herbert Simon over the mutual antagonism between the values of democracy and those of administration.[1] Whereas Simon championed the possibility of a science of administration based on facts and geared toward efficiency, Waldo questioned whether such a value-free science was possible; he argued that efficiency itself was a contentious political claim, a vision of the good life that is antithetical to democratic values such as deliberation and citizen participation. In Waldo's book, *The Administrative State*, he attacked the respective disciplines of public administration and democratic theory for failing to engage with each other, and he argued that because administration is or claimed to be at the center of modern democratic government, the two disciplines must address each other.[2] He reserved his strongest criticism for administrative theory: it needed to recognize its own underlying political philosophy and admit that its central principle of efficiency was neither value neutral nor easily reconciled with the principles of democracy.

The debate echoed earlier formulations of the tension by Woodrow Wilson, who promoted the politics–administration dichotomy as a solution to the (partisan) politicization of administration, and Max Weber, three decades later, who reiterated the need for a sharp distinction between politics and administration to prevent *Beamtenherrschaft* (rule by bureaucrats).[3] Although Waldo and Simon contended over the distinctions between facts and values, and between policy and administration, at stake lay a variant of the classic trade-off between democratic representation and efficiency. Democracies—especially a pluralist democracy in the American tradition (i.e., a polyarchy)—need to provide citizens and groups the opportunity for direct engagement in the processes of the polity, including elections, deliberation, policy creation, and the maintenance of accountability. But because such processes are time-consuming and inefficient, bureaucracies are delegated policy-making authority without being held to account through regular elections or transparent practices, and this leaves citizens unable to influence the way they are governed.

If these anxieties concerned social scientists at the turn of the twentieth century, the growth of the administrative state—and in particular the advent of the welfare state—merely intensified policy-making delegation to nonmajoritarian institutions in the latter half of the century.[4] But do the exigencies of efficient decision making and policy implementation necessarily curtail citizens' opportunities to participate in the democratic process? Does the need for a growing, unelected bureaucracy to implement a nation's will undermine the fundamental democratic principles of equality, liberty, representation, and participation? Does the "science" required to fashion an efficient bureaucratic machine preclude deliberation over the common good? Or is it possible for the competing and conflicting principles of administrative efficiency and democracy to be reconciled?

Despite its prima facie value conflict with democracy, public administration can also play a constitutive role in democracies by channeling public interests, protecting common values, formulating and executing policies, and bringing accountability and predictability to government activity.[5] The notion that bureaucratic structures might even foster democratic practices is not new. In his *Considerations on Representative Government*, J. S. Mill argued, "Freedom cannot produce its best effects, and often breaks down altogether, unless means can be found of combining it with trained and skilled administration."[6] This refining function, potentially carried out by expert administrators, provided a resource for would-be reformers faced with patronage-ridden politics. After Wilson, Progressive-era reformers championed a "politics–administration dichotomy" as a tool for reforming politics at the national level.[7] According to American political development scholars Desmond King and Robert Lieberman, one key irony of the American state is that bureaucracy has proven to be a precondition for democratization: "American experience differs from continental European trajectories in that a comprehensive democratic framework as a set of procedures was established before the expansion of national federal bureaucratic departments of the sort compelled upon politicians from the Civil War."[8] This alternative historical trajectory affected the character and resources of bureaucracies as well. In contrast to their European counterparts, bureaucracies in the United States built their own networks outside the government apparatus for program implementation and encouraged individual enterprise in building power.[9] In part it has been precisely the freedom to develop autonomous bureaucratic structures and to take recourse to extrastate actors that has allowed democratic ideas and interests to penetrate the American state apparatus. This phenomenon had a European correlate, too, for as Mark Warren notes, "The more functional democracies were built within relatively high-capacity states, in part because these states provided a locus for accountability demands as part of democratization struggles."[10] These experiences demonstrate that a tension between two seemingly irreconcilable principles can generate change and inspire new forms of democratic participation.

Yet how and to what degree can this occur? Over time, a number of democratic and legal theories have proposed ways of resolving, explicitly or implicitly, the value tensions between administration and democracy. Though they do not always use the term directly, these approaches favor coherent accountability structures to preserve certain principles of democracy and representative government.

Even before the modern state provoked questions of administrative accountability, classic Madisonian constitutionalism provided an overall political framework designed to counter the potential abuses of power in a democracy and representative government. Although the writers of the *Federalist Papers* gave little direct attention to the problem of administration as such, they devised a constitutional system intended to forestall the pathologies of democracy, namely the concentration of power in the hands of a single office or group. The framers of the Constitution pitted "ambition against ambition" and constructed a system guided by, among other principles, the separation of powers and of checks and balances. The separation of powers is not given explicit legal legitimacy in the American constitutional system (in the sense of being codified as such), but the Constitution nonetheless embodies this principle through its clear separation of government functions.[11] It reflects Madison's view that "the accumulation of all powers, legislative, executive, and judiciary, in the same hands, whether of one, a few, or many . . . may justly be pronounced the very definition of tyranny."[12] The Constitution, moreover, implants various checks and balances in the relations between the branches: Congress checks executive action with its control over the purse strings of government and exercises its oversight authority through committees. This echoes the belief that "the great security against a gradual concentration of the several powers in the same department, consists in giving to those who administer each department the necessary constitutional means and personal motives to resist encroachments of the others."[13] Here Madison acknowledges the jurisdictional battles that might compromise the execution of government from within the executive branch and applies his principle of accountability through separation and competition to the various administrators (and by extension to what would eventually become the administrative apparatus). These constitutional arrangements prescribe a mode of governing with certain pragmatic consequences insofar as they encourage, at least in theory, the efficient running of government and have the normative function of promoting a particular vision of political liberty.[14]

Madison failed to anticipate the emergence of the administrative state and of "emergency governance," as well as the challenges to democratic integrity they would pose. Later American democratic theorists countered that the classic Madisonian view provides an insufficient account of the sources of accountability and political equilibrium because it fails to include the full scope of political activity in the public realm. For classic pluralists such as Robert Dahl, the balance of competing centers of power—interest groups, branches of government, parties—serves to temper the tensions between efficiency, deliberation, and participation. In this view, ensuring a healthy balance of power and preserving democratic rule necessitates a particular institutional design (i.e., pluralism) not only to equalize citizen participation and representation but also to correct the inherent tendency of democracies to bend toward a tyranny of the majority. Here bureaucracy is a positive feature within a pluralist system, one locus of power among many, and an important actor in the separation of powers system. Similarly, for David Truman, the bureaucracy provided yet another access point into the policy-making process; it exists as simply one political actor among many in a system of group pluralism.[15] Dahl also viewed the growth of the bureaucracy as a natural and unexceptional component of the welfare state.[16] However, the implicit trust these theorists had in the democratic integrity of existing arrangements was so great that they give little attention to the problems generated by bureaucracy, and like many normative strands of democratic theory, they offered few prescriptions for ameliorative administrative design.[17]

Most recently, legal scholars have proposed legal and institutional solutions to the antidemocratic tendencies of the administrative state. The legal literature on executive constraint and emergency powers provides a slightly different perspective on the problem of administrative discretion from the perspective of pluralists such as Dahl and Truman: its theorists are concerned with the consequences of building provisions into the legal order for emergency powers and the suspension of democratic politics. Critics argue that doing so would legitimate undemocratic decisions and thus undermine the very foundations of the liberal order; in times of emergency, the sovereign must simply exercise power to preserve the integrity of the legal order ("Schmittian exceptionalism").[18] Others contend that the liberal order must accept the necessity of "exceptional" (i.e., extralegal) politics and provide legal and institutional guidelines for how and when this power can be used, so as to keep it in check ("liberal legalism").[19]

Although its focus is on an extreme case—discretion in a moment of emergency—the legal literature's insights about what Carl Schmitt calls "the exception" are also relevant to the quotidian cases of routine administrative decision making, and thus to the underlying tension between administration and democracy. Fundamentally, they ask whether there should be structures and practices within the administrative state to temper its undemocratic tendencies, or whether its regulation should be left to competing power centers or political checks. Much of the legal literature remains divorced from systematic empirical evaluation of routine administration, and moreover, it fails to consider the mutations in democratic practice—the side effects, as it were—that these checks on administrative discretion provoke. Can there be an institutional corrective to a structural problem in modern constitutional democracies? What changes do such frameworks provoke in the practice of democracy?

These approaches to democratic accountability have built on one another over time, refining the broad Madisonian constitutional framework in such a way as to accommodate the exigencies of the expanding administrative state and of emergency governance. Yet the efficacy of their solutions, and the political dynamics they provoke, remain in question.

Research Question

This volume is a historical inquiry into the sources and development of one such institutional solution to the administrative-democratic paradox: US federal inspectors general (IGs). IGs are auditor-investigators placed in nearly every federal department and agency who are tasked with ferreting out fraud, waste, and abuse in the federal bureaucracy. Do they restore the democratic integrity lost in the administrative state, or do they merely exacerbate its antidemocratic tendencies?

My argument focuses on one particular statutory framework—the Inspector General Act of 1978—and its interaction with other political processes.[20] Administrative accountability, where it has prevailed, has been the result of a growing reflexive bureaucratic capacity to self-correct, reform, and generate endogenous change.[21] In the modern state, apolitical, scientific-rational processes (e.g., audits) often replace politics as a mode of accountability and as a safeguard of democratic values. But do IGs temper this tendency or exacerbate it? In practice, the IGs' effects on bureaucratic behavior and democratic practice vary widely. At its most successful, the IG model can improve the quality of democracy by providing basic administrative and political accountability, and by enhancing some of the prerequisites for citizen participation: providing transparency and information, and strengthening the rule of law. At their worst, the IGs can be complicit in the same fraud and abuse that they were mandated to eradicate.

Unlike other frameworks intended to curb executive discretion, such as the Administrative Procedures Act, the National Emergencies Act, or War Powers Resolution, the IG Act has had a generative institutional effect, spawning, through periodic amendments, a growing army of IGs with expanding authority. IGs pursue accountability by providing an authoritative narrative to be disseminated to the Congress, the courts, and the public. In tandem with these external actors, the IG system is an attempted corrective to the undemocratic tendencies of the bureaucracy. It is my contention that the growth of this internal checking mechanism has altered the structure of executive accountability and political deliberation and has provoked dynamics in the wider politics of executive power. Although the IGs are far from the only institutional source of executive or bureaucratic accountability, they provide a glimpse into the microfoundations of this developing democratic function.

Although I call the IG phenomenon the "accountability state," in American political development fashion, IGs are only one mechanism of accountability among many. For a full elaboration of the concept of accountability, a wider-ranging treatment of all accountability mechanisms would be necessary. This would be a fruitful path for future research; it would include careful consideration of the role of the courts, congressional oversight committees, a strong and independent press, and government watchdog groups, as well as statutory frameworks such as the Administrative Procedures Act and oversight bodies such as the Office of Special Counsel, in checking executive growth and activity. Most importantly, such an approach (if pursued comprehensively, taking into account the way these various institutions interact) would expose the redundancies and gaps in the overall architecture of accountability. However, the work of the IGs extends beyond accountability tout court and contributes to broader processes in democracy, such as public deliberation, information dissemination, and the forging of links between civil society and government.

It is important to underscore that the development of the IG as a mechanism of accountability is not a uniform one; it must be understood as a product of its historical context as something that has grown alongside of and in reaction to the expanding administrative state and the growth of emergency executive powers. Drawing on insights from theories of democracy, administration, and institutional change, I document the emergence of an internal mode of democratic accountability that has evolved differentially across the state and that has contributed to the emergence of new democratic forms.

Preserving Democratic Integrity and Curtailing Executive Power

This study constructs its object of analysis at the intersection of multiple literatures: democratic theory, accountability studies, and the public administration literature on IGs. I start by framing my investigation with the questions prompted by democratic theorists and public administration scholars on accountability. I then address empirical deficits in the scant literature on IGs. Below, I briefly outline my analytic approach. I then review the literature and draw from it the questions that shape my enquiry.

Analytic Approach

I take an unorthodox analytic approach in this study with the aim of responding to analogous calls from within two fields of scholarship. Scholars in both democratic theory, broadly speaking, and accountability studies have lamented the chasm within their subdisciplines that exists between the empirical and the theoretical, the institutional and the philosophical. Efforts to place these approaches in concert often run afoul of the methodological conventions and strictures that can serve to limit, rather than to refine, the conclusions of scholarship at either end of the spectrum.

However, in both fields, efforts have been made to bridge this gap. Political realism, an important emerging school within political theory, posits the need for precisely this kind of methodological shift. It argues that, rather than start with prior normative commitments, political theory should begin with the here and now—that is, with the institutions that exist—and from there order the normative guiding principles of a theory of democracy.[22] In short, it demands a methodological inversion from top-down theorizing (i.e., deriving theories from abstract principles) to bottom-up theorizing (taking existing political institutions as the basis for building theories of democracy). This move cannot be reduced to the traditional distinction between deductive and inductive reasoning. Rather than beginning one's inquiry with an abstract principle—say, a Rawlsian conception of justice—and then deriving the best possible institutional arrangement to achieve that end, without regard to the practices and institutions that exist now (and without regard to the institutional exigencies of the present era), we must first take into account the constraints of existing, historically specific political and institutional conditions. In this case, given one demand of modern democracies—the need for large-scale apparatuses of administration—what are the features of contemporary political institutions such that classic democratic values can be preserved?

A similar drive toward methodological hybridity has been apparent in the field of accountability studies. Dubnick calls for a blend between two different "ontologies" of accountability studies, the institutional and the relational. Whereas an "institutional" focus highlights the precise structures and mechanisms of accountability in governance—audits, compliance measures, public disclosures—a "relational" approach examines the link between practices of accountability and questions of moral philosophy and identity.[23] The main limit of a purely institutional approach to accountability mechanisms is that the singular focus on audits or investigations neglects the relationships that underpin these practices. Dubnick comments, "Once a relationship becomes structured, formalized, and/or mechanized [through audits or performance measures], the social dynamic that underpins account-giving relations and behaviors is altered."[24] The advent of the audit society has left its mark on bureaucratic behaviors and expectations, and thus on the way that governments and legal systems are fundamentally structured. However, an empirically rich study of specific accountability mechanisms in their historical context can illuminate much about the underlying relationships within bureaucracies, between rival bureaucracies, between branches of government, and between the government and the citizenry. The dynamics and quality of these relationships not only affect the immediate outcomes of governance but also go to the heart of such fundamental principles as the separation of powers.

Through my hybrid empirical and philosophical approach, I attempt to contribute to both of these conversations. My effort to establish the narrative setting of accountability practices and chart their development over time aims to weave the empirical insights of the institutional approach to accountability studies with the broad perspective of the relational option. This methodological movement parallels the political realists' urge to take empirical data as the starting point for building theories of democracy. To the political realists, I offer concrete empirical evidence, through historical analytic narrative, so as to inform debates about the changing nature of democracy. Here the aim of the study is to begin with an empirical account of the way existing institutions deal with certain recurring democratic problems, then to offer preliminary thoughts about what these institutions and practices tell us about new modes of democratic engagement, and about the concept of the political when key components of citizen participation are delegated to the state. The following narratives focus less on the specific outcomes, strengths, and weaknesses of particular reviews than on how the account-giving relationship is affected by these practices and on what the consequences might be for the democratic legitimacy and the forms of democracy articulated in the American state.

The Argument

My primary analytic question concerns what kinds of contributions, and with what effect and consequence, IGs have made to democratic processes. This question has both a first-order, specific response in the form of concrete results from IG work and a more general, second-order response framed in terms of broad, democratic forms.

On a basic level, the narratives that follow demonstrate that federal IGs have contributed to effective governance and democratic integrity in much more diverse and unexpected ways than early observers would have predicted, and that they bear the imprint of multiple normative visions of accountability. Yet institutionally, their impact is still uncertain; it varies from one bureaucratic context to the next. Thus no broad generalizations can be drawn about the overall value of their effects, either positive or negative, on the state and on democratic functioning. However, certain conclusions can be drawn concerning the way that the IG phenomenon has slowly altered the structure of the accountability relationships—bureaucratic and political—that condition the way the state governs. The IGs' ascendancy points to a new form of delegation—the delegation of citizen participation to unelected officials in the form of accountability holding—and suggests that the exigencies of the administrative state are transforming the nature of the political in contemporary democracies. Equally important, IG work instantiates a novel form of democratic legitimacy produced through continuous monitory practice.

Democratic Theory: Preliminary Considerations of Accountability

The resolution of the tension between administrative discretion and democratic values lies in the concept of accountability. John Dunn makes this basic argument: "In the states of today, practices of democratic accountability form the key site of putative reconciliation between the norm of democracy and the apparently antithetical implications of state authority."[25] Jeremy Waldron echoes this insistence on the necessity of accountability for democracy by rooting the practice of public account giving in the traditional republican concept of the res publica, the idea that "the business of government is public business."[26] Yet despite its "necessity" to democracy, and despite a certain vogue in many social scientific academic circles, modern democratic theorists have typically marginalized accountability in favor of other democratic principles, such as participation and representation.[27] Historically, accountability has been approached implicitly, as the by-product of structural arrangements or electoral systems. Indeed, the term "accountability" itself was hardly used by theorists and philosophers before the mid-twentieth century.[28]

Part of this neglect, and the related conceptual confusion, have to do with the term's imprecision.[29] Much contemporary scholarship works to pin down its various meanings, narrowing the term and differentiating it from its use in the vernacular as something akin to punishment.[30] Political scientists often reduce the concept to, or at least focus on, elections as the most fundamental mechanism for preserving democratic accountability.[31] Yet such periodic forms of accountability hardly provide statewide accountability, not least for the legions of unelected career bureaucrats directing the administrative and regulatory states. Legal scholar Edward Rubin goes further, arguing not only that elections are not primarily mechanisms of accountability but also that the concept of accountability is "intrinsically bureaucratic or administrative in character" and cannot be understood without reference to the administrative state.[32] Only administrative oversight and hierarchies provide true accountability; elections as a source of accountability are a myth. Given the necessity of a large-scale administrative apparatus with which to run modern states, returning full policy-making authority to the legislative branch on the principle of nondelegation would simply force the legislature to build an equally large—and unaccountable—infrastructure of unelected officials in order to carry out its tasks. Rubin's formulation serves as an argument against the accountability-enhancing impulses toward nondelegation, the devolution of central government, and a unitary executive, and it roots the source of accountability in administration itself.

If this is correct, the microprocesses of bureaucratic accountability play a crucial role in generating democratic legitimacy. The decisions of a politician are (in theory) legitimate because the official is held to account through periodic elections. The decisions of unelected bureaucrats are (in theory) legitimate because representatives have delegated them decision-making authority. In practice, however, their actions are deemed legitimate insofar as they are continuously scrutinized with audits, investigations, and inspections. If authority in a representative democracy traditionally rested on the legitimacy of the electoral process, then these new accountability practices underpin the legitimacy of what John Keane calls a "monitory democracy": the set of "power-monitoring and power-contesting mechanisms" of continuous oversight that characterize post-1945 liberal democracies.[33] (The profound implications of this shift in the basis of democratic legitimacy are discussed further below, especially insofar as IGs instantiate a novel democratic form by furthering the production of this legitimacy.)

Aside from its frequent equation with elections, discussions of accountability are dominated by principal–agent (P-A) frameworks, which comprise the chief analytic lens used for understanding accountability.[34] P-A theories frame the stakes of accountability in the following way: democratic accountability implies that a principal (the public) can sanction an agent (a public official delegated some sort of responsibility) for failing to represent its interests or respond to its demands. Mechanisms of accountability are thus ways of limiting the discretion of public officials.[35] However, such frameworks suffer from numerous deficits with regard to accountability. In addition to oversimplifying the multiple relationships that constitute a system of accountability, they often imbue a fundamentally political dynamic with normative principles inherited from economics.[36] As Philp argues, it is erroneous to assume that the interests of a particular group are identical to those of the people. Holding an actor to account in the name of the people does not ensure that the aggregate interests of the people are the primary criterion for evaluation. Using P-A frameworks becomes even more problematic with regard to IGs: their interests are not synonymous with their two direct principals, Congress and their department heads (who have, moreover, very different, often opposing interests). Nor are they synonymous with their indirect principal's interest, the people's interest (a plural and incoherent notion to begin with).

Nonetheless, a P-A account such as Waldron's offers the analytic advantage of highlighting the specific duties associated with each role. He too argues that democratic accountability must be at least partly divorced from its singular association with elections and that it ought to be retheorized as an integral component of a continuing political relationship. His version centers on the duty owed by the agent to the principal to give an account of its actions; he distinguishes it from other conceptions by emphasizing that there must be a specific actor to whom accountability is owed, and that the principal can determine the standards to which the account giver is to be held (as opposed to an objective legal standard administered by a tribunal).[37]

Though Waldron does not argue it explicitly, the implications of his account are profound. In this argument, accountability becomes a permanent activity that impresses on the government (the agent) the duty to narrate and justify its actions regularly. This inserts a radically modern principle into a classic state function: ritual self-justification, not with reference to divine right, reason of state, or even the will of the people, but to a set of substantive values increasingly articulated in administrative and economic language. The state justifies its actions with reference to efficiency, effectiveness, and accountability (often vague and imprecise in its invocation), and most important, it derives its legitimacy from its perceived conformity with these principles.

Waldron's account also underscores the precept of political accountability according to which the principal can determine the standards by which the agent (government actor) is to be judged. These standards can be procedural or substantive (a point that Rubin also makes), but crucially, they are set by the principal. For my purposes, the IGs are a kind of intermediary interpreter, at once the account giver (as the narrator of the state's activity) and the account holder (as the implicit judge, able to choose and craft the standards by which the state's actions will be judged). With the latitude they have to choose which actions are worthy of being investigated, and able to select the terms in which to narrate them, the IGs set the moral and ethical standards by which the government must then act.

The contributions of Philp, Rubin, and Waldron suggest that the dynamic of accountability inherent in political and administrative relationships is part and parcel of democracy tout court. Accountability denotes not merely a relationship but also a repeated action called into being by that relationship. Many of those critical of the P-A approach (and even some who espouse it, such as Waldron) emphasize the need to return to the earlier narrative roots of the term as one meaning to give an account, rather than focus on the sanctions or punishment associated with the exchange.[38] Insofar as democracy is a practice rather than a state of being, it requires continuous reenactment of the ritual of account giving. But if accountability holding is a fundamental part of the practice of democracy, it follows that who performs it is a matter of utmost importance, one that goes to the heart of the question of democratic participation. Dunn places the onus of accountability on the citizen, claiming that "most of the weight, in seeking to secure accountability, has to be carried by the vigor of citizen participation and by the scope of rights and liberties open to citizens."[39] This echoes a traditional conception of democratic participation according to which the vibrancy of democracy depends on citizen activity. However, Waldron's argument transfers this duty to the agent—that is, the state—itself.

IGs fit uneasily with these considerations. If the principal (the people) should set the standards of assessment in a democracy, then what happens to the integrity of democracy when that task is delegated to part of the state apparatus itself? The IGs' emergence thus prompts questions about the unintended, and potentially negative, consequences of accountability for democracy. (Philp also calls attention to the way certain kinds of accountability can have potentially negative consequences, as when demands for accountability diminish the government's latitude for exercising judgment, or when calls for accountability serve only to legitimize preexisting substantive outcomes.) IGs perform what Warren calls mediated accountability— an arrangement in which one agent holds other agents to account on behalf of principals—and forms a part of the overall division of labor of accountability, but which complicates the simplistic P-A model and diminishes its explanatory power.

Accountability Studies: The Public Administration Approach to Accountability

Understanding accountability in the abstract through P-A frameworks, or as a state function, goes only so far toward explaining its effects on democracy. If we shift analytic registers from the theoretical to the institutional to understand how the mechanics of accountability work, we gain purchase on how, and to what effect, they affect the quality of governance.

Just as in democratic theory, the tension between the sanction/punishment and narrative-giving dimensions of accountability dominates the myriad ways of disaggregating the concept of accountability from a public administration perspective. Indeed, this conceptual distinction has mirrored, and in turn given rise to, multiple mechanisms of public accountability that often work at cross-purposes. Depending on how such mechanisms are deployed and managed, the two approaches (for instance, the "sanction-based" and "trust-based" accountabilities described by Jane Mansbridge) can foster governing contexts of either suspicion or trust, and so lead to vastly different outcomes.[40] This underscores a second dominant theme in the public administration literature: the unintended and often negative consequences of accountability and accountability-related public reforms.

A small sample of the concrete paradoxes that plague accountability reforms suffices to illustrate the underlying conceptual puzzle. First, it is a widely contested claim that performance management systems actually improve agency accountability.[41] Second, some public sector reforms aimed at depoliticizing public management by delegating more responsibility to specific bodies result in more intense politicization as elected officials vie for control over the locus of policy implementation (Moshe Maor's "managerial paradox").[42] Third, heavy responsibilities levied on administrative bodies impede the process of learning and development.[43] Finally, Dubnick's "reformist paradox" calls attention to the way in which any reform geared toward increasing accountability inevitably undercuts existing accountability arrangements.[44]

The phenomenon of unintended, even contradictory effects of reform measures goes by many names, including "multiple-accountabilities disorder" and "bureaupathology."[45] As discussed above, oversight mechanisms can contribute to the very problems they were intended to solve. In the case of IGs and other bureaucratic oversight mechanisms, this includes adding to the size, complexity, and unaccountability of a bureaucracy that they were designed to shrink and hold to account. Light frames the paradox in the following way: "By increasing the ratio of reviewers to doers, Congress and the president work against the accountability they seek, causing an impact never imagined by the IG founders. As the IG numbers go up, effectiveness may go down."[46] Here he highlights the IGs' role in exacerbating a form of bureaupathology, the phenomenon of organizational dysfunction that results from excessive bureaucracy. According to this logic, government expansion occurs both in size and in layers, multiplying and obfuscating the lines of accountability. Reforms for accountability are reactions to this, but they also contribute to a vicious cycle by making government bigger and less accountable. IGs diminish administrative efficiency and accountability by increasing government outlays and contributing to additional regulations.[47] In other words, bureaupathology breeds a form of negative policy feedback.[48]

A common feature of these paradoxes is that each reform prompted an unintended alteration of the underlying incentive structure for public officials, causing the actors in question to craft behavioral strategies in tension with what reformers intended. Hood provides a basic theory and mapping of such strategies: through a series of blame avoidance strategies, public officials and bureaucrats can avoid responsibility (in what American children might recognize as a game of ministerial dodgeball) by doctoring the presentation of their actions, by strategically distributing responsibilities within an agency, or by manipulating policy options and altering the process or the substance of government activity.[49] These behavioral strategies have grown in conjunction with—and cannot be considered apart from—the coeval management reforms of the late twentieth and early twenty-first centuries. With the restructuring associated with New Public Management (NPM) doctrines, including those that promoted public–private partnerships, responsibility could easily be passed on to other actors with no end point in sight.[50]

But in part because of this widespread tendency toward blame avoidance, the state's arsenal of instruments of accountability—under the principles of hierarchy, mutuality, competition, and contrived randomness—has grown.[51] Many instruments incorporate elements of more than one of these principles. IGs, for instance, blend elements of mutuality (civil servants monitoring civil servants) and contrived randomness (launching unexpected audits and investigations). Analytically, too few studies have explored the hybrid forms of these instruments and explained how one particular mechanism interacts with and affects the others. Again, in the case of IGs: though they are often dismissed as being merely a form of auditor or ombuds and limited to compliance monitoring, IG work contributes to a range of parallel processes of accountability including transparency, watchdog journalism, and performance reporting, in addition to the accounting and rule compliance for which they are better known.

It is necessary to survey the state of scholarship on the IGs themselves to understand how they suffer from, overcome, or transform these paradoxes, and in so doing, how they contribute to ever-evolving, newly configured accountability regimes.

Inspectors General

Congress established the IG framework in 1978 as a corrective to administrative discretion. I give a more detailed description of the IG Act's remit in Chapter 2 and a historical account of the IG's origins and development in Chapter 3. In the following section, I review and highlight the limitations of the existing literature on the IGs, nearly all of which issues from a public administration perspective. A brief caveat on the manner in which IGs have received scholarly attention: offices of the inspector general (OIGs) are not equivalent to bureaucracies; they do not provide services that gather coalitional support, and they are the agent of two opposing principals (Congress and their agencies). Moreover, the IGs themselves do not have the same incentives as other political appointees: they do not make policy, and they are not, at least in theory, political. IGs cannot receive bonuses and operate on a pay scale separate from that of other federal employees. In other words, the dynamics governing their development should not necessarily be the same as a service-driven bureaucracy. But in many ways, OIGs are organized as bureaucracies and behave as such. Their performance depends partly on the extent of their traditional bureaucratic capacities. Most of the literature on IGs has treated them as bureaucracies and frames its analysis with the questions and narratives that emerge from that field.

There is a striking dearth of research on the IG itself, and much of what does exist is limited in scope to the IGs' immediate effect on bureaucratic waste, fraud, and corruption from a public policy or public administration perspective. The primary study of IGs remains Paul C. Light's seminal 1993 monograph on the history of the IGs and their performance, *Monitoring Government*.[52] He builds his argument around the IGs' structural predisposition toward compliance monitoring over that of capacity-based or performance-based conceptions of accountability; this distinction has largely served to structure the terms in which IGs' effects have been debated.

The public administration literature revolves around two main themes: IG effectiveness and independence. Much of the existing literature, especially the early work, emphasizes the IGs' limitations and failure to provide a truly effective check on executive action. The National Performance Review (NPR) of 1993 (Reinventing Government Act) suggested that IGs restrained innovation and thus limited departmental capacity. Consequently, evaluation of their effect on the polity has been limited to public administration categories—frequently of the IGs' own creation, such as savings, successful prosecutions, reports issued, and investigations opened and closed—and judges according to the accepted values of public administration itself: efficiency and managerial reform. Although my aim is to move away from this line of analysis, the conclusions of the public administration literature are not inconsequential for the present study. Indeed, they have shaped the research agenda and the standard evaluative categories for understanding IGs. Initial scholarly studies in the early 1980s focused primarily on the history of the IGs without situating them in relation to models of policy formation or institutional development.[53] Later literature of the 1990s still remained largely atheoretical, but it reflected the influence of NPM principles and the Reinventing Government movement in administrative design.[54] These strands of thought influenced IG development in two ways: NPM stressed the importance of market principles and the customer model in structuring bureaucratic relationships; and Reinventing Government (as laid out in the NPR) outlined specific methods to improve government performance. The latter movement urged a shift from compliance monitoring to proactive, ongoing evaluation, and expanded IG responsibilities to include performance-monitoring reviews.[55]

Extensive qualitative reports that suggest management reforms by one OIG might be appropriate for its particular agency, but a different agency might benefit from many, smaller, technical audit reports. Comparing two such OIG outputs leaves the analyst at a loss because simple numbers of reports generated or cases closed fail to indicate the qualitative effect that the IG reviews have had on agencies.[56] Moreover, within the context of emergency, there is more at stake in executive overreach than financial waste or fraud: civil rights and liberties are often the first casualties in times of crisis, and their curtailment by an unchecked executive is one of the most significant challenges to a well functioning democracy. For instance, Central Intelligence Agency (CIA) IG John Helgerson's report on the use of torture by the CIA "didn't fit the metrics of an IG's semiannual report, but it had big weight and impact."[57] Thus, charting the effects of the IG moves from being a quantitative calculation to being an appraisal of the IG's effect on legal structure, on administrative procedure, and on participation in processes of accountability.

Since the turn of the twenty-first century, individual in-depth studies have focused on the performance of state and local IGs;[58] the performance of single federal OIGs;[59] IG effectiveness;[60] IG independence;[61] and phenomenological accounts of the IG experience.[62] IG reviews also vary in their rigor and consequence. Whereas IGs initially focused solely on compliance monitoring—that is, adherence to bureaucratic rules and laws—their consequence can differ depending on the nature of the recommendations they give and the willingness of external actors to implement them. By focusing only on conformity with existing rules, the IG model neglects other strategies for accountability, such as the use of positive sanctions and the development of infrastructure.⁶³ Similarly, Robert Behn suggests that, historically, IGs have suffered from an "accountability bias" from focusing on objective rule compliance because they "have a better chance of catching a [guilty party] when they concentrate on finances and fairness," rather than on more subjective conceptions of accountability or performance.⁶⁴ If the assertion that IGs have an accountability bias toward compliance monitoring is correct, then it remains a puzzle as to how IGs could expand their remit or influence, or make a meaningful contribution to improving the quality of democracy.

If academics have ignored the IGs, then the public sector has more eagerly passed judgment on IG performance. The NPR, led by Vice President Al Gore in 1993, played a decisive role in reorienting the trajectory of the IGs. Gore, a skeptic of the IG model and one of only six senators to vote against the original 1978 act, took the IG community to task in his appraisal and suggested that IGs fundamentally alter the aims and methods of their work. The study claimed that Gore "heard Federal employees complain that the IG's basic approach inhibits innovation and risk-taking. Heavy-handed enforcement—with the IG watchfulness compelling employees to follow every rule, document every decision, and fill out every form—has had a negative effect in some agencies."⁶⁵ The review encouraged the IG community to "change the focus of Inspectors General from compliance auditing to evaluating management control systems" and, "in addition, recast the IGs' method of operation to be more collaborative and less adversarial."⁶⁶ Though the review ultimately served as an authoritative directive to change, it also provided phenomenological evidence to support the negative claims of many scholarly studies until that point: IGs often created more problems than they set out to solve.

The government watchdog group Project on Government Oversight (POGO) has also produced many analyses—in many ways among the most rigorous social scientific evaluations—of the IGs. Since it first began to investigate federal governmentwide corruption and misconduct in 1990, POGO's reports have addressed both individual and systemwide problems in the IG community. Though many of its actions concern individual OIGs—such matters as excessively long vacancies or misconduct within an OIG—POGO has issued periodic analyses of the entire IG model. Its most comprehensive, a two-part review of the IGs to date published in 2008–2009, focused on their independence and accountability, and it affirmed the overall value of the IG system. In short, POGO rejected the claim that IGs' limitations outweighed their benefits.⁶⁷ Drawn largely from survey and interview data, the most valuable contribution of the study was the isolation of independence, above and beyond resources, as the most salient variable in determining an IG's success. However, the review also cautioned that by its very nature, independence makes the IG community vulnerable to accountability problems of its own.

Yet this positive view remains the minority position. Other discussions of the IG model, from Moore and Gates's early (1986) historical account to more recent analyses of the growth of government, interpret the IG phenomenon as a potential liability for government. By these accounts, IGs merely contribute to the size of government and thus make it even more difficult to ensure accountability.[68] Much of the scholarship with positive assessments of IG activity limits analysis to what IGs themselves target: for instance, Apaza's study of the Department of Homeland Security (DHS) OIG's effectiveness judges it by its own categories from within a public policy framework, and thus has difficulty rating the IGs' wider effects on political life. For instance, Apaza concludes that at least one OIG has (among many indicators) recovered a considerable sum of monies and produced a significant number of criminal convictions, and that this demonstrates, at least in part, the effectiveness of that IG's work. However, these criteria for success say little as to whether or not these targets are rigorous to begin with. Questions abound: does the work of IGs deter future wrongdoing? Are their targets reasonable? Are their recommendations rigorous? Do the categories omit other systemic sources of departmental dysfunction? At what point do the ever-higher rates of funds recovered indicate success or accountability in government? Or do these figures merely indicate an increasingly corrupt government bureaucracy? Overall, the literature on IGs is circumspect about their historical record and their effects on bureaucratic efficiency while allowing for limited success and future potential in curbing fraud, waste, and abuse.

The themes highlighted in the preceding (selective) survey of various accountability literatures point to the need for a broader perspective that incorporates the wide purview of the democratic theorists with the empirical rigor and detail of institutional case studies. What is needed is a synthetic approach that connects these different analytic registers. The broad treatments of accountability by legal and democratic theorists establish that the activity of accountability is a fundamental and inevitable part of democracy. Yet the public administration literature demonstrates that in practice, this activity—as integral to democracy as it might be—does not always enhance democracy. Distinguishing its beneficial from its noxious effects demands a careful empirical treatment of the mechanisms of accountability, both in an isolated fashion and as part of accountability regimes. To address this question, we must turn to detailed institutional studies for indications of each mechanism's dynamics. Here the limits of the existing IG literature are clear: its limited, self-contained evaluative parameters fail to link it to the broader concerns of democratic theory, or even the more philosophical considerations of public administration. This study assumes this mantle.

CHAPTER TWO

"ONCE YOU'VE MET ONE IG, YOU'VE MET ONE IG"

Modes of Monitory Democratic Practice

CHIEF JUSTICE: I then did use the person of your father.
The image of his power lay then in me;
And in th' administration of his law,
Whiles I was busy for the commonwealth,
Your highness pleased to forget my place,
The majesty and power of law and justice,
The image of the King whom I presented,
And struck me in my very seat of judgement;
Whereon, as an offender to your father,
I gave bold way to my authority
And did commit you.
[. . .]
PRINCE HENRY: You are right Justice, and you weigh this well.
Therefore still bear the balance and the sword.
—William Shakespeare, *Henry IV, Part 2* (1600)

Who Are the IGs?

Accountability and the democratic integrity that it furthers have traditionally been a structural feature of the American state; the 1978 IG Act is a direct reaction to the concrete failures of the separated system. As the chapter title implies, IGs comprise a diverse population of bureaucrats, with varying statutory responsibilities and limitations, staffing levels, and focuses. Despite the common general framework of the 1978 act and increasingly standardized training, IGs still retain much discretion as to how they organize their offices and what strategies they use in fulfilling their mandate. The differences give rise to different types of accountability that make both normative and empirical comparison difficult.[1] Although I will provide a fuller account of the IG category and history in Chapter 3, a brief description of the 1978 act and the circumstances of its birth is necessary.

IGs are a key mechanism of bureaucratic oversight that combines audit, investigative, and inspection functions. Though embedded in the executive branch, IGs report to Congress at least semiannually on their continuing investigations of fraud and abuse in the general workings of government. In doing this, they follow standardized procedures set out in what are known as the Yellow Book (for auditors), the Blue Book (inspectors), and the Quality Standards for Investigation. Statutorily, the purposes of the IG are:

(1) to conduct and supervise audits and investigations relating to the programs and operations of the establishments;

(2) to provide leadership and coordination and recommend policies for activities designed (A) to promote economy, efficiency, and effectiveness in the administration of, and (B) to prevent and detect fraud and abuse in, such programs and operations; and

(3) to provide a means for keeping the head of the establishment and the Congress fully and currently informed about problems and deficiencies [. . .] and the necessity for and progress of corrective action.[2]

Thus, in addition to its audits and investigations, the IG has a both positive (leadership) and negative (preventative and punitive) role. Most important is the third provision, which establishes the IG as a kind of information conduit between Congress and the executive, permitting the former to perform its oversight role. The IG's duties include reviewing existing policies, recommending policies, and keeping the head of its establishment and Congress informed.[3]

As of 2016, IGs number seventy-three across the federal bureaucracy and many hundreds in state and local governments. Beyond their mandated semiannual reports, IGs respond to specific requests from Congress or from within their departments to conduct reviews of particular instances of fraud and abuse. Each of the seventy-three IGs testifies regularly before Congress, at times only once or twice, but often at six or more hearings in a six-month reporting period. They operate within their host agency but coordinate with other OIGs within a framework for professional ethics, the Council of Inspectors General on Integrity and Efficiency (CIGIE).[4] In addition to special IGs, three main types of IGs populate the federal bureaucracy: federal establishment IGs, who supervise federal departments; intelligence entity IGs (CIA and director of national intelligence); and designated federal entity (DFE) IGs, who oversee many smaller federal entities.[5] Whereas the first two are presidentially appointed, Senate confirmed, and removable only by the president, the DFE IGs are selected and can be removed by the agency head, which affords them less independence.[6] These federal IGs are distinct from a host of other IG models, such as military and nonstatutory IGs, and from those used at the state and local level.[7] The incentive structure to pursue fraud, waste, and abuse in the 1978 act privileged compliance monitoring because it afforded numerous advantages to Congress.[8] Such a structure provides easily quantifiable findings—results that are visible and that lend themselves to claiming credit.[9]

How Do We Classify IG Effects on Democracy?

As outlined in Chapter 1, my primary concern is what kind of effects IGs have on democratic integrity and functioning. The questions are not simply, how efficiently is democracy functioning? How effectively? They are also, what kind of democracy? Which values and institutions are privileged and supported? IGs are an instance of monitory or monitorial governance, a historically novel form of democracy characterized by a "multiplication and dispersal of many different power-monitoring and power-contesting mechanisms" that complement or replace traditional forms of oversight such as legislatures and parties.[10] These mechanisms range from auditing bodies and citizens' juries to focus groups and think tanks. Within the government apparatus, along with other auditing, inspecting, and investigatory bodies, IGs provide (in theory) the accountability that is crucial to legitimate democratic governance. But within this broad monitory form of democracy, IGs can shore up the foundations of a range of modern democratic values in addition to accountability, such as representation, the rule of law, and responsiveness. They command a limited repertoire of instruments, but they have latitude in how and to what ends they deploy them. Understanding the variation in their effects demands attention to the mode of democratic practice that they employ and their institutional strategy.

Modes of Democratic Practice

IGs have a common set of legal and institutional tools, but they vary widely in the ends to which they direct those tools. This variation affects different democratic values and gives rise to different modes of democratic practice.[11] By mode of democratic practice, I signal the way that an actor can direct a set of practices and tools (e.g., audits and investigations) toward enhancing a particular aspect of democratic state functioning.[12] These include (but are not limited to) maintaining the political neutrality of the state bureaucracy, supporting constitutional rights, and enhancing the state's capacity to respond to emergency. The novelty of these modes, I argue, lies in the way they are pursued by apolitical, monitory actors rather than directly through the courts or the legislature. Their legitimacy thus rests on both merit-based expertise and the very methods and instruments they use to produce their narratives (e.g., audits and investigations).

IGs are not merely bureaucratic figures. They are also second-order political actors, key players in democratic governance.[13] Despite being unelected, the IGs play legislative, judicial, and executive roles; this requires them to straddle the divide between administration and politics. Staying wedded to a crude split between administrative and democratic values fails to do justice to the complexity of IG work. Indeed, democratic values can take on an economic valence, where, as Olsen notes, "responsiveness and accountability imply the ability to discover and accommodate market signals."[14] When IG monitory instruments and strategies are deployed by IGs, what kind of democracy is forged? Which values are supported and defended? I propose three modes of democratic practice that emerge from IG discontent: political democracy, constitutional democracy, and managerial democracy. I describe each mode in greater detail below.

A political mode of democratic practice tempers rather than stokes the effects of partisanship and political expediency on departmental outputs. An IG working in a political mode of practice would promote a political environment in which healthy partisan agonism can thrive and ultimately be resolved through the political process.[15] In short, a political mode of democratic practice preserves bureaucratic neutrality, which is necessary for the substantive resolution of value conflicts passed on to the administration from legislators.

An IG can practice such a mode of democracy by weighing in on political scandal in an impartial fashion, furnishing neutral but rigorous narratives that provide elected officials, the courts, and the public with the necessary information to begin their own processes of accountability. This IG unearths political scandals and corruption more than routine waste; the IG seeks to prevent ideology from entering bureaucratic decision making. A successful IG would rise above the partisanship of a given scandal or bureaucratic lapse and target the systemic or even cultural biases within the department that permit repeated lapses of performance or propriety. An unsuccessful IG operating in this mode would focus its recommendations and prescriptions on retroactive punishment for perpetrators and limit them to improving the gaps in departmental procedure that permit or encourage wrongdoing.

Such an IG would focus on behavioral impropriety and the uncovering of individual instances of fraud and moral wrongdoing (e.g., embezzlement or sexual harassment) more than on finding the systemic sources of wrongdoing or improving administrative performance.

At its most successful, an IG that crafts a political democracy heightens the bureaucracy's role as arbiter of the fundamental value conflicts that drive the politics of a plural society.[16] Ideally, this mode of democratic practice does not tame the agonistic dimension of the political completely but refines it by providing external actors with the legitimizing input of IG expertise. Ultimately it reinforces the ethical function of bureaucratic neutrality. Where the efficacy or legitimacy of departmental action is threatened by political scandal, an IG can offer correctives in the form of concrete institutional modifications (e.g., new rules) but also by providing neutral, informed narratives released into the public sphere. In short, such an IG manages the political impact of accountability breaches by reinforcing the legitimacy of the department.

An IG working in a constitutional mode of democratic practice orients its actions toward the statist and constitutional elements of agency work. If the judicial response to the growth of the administrative state has been to articulate constitutional rights and ease requirements to pursue these rights,[17] then the IGs have played a crucial bridging role in this process through their narratives and their choice of investigations. An IG operating in this mode frames its reviews as questions of moral wrongdoing or integrity. It does so in a number of ways. First, it focuses on the net power held by any given political entity by judging the scope of its actions, and it evaluates a given action by the degree to which it prevents or permits the concentration and abuse of power in a single institution. Such an IG also judges the propriety of the action, identifying wrongdoing whether or not it accords with existing law. In part, the expansion of the IGs' focus to include this perspective in their oversight was statutorily based: with the passage of the Patriot Act, the Department of Justice (DOJ) and DHS IGs were given a legal basis for investigating civil rights abuses, especially those related to the implementation of the act. But determining what counts as an abuse of rights is partly an interpretive act, and consequently different IGs' pursuit of such violations has varied considerably. A review guided by this perspective will frame the issue as one of propriety of government action or rights violations. Successful IGs practicing this mode will publicize their reviews, making narratives available for further citizen scrutiny and even judicial proceedings. In this way, the successful IG provides a link between the bureaucracy and the courts, reinforcing the judicial function of oversight, and plays a role in norm setting.

The IG's adoption of this mode of democratic practice can lend it a quasi-judicial role, passing judgment on the legality or appropriateness of an action regardless of its compliance with existing law, and even in such a way as to challenge the existing legal framework. Although many IG reviews target management structures in their recommendations, at their most active, the reviews can question the very legal framework underpinning the legitimacy of the actions in question. In addition to supporting the rule of law, much work done by constitutional IGs defends the "liberty" side of the liberty/security dichotomy in national security.

A managerial mode of democratic practice bears the imprint of the neo-liberal public reform movements (NPM and Reinventing Government), and the IG reforms of the 1990s reinforced this tendency by redefining the IGs' role as one of management consultant. (See Chapter 3 for an extended discussion of these reforms.) Despite its emphasis on administrative values of economy and efficiency, the managerial mode of democracy is not ipso facto opposed to classic democratic ideals such as representation. Not only do some IGs uphold a commitment to improving the performance of their agency, but they also concentrate on the broad structures—networks and incentives—that underpin that performance. IG reviews dictated by the managerial perspective will frame the issue under investigation as one of efficiency and effectiveness, and they will implicitly or explicitly pass judgment on the program's utility for the department's goals.

The "contemporary managerialist ideal," according to du Gay, comprises "market creation, entrepreneurial conduct; and performance measurement."[18] An IG can privilege a normative vision of accountability in which these administrative values mould the practice of bureaucratic oversight. This IG's strategies are similar to those of NPM: adopting a customer service model and working toward prevention rather than reaction. In alignment with its NPM orientation, it tries to move from hierarchy to teamwork and mutual participation as organizational principles. It works on building institutional structures within the OIG and in consultation with other OIGs, as well as developing ties with organizations in civil society, contributing to a web of accountability. In its assessments, an IG operating in this mode of democracy monitors not only compliance but also the department's reform strategies; in its recommendations, it proffers not only procedural remedies but also institutional innovations designed to improve performance and maximize oversight.

While some traditional democratic values, such as civil liberties and rights, can be undermined by the managerialist mode of democratic prac-

Table 2.1. Modes of Democratic Practice

Mode of Democratic Practice	Framing and Value Orientation
Political	• Corruption and scandal-driven focus. • Tries to ensure fairness or appearance of fairness. • Reinforces the ethical and refining function of bureaucratic neutrality. • Attentive to role of partisanship and ideology in wrongdoing.
Constitutional	• Norm-driven focus. • Frames as questions of propriety or rights violations. • Reinforces the constitutional and judicial function of oversight. • Targets legal structure.
Managerial	• Efficiency and performance focus. • Reinforces the responsive capacity of bureaucracy. • Targets management structure to improve performance.

tice, others are transformed or enhanced. The most salutary effects of this mode of practice are not only (or even primarily) in the direct outcome of the review, but rather in shoring up the foundations of future accountability when IGs build institutional capacity. However, because bureaucratic efficiency remains the overriding value, it can fall short when faced with rights abuses; in the context of national security, it falls on the "security" side of the liberty/security tension.

This typology of modes of democratic practice, all falling within a novel monitory form of democracy, calls attention to the varied bureaucratic arenas in which more abstract democratic values such as impartiality, liberty, and responsiveness can be instantiated. Analytically, it detracts undue attention from those values themselves (the object of many comparative studies of democracy) and reorients it squarely on the institutions in which the meaning of such abstract values is battled out and the cultural contexts out of which they emerge.

It is important to underscore that these ideal types serve as both independent variables (as modes of activity with effects on democratic practice and legitimacy) and as dependent variables (as the consequence of ideological, personal, and institutional factors). Moreover, they are primarily descriptive classifications based on empirical evidence rather than analytical categories formulated before the empirical work.

Institutional Strategies

The second factor influencing the effect that an IG has on democratic integrity and legitimacy is institutional strategy. This comprises the nature and targets of the IG's recommendations, its institutional innovations, and its coordination with external actors. It is best understood as a spectrum that spans from simple compliance monitoring on the one end to building capacity and infrastructure within the host department on the other end. In short, it centers on a tension between compliance and innovation in both agency performance and capacity building as strategies for oversight. At a minimum, IGs should assess compliance with existing rules and regulations, and they should try to deter future deviations from them with sanctions and punishment. The recommendations of an IG with this compliance monitoring orientation can target the procedures and management structures of the department and might point to some individual responsibility, but it does not address the underlying or systemic sources of the violation.

However, IGs can intensify their strategy and target the legal and institutional infrastructure through recommendations and through coordination with other offices and political actors. Recommendations can point out underspecified law or require the development of overall management plans (e.g., in times of emergency). Beyond its recommendations, the IG can build a web of accountability by cultivating networks with other OIGs and external actors so as to strengthen continuous, police-patrol oversight. Outside of individual reviews, it can develop competencies within the OIG to focus on particular areas or pathologies within the host department; this allows the OIG to target systemic problems on a continuous basis rather than single instances.

Two important caveats regarding classification are in order. First, OIGs issue dozens, sometimes hundreds, of audits, investigations, and other reviews each year. Some reviews issued from a single OIG might reflect a concern for the efficiency of a particular program, while others issued concurrently from the same OIG might reflect a concern with a constitutional value such as privacy rights. Moreover, the subcomponent heads within each OIG come with different professional backgrounds and training, and each sets priorities within the subcomponents. For example, the head of the audit division in an OIG will propose the priorities for audit reviews, while the head of the investigations division will choose which investigations to pursue. Thus, to draw a uniform conclusion about the fundamental orientations of an entire office over time based on a single review would be grossly misleading. Because of this, the characterization of any IG or OIG as demonstrating a mode of democratic practice is necessarily a glimpse in time and reflects only loose or broad trends. The cases that follow do assign these labels to specific OIGs, but the analytic value of such characterizations is not to fix a historical label definitively on a particular IG or OIG. Rather, it is to demonstrate the range of possible IG effects on democratic functioning and to identify the factors that condition these effects. In other words, each case study serves as a stylized example of the way that a variety of factors can push an IG to choose different strategies, to privilege different values, and to target different government functions.

Second, not all modes of democratic practice are equally common among IGs. Some OIGs serve departments that are more likely to experience financial corruption because of the types of programs they run, and they thus might have fewer rights violations with which to contend. In practice, since the 1990s, IGs across the federal government are encouraged through CIGIE, through governmentwide auditing standards, and through bureaucratic pressure, to conform to the principles of NPM and downsizing government, with a view to promoting efficiency. This provides the managerial approach to defending democracy with strong cultural and institutional reinforcement.

The three case studies demonstrate the ways in which the original IG model, which focused on compliance monitoring, has evolved and expanded, as well as how actors with the same set of basic tools can promote various aspects of democracy in diverse ways by adopting different institutional strategies and by operating in distinct modes or registers of democratic practice.

Explaining the IGs' Differential Effects on Democracy

Why do some IGs adopt different institutional strategies than others and operate with different modes of democratic practice? IGs are a form of bureaucracy, and bureaucracies need resources to carry out their tasks. On a basic level, IG work is grounded in material capacities and can be measured along classically Weberian indicators of bureaucratic power—material size, expertise, autonomy, coercive power, and reputation-based legitimacy. These dimensions are crucial to understanding the dynamics of the IGs' influence. Without resources, a robust organizational capacity, and the legitimacy underpinned by their reputation, the IGs' role as narrative builders would be ineffectual. Tracing the development of these dimensions requires attention to the budgets and personnel numbers (relative to their host departments), the type and distribution of their expertise, and their independence. Understanding the IGs' emergence, growth, strategies, and effects necessitates attention to bureaucratic form and organization.

However, as an explanation of the differential effect IGs have had on democratic functioning, these explanatory factors come up short in explaining the variation in the types of strategies that IGs use, in the substantive content of democratic accountability they pursue, and in the different norms related to the scope of executive action and bureaucratic behavior that they defend. Why, for instance, would an IG with limited resources choose to pursue an investigation of civil rights abuses over one that improves its host department's efficiency? In other words, how do IGs navigate the administrative-democratic tension? Beyond the material base, ideological, institutional, and functional considerations play important roles in influencing the marks that IGs leave on the state and on the quality of democracy. Although IG appointments are statutorily nonpartisan, ideological commitments can influence and compromise IGs' agendas and diagnoses. For instance, a strong commitment to improving certain departments' performance might be influenced by a strong ideological commitment to the war on terror and might lead an IG to privilege performance concerns over rights violations.

However, ideological influences are not limited to individual partisan commitments. They infuse theories of administration that in turn shape the possible options available to administrative reformers. Taking cues from academic and business wisdom, both congressional and administrative actors can variously push compliance, results, or performance. As the dominant academic theories of administration have changed over time, the standards and practice of the IGs have evolved accordingly. In the 1970s, during the development of the IG Act, and later in the 1990s, administrative reform proposals bore the marks of numerous strands of administrative theory. A common perspective suggests that the concepts of classic public administration remained in place until the late 1970s and were replaced by NPM and neoliberal principles over the ensuing two decades.[19] NPM, the dominant intellectual framework in Anglo-American public administration scholarship and practice, introduced a new focus in accountability measurement, an emphasis that replaced an earlier focus on corruption and based evaluation on the principle of the public good. It focuses on the efficacy and efficiency of a given action rather than its propriety. The NPM paradigm emphasizes a set of doctrines for the conduct of public management, including "hands-on professional management"; standards and measures of performance; output controls; disaggregation of units in the public sector; public competition; private-sector management practices; and parsimonious resource use.[20] However, especially from an international perspective, the view that NPM replaced the classic public administration paradigm is inaccurate.[21] Rather, competing and sometimes incompatible strands of theory often coexist in single bureaucratic settings, with the insights of NPM being layered onto traditional administrative arrangements. This layering of management ideas has given shape to IG practice but cannot alone account for the range of variation of IG effects on democracy.[22]

Despite a certain clarity in the schools of thought governing public administration and reform, the implementation of reform principles in practice is much less transparent. Bureaucracies are rarely pure incarnations of theories of administration; rather, they are hybrids of different models that reflect diverse and sometimes conflicting sets of values. The competing theories have influenced IGs' preferences indirectly through the practices encouraged in government agencies (for instance, best practices shared between departments and agencies, and governmentwide auditing standards such as the Yellow Book of auditing regulations). The theories have also influenced IGs through their professional training and experience. Personal professional backgrounds thus play a large role in determining IG strategy. IGs generally come to their positions with one of three professional backgrounds: legal training, law enforcement, and finance or accounting (auditing). IGs often cultivate the kind of expertise with which they themselves are most familiar, building institutional structures within an OIG to coordinate these skills. Their backgrounds frequently condition the development of institutional structures that underpin and predispose OIGs to conduct certain types of reviews. By defining a distinctive mission and fostering specialized competencies, IGs can give their offices the focus and institutional support needed for writing consequential reviews. The institutionalization of particular expertise entrenches an IG's tendency to pursue certain kinds of reviews and not to pursue others.

In addition to the intermediary institutional structures built by the IGs themselves within their offices, another institutional factor plays a significant role in affecting the strength and consequence of IG work: independence. This, along with material (budgetary) security, has been the primary target of congressional legislation aiming to shore up the IG model. Functional considerations on the part of the IG can also factor into choices about

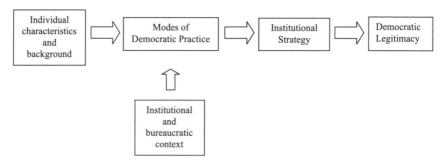

Figure 2.1. IG Effects on Democratic Legitimacy

the allocation of resources to different reviews; these can be deliberate choices based on the mission of a department or agency. According to this logic, the IG of, say, the Social Security Administration should focus primarily on auditing because the agency's raison d'être is to manage a high-budget program. In contrast, the Justice Department's IG might focus on legal issues because it represents the protection of the law at the federal level.[23] IGs might also choose to operate on the basis of a limited interpretation of their role for the sake of democratic integrity and restraint of power. For instance, an IG might believe its role to be advisory rather than productive or creative. It might also take seriously the separation of powers and decline to make judgments or take actions that would lend it a quasi-judicial or a policy-making role.[24]

Finally, individual relationships within the bureaucratic structure influence the capacity of IGs to do their work. According to the accounts of many former IGs, the personal relationship between an IG and the department head is often the determining factor in consequential IG reviews. Former Justice IG Glenn Fine opined, "I believe that any variance in the effectiveness of Inspectors General has been less the result of any deficiencies with the statute and more a function of the outlook and practices of particular Inspectors General, as well as the attitude of the agency or agency head toward the Inspector General."[25] Like others, he emphasized the contingent personal and contextual factors in shaping IG work and bureaucratic discretion.

The Process of Institutional Change: Exploiting Ambiguities

All of these elements have contributed to the variation in effects that IGs have had on democratic processes, to the expansion of the IG model, and to the expansion of the IGs' remit. Regardless of the substantive driver of change, institutional change requires the presence of discursive and institutional ambiguities that actors must exploit. These ambiguities will give rise to "layering," a form of institutional change in which "new rules are attached to existing ones, thereby changing the ways in which the original rules structure behavior." Through amendments and revisions of existing rules and capacities, actors can "alter the logic of the institution" and transform its original purpose.[26]

This institutional and substantive expansion has been spurred by four interlinked sources of ambiguity in the IGs' immediate context: a dual source of legitimacy; a dual set of incentives; multiple, competing audiences; and a dual function in government. First, IGs derive their legitimacy from Congress (through statute and through Senate confirmation) and from the executive (through presidential appointment). As presidential appointees, individual IGs rely on the executive for their survival and have incentives not to interfere with the president's agenda. However, the parent of the broader IG institution—the source of its mandate and the audience of its semiannual reports—remains Congress, a distinct source of pressure. Second, IGs are firmly located within the executive branch but are at the same time a creature of Congress, its eyes and ears within the executive bureaucracy. This position straddling two governmental branches establishes a dual set of incentives: on the one hand, the more waste, fraud, and mismanagement that IGs uncover, the more they are rewarded, and failure in this area will result in penalties or firing, but on the other hand, IGs must be heedful of the preferences of the executive because the president can remove IGs without cause.

Third, IGs have multiple, competing audiences whose relative importance shifts over time. Both Congress and agency heads receive the IGs' semiannual and special reports, but the IGs also serve as the president's police officers, keeping the bureaucracy in line; they use the media to give visibility to their reports and are used in turn by the media as sources of internal information; and finally, they have at times been "parented" by the Office of Management and Budget, which determines their levels of personnel and resources. The IG position is a fusion of two main distinct functions: an audit function and an investigative function. These two functions entail different bureaucratic orientations and cultures, and they focus on different types of problems. The language and bureaucratic cultures of each function differ, and the relative strength of each within an individual OIG makes a difference in that office's activity. The audit and investigative functions gradually expanded to include inspection and evaluation functions, but their relationship within each office has remained vexed. Because each function involves different methodologies and starting assumptions, IGs define problems differently and thus pursue different sorts of issues. Because it is the way that issues are defined that determines the types of solutions that are appropriate to correct them, the framing of each issue will determine what kind of accountability is effected by a given review.

IGs navigate these ambiguities through discursive interaction among actors—IGs, members of Congress, and groups in civil society—and continuously reforge the meaning of accountability. Although the term "discourse" has been tainted, from the perspective of some political scientists, by its association with postmodern literary theory, it has enjoyed recent attention as a result of the renewed interest in the explanatory power of ideas in institutional change. Vivien Schmidt, situating her work in the institutionalist tradition, has rescued the term and offered a framework, discursive institutionalism, in which discourse—understood as the representation of ideas and the interactive, dynamic process of coordination and communication—takes on causal and explanatory power.[27] In this framework, ideas, which operate at different levels of generality and are of different types, are the primary drivers of institutional change, and they do so thanks to interaction among policy makers and between policy makers and the wider public.

From this perspective, individual IGs, together with Congress and groups in civil society, generate, deliberate over, and legitimate specific conceptions of what a government bureaucracy should do and how it should behave. The range of potentially contradictory expectations and normative standards that IGs may privilege manifest themselves in the framing of problems and their solutions.[28] IGs also vary in their self-conceptions as well as in their views of what constitutes the appropriate object of an OIG's investigations and audits.

These ambiguities have permitted individual IGs ample latitude in how they interpret their role, and this has led not only to the variation in IG performance and impact, but also, mediated through organizational capacities, the extension from an early, limited focus on compliance monitoring to more consequential institutional strategies and a deeper effect on democratic processes.

Some Propositions Regarding IG Contributions to Democratic Practice

Above, I have outlined potential ways that IGs might affect democratic processes; however, considerable variation exists among IGs (and OIGs) in the way and the degree to which this occurs. The ambiguity of the IGs' mandate in its original formulation, coupled with multiple administrative reforms and individual latitude in interpretation, has given rise to an assortment of democratic values toward which IGs can direct their institutional strategies and correlate contributions to democratic integrity. This diversity goes to the heart of the administrative-democratic tension. I offer three propositions to explain the variation in the IGs' effects.

P1 (heightened effects)—Some IGs have transcended their structural bias toward compliance monitoring and have intensified the effect they have on democratic integrity and legitimacy.

The opposite proposition—that IGs continue to limit their scope to compliance monitoring and that IGs are a form of bureaupathology with negative effects on administrative efficiency and democratic integrity—dominated the scholarly literature surveyed above, and the burden of proof to demonstrate the IGs' consequence remains. My proposition suggests that contrary to earlier assessments, some IGs build organizational infrastructure, target the administrative legal structure, and, in expanding the purview of their values, protect democratic values previously unaffected by IG work. If this is true, evidence that IGs have pursued other modes of democratic practice begs the question of how IGs have expanded the scope of their work. Hence I offer the following two further propositions.

P2 (value variation)—Personal background and professional experience affect which modes of democracy IGs practice.

Legal backgrounds dispose IGs toward legal and constitutional concerns, while financial, auditing, and management backgrounds encourage attention to the efficiency and performance of a department, and diplomatic training inclines IGs toward the internal management of scandal. IGs with legal backgrounds tend to be sensitive to legal nuances and to the political and constitutional questions that arise in jurisdictional battles and in occurrences of moral wrongdoing. The skills some IGs develop as auditors give them knowledge of financial management and of ways to maximize the ratio of outputs to inputs (in profit or service provision). Finally, IGs with experience in diplomacy are alert to the effects of political scandal on bureaucratic reputation and performance and will concentrate their efforts on this type of mismanagement.

P3 (strategy variation)—The material resources of an OIG, the professional background of its IG, and independence influence institutional strategy.

Without sufficient resources, IGs cannot conduct audits and investigations with the depth and rigor needed to check anything beyond compliance with existing regulations, nor can IGs devote the time and staff necessary to design capacity-building or performance-enhancing reforms. Similarly, without independence, IGs are left hamstrung in their ability to conduct reviews that challenge the department head. Whether they are hampered by budget or staff limitations, lack of relevant experience, departmental interference, or by their own political ties to an administration, IGs who lack independence rarely risk more intensive forms of IG work, such as building legal and institutional infrastructure. The institutional strategy adopted by an IG strongly influences the intensity of its effects: targeting the infrastructure of accountability has a much wider-ranging effect on democracy than solely targeting administrative procedure and management practices; it requires sufficient material resources and the independence to pursue reviews without political or administrative pressure.

I evaluate these three propositions at the core of the book by assessing the outcomes of individual reviews, viewed in the context of the history, culture, and resources of the OIG. I then relate these conclusions to the broader question of the IGs' effects on democratic integrity, legitimacy, and practice—and ultimately on the way the IGs are forging a new democratic form through modes of monitory democratic practice.

Research Design

To understand the differential effects that IGs have on democratic practice and the distinct contributions they have made to a monitory form of democracy, I focus on the microfoundations of institutional growth and on their institutional links with other actors in forging administrative accountability. The puzzle of the IGs' uneven growth requires attention to traditional bureaucratic capacities and leadership on the one hand, and attention to the effects of the reviews themselves on the other—that is, attention to the various types of accountability and their effects on broader democratic processes. My analysis will operate on two levels. The first-order analysis consists of a concrete examination of individual IG projects using measures appropriate to the nature of IG recommendations, such as standards and institutional innovations. The second-order appraisal evaluates how these projects, taken together, contribute to distinct modes of democratic practice, thus addressing the question of how administration and democracy interact. I use a comparative-historical approach to explain how new modes of democratic practice have emerged from IG discontent.[29] This approach relies on a variety of methods to analyze processes across cases and within them over time: comparative narratives through process tracing, statistics, and legal analysis.

My goal is neither to test nor to build a comprehensive theory of a systematic mechanism. Rather, it is to explain a particular historical outcome, a single-outcome study: the success and differential development of a monitory body in forging different modes of democratic practice.[30] This involves concept clarification about new democratic forms and descriptive inference about a particular unit (the category of a neutral, independent bureaucratic office). In an initial overview of the IG category, I set out the legislative and political history of the contemporary IG community and highlight certain pressures that have transformed it. I then offer three cases, divided into two chapters each. In the first chapter of each case, I establish the bureaucratic context—the resources, internal structures, personalities, and political dynamics of each OIG over time—and provide a narrative of the political history of each individual OIG. In the second chapter, I provide an analysis of significant OIG initiatives (their immediate and long-term effects) and follow their historical implementation and use by other actors. I then use the cases to theorize more broadly about the effects that each OIG has had on democratic practice.

In selecting the departments to follow, I chose to limit the universe of possible cases to presidentially appointed, Senate-confirmed IGs in order to avoid structural variation in the level of independence (i.e., the statutory elements of independence such as role in the budget process or appointment by the president) and to standardize the statutory framework. Because the impetus to the "imperial bureaucracy"—that is, a proliferating, unaccountable bureaucratic apparatus—lies both in emergency politics and in the broader growth of the administrative state, I chose departments that have dealt with the effects of "emergency governance" (i.e., the national security state).[31] The departments of Justice, Homeland Security, and State were selected because of their dual role both in national security programs and in domestic administration. This choice permits a greater appreciation of the IGs' potential to monitor a range of problems, including rights violations.

To highlight the variation in IG work, I selected two successful cases (i.e., OIGs that produced consequential reviews with positive effects on democratic integrity and practice) and one unsuccessful case (i.e., an OIG whose reviews provided limited accountability).[32] Through a thorough preliminary investigation of the existing literature on IG performance, interviews, and familiarity with many individual reviews, I can place the chosen cases into a wider context that permits a consideration of the successful and unsuccessful cases. Moreover, the inherent diversity between OIGs—their institutional variation—also considerably mitigates this problem: a frequent comment within the IG community is, "Once you've met one IG, you've met one IG."[33] This observation underscores the variation in size, organization, purpose, and orientation of each OIG—even those operating within the same legal framework. From a methodological perspective, this choice maximizes the variation between cases and diminishes the severity of the charge of selection bias.

An organization premised on the development of special competencies and the recruitment of specific expertise led two OIGs—DOJ and DHS—to hold the executive branch to account by providing narratives to the wider public and Congress through frequent and consequential reviews of executive action over time. The capacity to hold the executive to account on display in the Justice and Homeland Security OIGs was not peculiar to these departments but was nonetheless far from the rule across federal OIGs. A third office, the Department of State, struggled to build office capacity and has issued few reviews of consequence. Common to Justice and Homeland Security but absent in State were long-term leaders who cultivated a specialized competency that focused material resources and expertise on a distinctive mission. In contrast, the State Department was plagued with long absences in the IG position and manifested the traditional split between the two IG competencies of auditing and investigating that precludes internal cohesion.

The success of Justice and DHS in issuing consequential reviews is also striking because of the institutional differences that existed between them. Whereas many of the DOJ IG's consequential reviews were primarily special investigations conducted by investigative lawyers, the DHS IG relied more often on its audit function to rein in administrative discretion. The precondition for this accountability was a specific analytic capacity, peculiar to each, and cultivated by individual IGs. In the State Department, there was no institutional framework that privileged expertise; nor was there an attempt to promote joint reviews that equivalently conjoined the audit and investigative functions. Indeed, in-house inspectors with little relevant expertise or experience were often privileged over more experienced personnel. Their reviews failed to create lasting state-building changes and accountability. However, the two successful cases differed in the type of accountability they brought to their host agencies. The institutional differences between DOJ and DHS were underpinned by different modes of democratic practice. Moreover, differences in the professional and political backgrounds of the IGs led them to follow different institutional strategies in pursuing accountability. In each of the successful cases, the IGs consistently delivered reviews with far-reaching consequences for the scope of government action, civil rights, performance, and law. But whereas many Justice Department reviews demonstrated a concern for constitutional and legal principles, the DHS reviews operated according to efficiency- and performance-based conceptions of accountability. The State Department reviews were limited to compliance and procedural accountability, and were often mired in political scandal. Each of the three cases thus manifested characteristics of a distinct mode of democratic practice: Justice contributed to a constitutional democracy; Homeland Security to a managerial democracy; and State, with little success, to a political democracy. The success of each OIG in practicing each mode of democracy, conditioned by a particular understanding of accountability, depended crucially on the types of capacity that each OIG had—the skills and expertise within the office—and the vision of the individual IGs.

In selecting individual reviews and projects from the hundreds produced by each OIG each year, I chose the most effective and largest reviews (in terms of length of investigation and cost) over time. This selection process was more problematic than the selection of OIGs because of the hundreds of reviews available and the difficulty of comparing them. The cases under review varied widely in size, nature, and severity. Individual reviews were chosen on the basis of the input of multiple OIG staff members and on the basis of the kinds of media attention to the events under review. Accordingly, the individual reviews cannot be taken to be representative of all reviews of a particular OIG; they can only be taken as illustrative of some OIG work.

I triangulated four major sources of data for this analysis: public records (including congressional debates and hearings, bureaucratic memos and letters, IG statistics, and policy reports); elite interviews; media, civil society, and academic reports on the IGs and their reviews; and secondary literature. The lack of secondary source materials proved challenging because no established administrative or political history exists of the IGs as a community or of individual OIGs. (There is one exception to this: the memoir of former IG Clark Ervin provides a single-perspective narrative account of some events in question.) The construction of the narrative was thus entirely novel and was based on primary source materials, interviews, and press accounts. To supplement the limited archival access and scant secondary material, I relied heavily on official IG documents in the public domain, the IG reviews themselves, interviews, and press accounts.[34]

CHAPTER THREE

AN INSPECTOR CALLS (WITH APOLOGIES TO J. B. PRIESTLEY)

The Inspector General Category

The Inspector General must have a horse allowed him and some soldiers to attend him and all the rest commanded to obey and assist, or else the service will suffer; for he is but one man and must correct many, and therefore he cannot be beloved. And he must ride from one garrison to another to see the soldiers do not outrage or scathe the country.

—*English Codes of Military and Martial Laws* (1629)

Introduction

The simple military model of the inspector general illustrated in the *English Codes of Military and Martial Laws* offers a glimpse into a predemocratic mode of accountability. The passage describes the inspector's resources, his authority, the organizational structure in which he operates, and his duties. It also articulates his role to protect the state from the very people who work for it and in its name. Roughly a century earlier, Machiavelli offered the first modern articulation of raison d'état, the legitimating principle that the preservation of the state trumps rival political values.[1] The prince must be willing to forego love in order to maintain the state (and therefore to acquire glory). Like the prince, the early military IG risks his authority when he allows himself to be loved, thus threatening the military and political order. However, the contemporary IG has acquired the congenial vestments of a management consultant rather than those of a reproachful police officer. Although in many ways unrecognizable from its early modern ancestor, the contemporary IG has now resurrected the security function from which it originated, albeit in a radically new form: an extraparliamentary, monitory body that ensures both the state's security and rights-granting functions, and one that legitimates the state's decisions. In this chapter, I provide an introduction to the contemporary IG model and trace an unlikely trajectory from its midcentury bureaucratic role to being an instrument of emergency governance in a twenty-first-century articulation of raison d'état.

The State of the IGs

Across the board, IGs' performances have been by many measures successful. Statistics for 2014 show that IGs' work resulted in $46.5 billion in potential savings and reported over 5,895 successful prosecutions, 1,827 civil actions, and 5,195 suspensions or debarments.[2] By their own account, as a community, the IGs produce an $18 return for every dollar of taxpayer investment in them.[3] But beyond the dollars saved, their growing capacity has led IGs to review other forms of administrative discretion, such as assertions of executive privilege and curtailments of civil rights and liberties. While some IGs serve agencies that manage large programmatic budgets, and thus are more vulnerable to fraud and waste, others, such as the national security IGs, monitor departments whose primary vulnerabilities to wrongdoing lie in their management of potentially rights-threatening activities. In the national security agencies, they have provided transparency, probed areas of limited or underspecified legal protection, and used their expertise to frame policy recommendations. These objectives provide a focus beyond the general standards of bureaucratic oversight (i.e., fraud and waste) and give IGs the authority to reshape policy and, indirectly, law.

IGs are growing in number as well (Figure 3.1). Their expansion in numbers must be taken in the historical context of an expanding federal government, which has steadily added both height and girth to its once modest ranks. Vertically, Paul Light notes that seventeen executive titles were available in federal departments in 1960; by 2004, this number was sixty-four. Horizontally, the senior titleholders jumped from 451 in 1960 to 2,592 in 2004.[4] The IGs have played no small role in this expansion. Finally, IGs have grown in reputation and visibility. Figure 3.2 provides a base indication of the degree to which the inspector general concept has grown in visibility and in public discourse. Visibility should not be confused with influence, and visibility does not always assist IGs; part of their legitimacy rests on the neutrality that comes from their relative anonymity, as well as the absence of any promise of personal recognition resulting from IG work. (This leads many in the IG community to look askance at postreview, tell-all memoirs.) However, IG reviews cited or discussed in the press often come to the attention of members of Congress with more fanfare and urgency that topics merely covered in the routine semiannual reports that are sent directly to Congress.

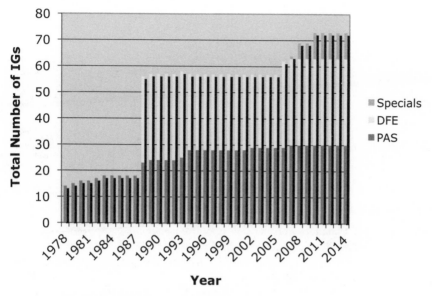

Figure 3.1. Growth of US Federal IGs by Type, 1978–2014

The visibility statistics demonstrate that media sources are aware of the IGs' work and use it as a legitimate source of data. Unless themselves embroiled in scandal, IGs are rarely the direct subject of media reporting. Rather, many references to IG work in mainstream media make no judgment about the accuracy of an IG's findings and cite the reviews as though the IG's narrative were fact. When an IG's findings are contested, media articles frequently frame the story as a battle between two narratives competing for truth or legitimacy, at times even suggesting that the burden of proof rests on the accused bureaucrats for offering a narrative at odds with that of the IG. The visibility statistics thus suggest a widespread public perception of IGs as neutral, authoritative narrators of government behavior.

Inspector General Category

After its statutory formation in 1978, the history of the IG community unfolded in three waves: the first, experimental decade, in which it rose to prominence, but soon stumbled with institutional hiccups and political challenges; its subsequent neoliberal reorientation and redefinition in the 1990s; and finally, after 9/11, its entry into an age of collaboration and its development into a web, using a distinct model of collaborative OIG: the emergency event-based, special IG. The international influence of recent

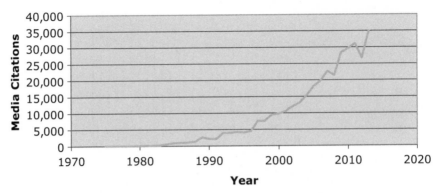

Figure 3.2. Media Citations in American News Outlets for "Inspector General,"
1975–2013. *Source:* Factiva. A Factiva search for the phrase "inspector general"
was conducted to determine its frequency in media reports and US government
documents between 1975 and 2013. Because the acronym "IG" is commonly used,
this chart likely suffers from a Type II statistical error (underrepresenting the
frequency of the concept in the news media). However, because the acronym "IG"
could have a number of meanings (and thus appear in articles unrelated to inspectors
general), I erred on the side of conservatism and limited the search to the full phrase.
It was also restricted to American news sources: all non-American sources with
more than 2,000 hits were excluded from the sample. The top sources (all with more
than 2,000 hits over this period) were: Associated Press; Fed News; *Washington Post*;
BBC—all sources; Targeted News Service; Dow Jones Newswires; *New York Times*—
all sources; congressional documents; Reuters—all sources; *Wall Street Journal*;
Agence France-Presse—all sources; *Federal Register*; CNN—all sources; PR Newswire;
Department of Justice documents; *Times-Picayune*; Platts—all sources; *NewsRx
Medical Newsletter*; *Aviation Week*—all sources; *Boston Globe*—all sources; *Tampa
Bay Times*; *Business Recorder*; *St. Louis Post-Dispatch*; *National Journal*—all sources;
LegAlert; and M2 Presswire—all sources.

public management theories, coupled with a post–Cold War tendency
toward emergency governance, has pushed the IGs' trajectory since the
early 1990s, paradoxically giving a highly neoliberal inflection to the early
modern security impulse underlying the raison d'état. I trace the history
of the IG model along two axes: first, bureaucratic and political identity,
from policing to management consultancy; and second, organization, from
fixtures in permanent bureaucracies to event-specific, time-limited entities,
based more closely on a logic of crisis than of routine bureaucratic oversight. This trajectory was shaped partly by the Reinventing Government
reforms of the 1990s and exhibits the institutional hallmarks of neoliberal

principles (inter alia, privatization, contracting, reorganized incentive structures, and lines of accountability).

Conceptual Origins

Though its roots lie in military regulation, with the first IG appointed by George Washington in response to unethical behavior by a general in the Continental Army, in its twentieth-century incarnation, the IG developed initially as a response to a Congress overwhelmed by its accounting and auditing role in the quotidian workings of government.[5] The Budget and Accounting Act of 1921 established the budget system, removed the accounting and audit function from the executive branch, and placed it within Congress's remit. Between the passage of the original Budget Act and its 1950 amendment, the staff of the Government Accounting Office (GAO) peaked at nearly 15,000, replicating the Treasury's own accounting function. The inefficient system also had the significant limitation that the audit and accounting functions were performed by the same entity, thus failing to provide a crucial check on accounting practices.[6]

Split between the need for information about the executive branch for oversight purposes and the overwhelming workload of accounting, Congress sought a mechanism within the executive branch for extracting information. Although the genesis of the move is hazy (as reflected in legislative reports), in 1959 Congress established an "inspector general and comptroller" for foreign assistance, housed in the International Cooperation Administration of the State Department and appointed by the secretary of state, in the Mutual Security Act amendments of 1959.[7] These amendments granted the IG access to any information that it needed to carry out its accounting and auditing function, but the means of that access remained underspecified. The crucial capacity on which these amendments hinged was the IG's access to information with which to report to Congress, and the multiple goals pursued by the framers of the bill would provide the interpretive latitude for the IGs later to expand their activities.

The Inspector General Act of 1978 and the First
IG Classes

In 1977, the House Government Operations Committee commissioned research to deal with the overall phenomenon of government fraud and waste. The commission reacted to the perceived lack of leadership, indepen-

dence, and effective channels of communication with Congress and proposed combining the audit and investigative functions of each department
under an IG.[8] Before the IG Act's passage, the executive branch strongly
opposed the creation of a set of statutory IGs that reported independently to
Congress.[9] On the grounds of the separation of powers and executive privilege, the Office of Legal Counsel (OLC) argued that the president reserved
the right to decide when and how executive employees could report to Congress.[10] Although the House bill had originally granted IGs the authority to
report "particularly serious or flagrant concerns" directly to Congress without the approval of the agency head, the Senate version took into account
the administration's protests by making agency heads provide consent and
giving them the authority to edit the reports before submitting them to oversight committees.[11]

Despite some concerns that the IG Act would be unconstitutional, the act
passed on October 12, 1978, and established a system of twelve IGs based
on the model of the Department of Health, Education, and Welfare IG.[12]
The act was part of a package of post-Watergate reforms aimed at curbing
executive overreach and improving accountability. Alongside the Civil Service Reform Act and the Ethics and Government Act (which established the
Office of Government Ethics), the act established the Office of the Inspector
General and created twelve statutory IGs for executive departments.[13] Significantly, the IG Act of 1978 did not include any IG from a national security-
related department or agency. It was both department based and excluded
from the realm of emergency.

IGs were beholden to both branches through exhaustive reporting
requirements in the form of semiannual reports to Congress and to agency
heads; IGs could make use of a variety of provisions to balance their competing allegiances to each branch, such as a strict seven-day window in
which to report to Congress special abuses discovered within the agency.
Their independence was supported by a presidential appointment and Senate confirmation, as well as by the statutory requirement that they be chosen
"without regard to political affiliation and solely on the basis of integrity
and demonstrated ability."[14] These provisions distinguished IGs from
other presidential appointees because the incentives for accepting a usual
appointment—for instance, policy-making authority and the advantages of
political affiliation—do not apply.

Although it met with indifferent reception, the institutional reorganization and authority granted to the IG was significant. The act combined audit
and investigative functions; it insulated the new position from administra-

tive politics through the condition that appointees be selected regardless of political affiliation and through a dual reporting requirement to Congress and agency (department) heads (including both regular and special reports); and by granting IGs access to all documents and information necessary to complete investigations.[15] Famously described by one former IG as "straddling the barbed wire fence," the position required the IG to split loyalty between Congress and its agency or department.[16] "The Hill is always thinking we can go to our agencies, [and] our agencies always think we're finking to the Hill," said IG Sherman Funk.[17] IGs were given functional independence within the executive branch and additional responsibility to Congress in the form of semiannual reports. Finally, they were invested with investigative power: they could issue subpoenas and initiate proceedings in the Justice Department.

Controversially, in 1981, President Reagan summarily ejected all of the incumbent IGs from their positions—a move that was quickly investigated and condemned by the Committee on Government Operations. This controversial decision was meant to give the appearance that Reagan was committed to building a strong corps of IGs and to "weed[ing] out" some of Carter's alleged political appointments.[18] Later that year, with EO 12301, Reagan instituted the President's Council on Integrity and Efficiency (PCIE), a professional standards board for the IG community that brought IGs together with members of the Office of Management and Budget.[19] It served as "a kind of executive branch trade union," and its aims were to bolster further coordination and to develop common standards for the oversight of government departments.[20]

In their first decade, especially after the first three rocky years, the IGs knew they could follow a clear script to win the resources they needed: hit the numbers in the war on waste through rigorous compliance monitoring.[21] The majority of them quickly set up shop, organized their offices, and developed strong relationships with Congress and the Office of Management and Budget. But the mounting excitement surrounding the IGs' potential would come to a close with a major reform to the act in 1988. Ten years after its passage, the 1978 act received an update that expanded reporting requirements for IGs. The 1988 amendment also created a set of thirty-three DFE IGs, nondepartmental entities, and thus vastly expanded the size of the IG community. (DFEs were regulatory agencies of the federal government whose budgets were over $100 million annually in federal funds.[22]) Unlike the "establishment" IGs, DFE IG appointments were not political; instead, IGs were selected by agency heads. The act also added three "establishment" IGs: to the Federal Emergency Management Agency (FEMA), the DOJ, and the Treasury. (The Department of Defense [DOD] had been added in 1981 and the State Department in 1985.) Two years later, President George H. W. Bush added a body parallel to the PCIE for the DFEs, the Executive Council on Integrity and Efficiency (ECIE).

The Neoliberal Reinvention (1993–2001): From Policing to Management Consultancy

In the early 1990s, the newly expanded IG community found itself adrift. In 1993, both Congress and the White House, through the Government Performance and Results Act and the NPR, respectively, promoted a shift from procedural accountability (compliance monitoring) to performance-based evaluation. But the shift was not clear-cut, and IGs expressed concern over the ambiguity of their roles.[23] The NPR also "broaden[ed] the focus of the inspectors general from strict compliance auditing to evaluating management control systems."[24] The PCIE and ECIE responded to the NPR and to the developing field of IG activity by crafting a set of revised principles as the basis for a proactive, rather than a limited and reactive strategy, which privileged "a more consultative approach" between the main actors.[25] The report suggested a ready new identity for the IG community as management consultants, substituting for the less appreciated police function hitherto associated with IG inspections. But the NPR also provided fodder for dramatic transformations to the IG model's organization. It encouraged a movement from a hierarchical to a network-based management structure, a shift that would be a precondition for the appearance of temporary event-based IGs a decade later.

Though the NPR presented IGs in a dubious light, suggesting that their work more often stymied innovation than improved efficiency, DOD IG Eleanor Hill would later suggest that NPR's criticism had a transformative effect on the IG community, forcing it to reckon with its role and to seek a greater balance between strict rule enforcement and constructive criticism akin to consulting.[26] In short, the NPR's analysis promoted the capacity building and performance accounting whose absence earlier observers had lamented. Gore's report specifically addressed the role of the IGs and recast their relationship to their host agencies as one of service provider to client; the report envisaged the citizen groups with stakes in each agency as "customers" (with "customer" notably replacing "citizen").[27] In the government as a whole, the NPR pushed for an elimination of traditional bureaucratic hierarchies in favor of an entrepreneurial "committee approach," in which the lines of accountability would become diffuse.[28]

This neoliberal paradigm shift, according to its critics, had the potential to make the classic conception of public accountability evaporate. Although one of the goals of many NPM-style reforms (of which the Reinventing Government movement was one) was to increase accountability, in practice, it made accountability relations more nebulous by diffusing responsibility among many actors, especially by making bureaucrats responsible both to politicians and to their "customers."[29] Paradoxically, the drive to promote horizontal accountability within the bureaucracy might enhance an agency's capacity to learn and increase efficiency, but not necessarily permit greater democratic control. As one critic articulated the problem, "Efficiency is no guarantor of good political and social judgment, which is essential in securing genuine political accountability and legitimacy in a democracy."[30] The mistake of NPM-style reforms, in this view, is to elide the distinction between private and public accountability. Whereas the former aims to maximize profit, the latter aims to preserve public values such as representation, participation, equality, fairness, impartiality, and justice—in short, the values of democracy. The administrative-democratic tension reared its head once again.

In addition to altering the IGs' identity, the reforms also affected their tools and the shape of their organization. The downsizing associated with these reforms trimmed an entire layer of administrators (midlevel managers), and this handed communication responsibilities to higher administrators who lacked coordination experience and expertise.[31] IGs struggled to adapt to this change not only in their own offices but also in the offices they oversaw. The pressure to privatize challenged the IGs' tools because their access to information outside of the public sphere is sharply delimited. Finally, the reforms radically affected the distribution of expertise in the public and private spheres—and even the very conception of expertise. Public sector workers, who had once held a substantive expertise (for instance, about education or health care), began to cede authority to private sector experts despite their lack of institutional knowledge. Privileged instead in government agencies was the procedural expertise of a contract manager.

Whereas IGs would have in theory been the front line of (traditional) accountability holding, their new role as management experts elided the idea of holding actors to account for wrongdoing and reframed the concept in economic terms. However, like other NPM-inspired reforms in the international arena, the NPR did not have the wide-ranging, transformative effects to which it aspired, and the IGs did not (entirely) abandon their role in compliance monitoring.[32] In its 1995 annual report, the PCIE/ECIE "emphasize[d] two principal themes: how the IGs serve as 'agents of positive change' and how they make effective use of 'multidisciplinary teams,'" and proclaimed that "these efforts demonstrate how the IGs are not merely riding the train of the Reinventing Government movement, but are also helping to stoke the engine. At the same time, the IGs remain vigilant in fulfilling their statutory mandate to prevent and detect fraud, waste, and abuse."[33] Despite its potential to muddle the lines of accountability and ultimately compromise democratic legitimacy, this new form of straddling—or ambiguity of mission—was to provide the opportunity for different actors to widen the IG model in ways that enhanced its potential to protect rights and democratic integrity.

In the 1990s, the community as a whole suffered from the general climate of government downsizing and budget cuts. The added responsibility of the Chief Financial Officer Act, along with the IGs' informal aid in carrying out the performance measurement of the Government Performance and Results Act, meant that IG capacity and independence came under threat. Between 1992 and 1996, 65 percent of presidentially appointed, Senate-confirmed OIGs lost staff, and 39 percent operated with a reduced budget. Over 61 percent of the entire community rated a "lack of resources/ staff" as the most important challenge facing their respective offices.[34]

The IGs' budding role in national security monitoring also provoked new challenges. A 1998 amendment, known as the Intelligence Community Whistleblower Act of 1998, instituted the inspectors general as the compromise between a recalcitrant administration and a Congress eager to curb problems within the intelligence community.[35] The debate was merely a reworking of the question of balance between secrecy and transparency, but the Senate bill ultimately reaffirmed the arrangement reached in the IG Act of 1978: a system of "complex and longstanding accommodations between the legislative and executive branches," in which Congress reacts to informally reported violations through budgetary reprisals.[36] The act stipulates that whistle-blowers must receive permission from their agency head before submitting complaints to congressional committees, and they are not necessarily guaranteed protection from retaliation.[37] The act did, however, make the pathway for whistle-blowers clearer by permitting, but delimiting, their access to Congress through the intelligence committees. Finally, the Reports Consolidation Act of 2000 introduced a statutory requirement for each IG to provide an annual list of its department's top management and performance challenges, with an analysis of the department's success in resolving them.[38]

As IG powers grew, the national security agencies lagged in their willingness to be placed under such constraints for fear of compromised security. By the end of the Reagan administration, however, all of the related departments (Justice, CIA, State, Treasury, Defense, and the National Security Agency [NSA]) had an office of inspector general. The IGs' role was decisively amended in the aftermath of 9/11. The first change was that rights monitoring became an integral component of national security IGs' role. The Patriot Act established a new position within the Justice IG's office and in the new DHS specifically to oversee violations of rights and liberties.[39] These positions were independent of, but coordinated with, the offices for civil rights within their respective departments.

The second development was that the IGs' authority was clarified, formalizing an ambiguous authority that IGs had developed over time. Although the matter had been on the congressional agenda for some time, the Homeland Security Act of 2002 amended the IG Act to grant most establishment OIG special agents full law enforcement authority. This included the capacity "to make an arrest without warrant while engaged in official duties, and execute warrants for arrest, search of premises, or seizure of evidence upon probable cause to believe that a violation has been committed."[40] This capacity had previously only been given explicitly and permanently to four OIGs. However, the ability of any IG to "access" such authority was not novel:

> As the role of the Inspector General has evolved, the need for such appointments became so consistent, and the volume of the requests so large, that "blanket" deputations evolved. Since 1995, virtually all criminal investigators in the offices of the twenty-three covered Inspectors General have exercised law enforcement authorities in cases under office-wide deputations. Thus, the grant of statutory law enforcement authority would not extend new authorities to IG personnel, but would merely recognize the authorities that are already in place.[41]

If the practice was already standard, then the new statutory basis lent the IGs' work legitimacy. Since 9/11, Congress has capitalized on the IGs' law enforcement power, directing them to investigate specific programs in the war on terror, including assessing many of the Federal Bureau of Investigation's (FBI) investigative tools, President Bush's warrantless surveillance program, and surveillance policies on US citizens.

The 2000s: The Age of Collaboration and the
Emergency, Event-Specific IG Model

In the first decade of the twenty-first century, the United States experienced a series of emergencies, beginning with 9/11 and the subsequent wars in Iraq and Afghanistan, then hurricanes Katrina, Rita, and Wilma, and finally the economic recession of 2008. Emergencies demand an immediate but often temporary mobilization of resources to manage them. The exigencies of these multiple emergencies in the 2000s had a profound effect on the way that the IG community structured its approach to accountability. The first change was a shift in the organizational model and coordination of the IGs; the second was substantive, introducing an explicit focus on rights (and national security) that complemented—or countered—the neoliberal turn of the 1990s.

From its inception, the IG community occasionally pooled resources to conduct joint reviews that crossed into multiple IGs' jurisdiction. According to one 1995 PCIE report, "On average, in FY 1995, OIGs conducted fewer than 7 percent of their investigations with other OIGs and more than 19 percent with non-OIG investigative agencies."[42] By 2000, all of the PCIE OIGs had conducted at least one investigation with another non-OIG investigative unit, with some OIGs collaborating as much as 60 percent of the time (Housing and Urban Development); 42 percent (Labor); 36 percent (Defense); 32 percent (State); and 24 percent (Justice). In addition to these interagency investigations, the DOD OIG performed 19 percent of its investigations with another OIG; the Office of Personnel and Management, 55 percent; and National Aeronautics and Space Administration (NASA), 25 percent.[43] (In contrast, very few of the ECIE OIGs engaged in any joint reviews.) In 2004, the PCIE saw a jump in joint investigations, noting that of the twenty-five PCIE OIGs, "The highest portion of joint cases reported by an OIG was 74 percent . . . [which] indicate[s] a substantially higher level of joint case activity than in FY 2003."[44] Joint OIG investigations are a reaction to, and a mirror of, governance trends of service provision through integration and horizontal coordination, known internationally as "joined up governance" or "whole-of-government" approaches.[45]

While not a uniform trend upward in these years, the difference between these statistics and the figures for 1995 are striking. Further, in these years, at least one OIG reported that joint reviews comprised 74 percent (2004), 73 percent (2005), 61 percent (2006), and 96 percent (2007) of total reviews. (Since 2008, CIGIE has not published statistics on joint reviews.)

Table 3.1. Number of OIGs Conducting Joint Reviews

Year	<10 Percent of Total Reviews	10–50 Percent of Total Reviews	>50 Percent of Total Reviews
2004	7	14	4
2005	5	16	4
2006	8	16	2
2007	10	15	2

Source: PCIE Annual Reports FY 2005–2008.

The joint reviews are organized when assessing a program run by one department but funded by another (or jointly run by two agencies); when a review requires other federal law enforcement support; and when programs cross departmental boundaries (such as programs run in Iraq, which often require coordination between the departments of State, Homeland Security, and Defense). They often concern international trade (for example, helping multiple agencies coordinate trade promotion activities) and joint military–civilian programs (such as monitoring US controls on defense-related exports). However, domestically, they can assess activities such as collaborations between the Agriculture Department and the Environmental Protection Agency in implementing conservation practices.

Although the community had experimented with performing joint reviews in the 1990s (collaborations between two or three OIGs, or between one OIG and another government agency such as the FBI), the intentional model of joint, collaborative reviews took hold after 9/11 and was even formalized as a new type of self-contained OIG. After the terrorist attacks, not only did the community grow in numbers and responsibility (with a number of OIGs receiving explicit mandates to monitor potential civil rights and liberties abuses in addition to the usual fraud, waste, and abuse), but also Congress and the central IG coordinating bodies (PCIE and ECIE, and later CIGIE) began to promote an event-specific, collaborative model of OIG. These temporary IGs drew resources and expertise from multiple established offices with the purpose of monitoring specific, emergency-related recovery events, and they received their own budget from Congress. After the communitywide IG collaboration overseeing the 9/11 recovery process, Congress set up the Special Inspector General for Iraq Reconstruction (SIGIR) in 2004, as well as one for the oversight of Hurricane Katrina in 2005. Later it established both the Special Inspector General for Afghanistan (SIGAR) and SIGTARP (for the administration of the Troubled Asset Relief Program funds) in 2008.

The new model of special IGs has not replaced the permanent, agency-based system—indeed, that network has only grown in size, with sixteen IGs added between 2000 and 2014—but it has also made the IG a more adaptive instrument for government oversight, and thus an easier tool to which legislators can have recourse. The federal IG model even spread beyond the executive branch proper with the so-called legislative IGs: the GAO, US Capitol Police, Library of Congress, Architect of the Capitol, Government Printing Office, and US House of Representatives all received an IG during the 2000s. In 2006, the House Judiciary Committee approved a bill for the creation of an IG for the federal courts, though it never came to fruition.[46]

Because of its novelty, the emergency-event special IG model also begs the question of how and when it will be used. Some legislation has been drafted to authorize CIGIE to identify a lead IG, or contingency IG, when an emergency event reaches a certain financial threshold.[47] The special IG model contributes to the routinization of emergency as part of the administrative state's modus operandi, and the rules by which it comes into existence—financial limits—determine the state's own definition of emergency. Organizationally, special IGs share the temporary, specific focus of independent counsel (IC) investigations, a similar instrument of executive oversight that underpinned the investigations into the Iran-Contra, Whitewater, and Monica Lewinsky scandals. However, in contrast to the IC statute, special IGs have until now been used primarily in reaction to emergencies—larger, systemic crises stemming from unexpected, exogenous shocks rather than the scandals of particular public officials. Special IGs lose the advantage of permanent OIGs, which develop location-specific competences, and moreover must contend with the large amount of contracting used in emergency management—a factor that can limit IGs' legal access to documents, thus impeding thorough investigations.

Alongside these reforms internal to the IG community, a battle waged in Congress over which tools were needed by the IGs to both strengthen them and keep them in check. In response to the prodding of individual IGs and POGO, Representative Jim Cooper (D-TN), first introduced inspector general reform legislation in 2003.[48] Five years of debate led to the first comprehensive reform of the Act since the 1988 amendments. The 2008 IG Act largely shored up the statutory bases for IG independence by requiring an independent budget line for the OIG; requiring the administration to notify Congress thirty days before attempting to remove or transfer an IG; and reaffirming the requirement for IGs to be chosen on the basis of quali-

Table 3.2. Overview of Special OIGs

IG	Years in Operation	Associated OIGs	Budget History (in Millions)	Staff
SIGIR	2004–2013	State and Defense (reports directly to)	2006: $24 2007: NA 2008: $28.8 2009: $37.9 2010: $29.4 2011: $22.1 2012: $18.5	2006: NA 2007: 99 2008: 131 2009: 138 2010: 100 2011: 95 2012: 86
SIGAR	2008–present[a]	State, Defense, and USAID (reports directly to)	2009: $7 2010: $26.5 2011: $32.7 2012: $44.4 2013: $49.9 2014: $49.7	2009: 57 2010: 117 2011: 138 2012: 185 2013: 193 2014: 198
SIGTARP	2008–present[a]	Treasury, Federal Reserve, FDIC, SEC, Federal Housing Finance Agency, HUD, Tax Administration, GAO[b]	2009: $50 2010: $33.5 2011: $39.1 2012: $41.8 2013: $41.1 2014: $43.1	2009: 60 2010: 135 2011: 155 2012: 164 2013: 169 2014: 165

Sources: SIGAR Quarterly Reports to Congress FY 2009–2014; SIGIR Annual Budget, FY 2010–2012; SIGTARP Quarterly Reports to Congress FY 2009–2014. NA = not applicable.
[a]As of December 2015.
[b]Unlike SIGIR and SIGAR, the OIGs associated with SIGTARP do not provide direct supervision of the special IG, but they all form part of the TARP oversight council.

fications, without regard to political affiliation. The act passed after Republican reluctance regarding the potential seven-year term limit and stricter controls on the requirements for IG dismissal.[49] Its most significant provision was the inclusion of independent legal counsel for all IGs (particularly important, in the eyes of Congress, for the DOD IG).[50]

The second major effect of the 2008 act pertained to the reorganization of the IG ethics councils. The PCIE (for the major departmental IGs) and the ECIE (for the DFE IGs) were established by executive order in 1981.[51] These were consolidated into the Council of Inspectors General on Integrity and Efficiency (CIGIE). The aim of this reorganization, according to its mission statement, was to permit the IG community to "address . . . issues that transcend individual" agencies and departments.[52] CIGIE became the institutional backbone of the emerging IG model and the link between the branches that facilitated Congress's use of the special IG. It also began the process of standardizing the IG as a role—"building a profession," in the words of the head of the training institute—by establishing an institute for the training of IGs and dissemination of best practices.[53] The act also made provisions to extend some protections previously enjoyed only by establishment IGs to DFE IGs. This included codifying the nonpolitical nature of DFE IGs' appointments (previously stated only as an intent in the conference report of the IG Act amendments of 1988) and permitting them law enforcement authority (including the ability to make arrests without warrants).[54]

In addition to these amendments, the 2008 act supported the IG model's use as an instrument of emergency governance. It streamlined funding procedures and made them more transparent by requiring a separate and more detailed budget request for the IG; expanded its power of subpoena to electronic and tangible items; and granted explicit law enforcement authority.[55] However, President Bush's subsequent signing statement effectively nullified the budget provision, prompting an angry retort from the Senate Committee on Finance, signed by senators Grassley (R-IA), McCaskill (D-MO), Lieberman (I-CT), and Collins (R-ME). Section 8 of the act had required the president to "include a line item detailing the President's budget request for each IG, as well as the IG's budget request."[56] As they argued in their rebuttal letter, "Congress included Section 8 in the law to prevent the use of the budget process to inappropriately influence, marginalize, or prevent important investigations initiated by IGs."[57] Despite the signing statement, the overall effect of the 2008 Reform Act was to bolster IGs' independence.

The Dodd-Frank Wall Street Reform and Consumer Protection Act of 2010 also included a number of provisions to bolster DFE IGs' independence, including the requirement of a two-thirds majority vote for IG removal in DFEs, as well as the use of boards and commissions (rather than agency heads) to designate DFE IGs.[58] A GAO assessment a year later offered a positive review of the reforms' implementation and, similarly, of the reforms of the 2008 reform act.[59] The act also established a joint consortium of nine financial regulatory IGs, the Council of Inspectors General on Financial Oversight, to monitor the broader financial sector, thus spreading the model's remit into the realm of economic emergency.

The organizational shift toward event-specific monitoring mirrored a substantive shift in the IGs' focus. Though rights were not explicitly omitted from their job description, the original IG statutory framework did not lend itself to rights monitoring. Sensitive information and national security have always provided a rationale for exceptions to the IGs' authority, codified as "Section 8" exceptions: under Section 8 of the act, the heads of the Defense, Justice, Treasury, and Homeland Security departments may all suspend IG investigations in the name of national interest or of national security. Moreover, "sensitive information," which includes undercover operations; the identity of confidential sources; intelligence or counterintelligence matters; and "other matters the disclosure of which would constitute a serious threat to national security,"[60] are also exempted from the blanket requirement that "neither the head of the establishment nor the officer next in rank below such head shall prevent or prohibit the IG from initiating, carrying out, or completing any audit or investigation, or from issuing any subpoena during the course of any audit or investigation."[61] These statutory limitations on IGs' capacity to monitor rights violations and bureaucratic activity in the national security context are coupled with other factors. Budgetary control, dismissal procedures, the scope of the IG's jurisdiction (especially in rights monitoring), politicization, and inability to hold offenders to account all deter IGs from pursuing this type of abuse. IGs' independence can be curtailed through budget decisions that compromise their capacity to carry out investigations, and IGs have often cited budget constraints as a hindrance to their effective performance.[62] In addition, IGs face the possibility of presidential dismissal, and although the president must report the reason for dismissal to Congress within thirty days, this opens considerable scope for political interference (for instance, with President Obama's controversial dismissal of AmeriCorps IG Gerald Walpin, a Republican, in 2009 on dubious grounds of "loss of confidence").[63] In his first meeting with Secretary of State Jim Baker, Sherman Funk informed his new boss, "You can't fire me, only the President can."[64] According to Funk, "[Baker] looked startled, and I said, 'But don't get bent out of shape, all it takes is a phone call from you, I'm sure.' Then he smiled, and after that we had no problem."[65] This limitation is compounded by the working relationship between the IG and the agency (department) head.

Third, the fact that IGs focus on statutory concerns, leaving constitutionality to the courts, means that the attention they pay to certain types of abuses is limited. This state of affairs makes the IG in some ways a positive complement to the courts, but it also delimits the IGs' jurisdiction in a way that could miss rights violations.[66] In short, it is precisely the area in which IGs might function as a corrective to the courts' traditional deference to the executive—constitutionality—that lies outside of their jurisdiction.

The politicization of IG appointments, irrespective of the statutory prohibition of political appointments, has also plagued certain administrations. Although the Clinton administration largely selected career public servants as its IGs, 60 percent of George W. Bush's appointments had experience on a Republican staff, whereas only 20 percent had auditing experience.[67] Direct political interference also reared its head in the Bush administration, with Vice President Cheney's interference in the IG's office. The *New Yorker*'s Jane Meyer quoted one official as reporting that "the whole IG's Office was completely politicized" and cowed into bending to the vice president's wishes.[68]

The turn toward rights monitoring and national security was thus not an evident one, and it is one that demands explanation. After 9/11, the government's use of National Security Letters (NSLs), its immigrant detention policies, its coercive interrogations, and extraordinary renditions all received IG attention. Despite the executive branch's resistance to national security IGs, congressional pressure to monitor security agencies gradually made its mark, with qualifications. The DOD acquired an IG in 1982; State in 1986; Justice and Treasury in 1988; and the CIA in 1989. Since the time of the 1975 Rockefeller Report on the CHAOS program, in which the CIA spied on American citizens to monitor antiwar mobilization, Congress supported a strengthened internal IG in the CIA, but it was not until the aftermath of the Iran-Contra scandal in 1986 that Congress turned to an independent, statutory IG as a solution to abuse within the intelligence community.[69] With the passage of the Patriot Act, an IG was placed in the newly established DHS, and the IGs in both that department and in Justice acquired the responsibility of investigating abuses of civil rights and civil liberties above and beyond violations related to the Patriot Act itself.

One of the murkier objects of IG investigations occurs when technically legal or congressionally approved actions potentially violate basic rights. When legal provisions permit rights violations, such as detaining terrorist suspects or detaining immigrants past a statutory period, IGs have the authority to initiate reviews of government conduct and hold them to account on the basis of civil liberties, and thus challenge their legality. In the case of post-9/11 immigrant detentions, the DOJ IG initiated a review that ultimately contested and publicized the DOJ's detentions. Similarly, CIA IG John Helgerson contested the CIA's use of enhanced interrogation techniques even though OLC member John Yoo had declared these techniques legal.[70] Thus, although IGs have come under criticism for "address[ing] rule-based compliance without engaging broader conceptions of accountability," the IGs' expansion into the domain of rights monitoring has challenged this conception of IG performance.[71] In short, IGs have the potential to review government actions not only for their accordance with the letter of the law but also with their spirit.

In their role in the national security state, IGs negotiate the question of which powers the state should have, and through their reviews and inter-agency coordination, they develop standards for the regulation of these powers. By passing judgment on what counts as rights abuse, and by making recommendations on the basis of the standards they themselves have helped to develop, they exercise a kind of discretionary power that contributes directly to the codification and inscription of emergency measures into the rule of law.

IG reviews have complemented, and provided parallel paths for, congressional and executive oversight of national security, especially when the executive branch proves slow or incompliant during an executive–legislative standoff. For instance, in early 2014, a Senate Intelligence Committee's investigation into an allegedly illegal CIA program uncovered unconstitutional CIA interference into the congressional investigation itself. In a speech to the Senate, Senator Dianne Feinstein (D-CA) charged that the CIA effectively spied on Congress during the investigation, breaching the Fourth Amendment, the Computer Fraud and Abuse Act, and Executive Order 12333, which makes domestic surveillance by the CIA illegal.[72] Although the Senate investigation had been compromised by CIA interference, the IG was able to refer the matter to the Justice Department for potential criminal violation. The IG report, when released, would serve as the basis for arbitration between the two branches, a role based on a position of neutrality from which the Senate committee could not operate.

Within the security state, legislation has both supported and curtailed the IGs' independence and authority. National Security exemptions—Foreign Intelligence Surveillance Act (FISA) regulations in particular—have been a permanent battleground for IG authorities. Support for the 2008 FISA bill rested in part on the reassurance that IG oversight would prevent national security programs (notably the warrantless surveillance program) from violating civil liberties. However, critics argued that the IG framework (at the time) was insufficiently robust to provide effective oversight.[73] (Until 2014, the NSA IG was appointed by its own agency head [and was not statutorily independent]; Public Law 113-126 made this IG and the National Reconnaissance Office IG both presidential appointments.) The intelligence community IGs lacked the resources and authority to investigate these programs

Table 3.3. Academic and Professional Backgrounds of Selected National Security Inspectors General, 2014

Department or Agency	IG	Academic Background	Professional Background
Central Intelligence Agency (CIA)	David Buckley	Military	Air force investigator; Senate investigator; defense OIG; national security consultant (private sector)
Defense	Jon Rymer	Economics; business administration	IG (FDIC); private sector management; auditing; accounting
Homeland Security	John Roth	Law	AUSA (MI); federal investigator; attorney general's office
Intelligence Community	I. Charles McCullough III	Law	Special agent (FBI); senior counsel for law and intelligence (Treasury); NSA OIG
Justice	Michael Horowitz	Law	DOJ criminal division (various posts); deputy assistant attorney general; AUSA (Southern District of NY)
State	Steve Linick	Philosophy; law	AUSA (CA and VA); DOJ criminal division (various posts)

comprehensively, including subpoena power beyond their host department. Although the IGs of the intelligence community are required (per the 2008 FISA amendments) to submit comprehensive annual reviews on the implementation of FISA regulations, attempts by senators Rob Wyden (D-OR) and Mark Udall (D-CO) of the Senate Intelligence Committee, and later Patrick Leahy (D-VT) of the Judiciary Committee to mandate reviews of government surveillance programs all failed.[74]

Moreover, some institutional innovations linked to homeland security, such as fusion centers, evade clear lines of accountability and authority and fall outside the IGs' sphere of responsibility. Fusion centers, which channel counterterror information from multiple departments, agencies, local police, and the private sector, fall under the remit of no single IG. Individual IGs may be able to oversee limited components of fusion center work, but their investigative powers end at the boundaries of their own host departments. The use of special IGs might prove to be at least a partial corrective to this challenge.

IGs in the Overall Web of Accountability

Where do IGs fit in the broader federal system of accountability? The IGs have grown into their own coordinated web of accountability, but they work in tandem with other mechanisms of executive accountability. The GAO, congressional committees, ICs, and whistle-blowers often investigate or identify the same types of problems, and in relation to this constellation of monitors, the IGs are at times a complement and at times an overlap. It is useful to highlight the differences and overlaps between these various mechanisms of accountability to understand how they fit as part of a broader architecture of accountability.

The GAO, Congress's own accountability agency, and the IGs maintain a relationship that is at once conflictual and complementary, and their work as congressional watchdogs can overlap. Although the GAO's origins lie in financial oversight of the federal government, "primarily scrutiniz[ing] government vouchers and receipts," the scope of its current activities extends to performance audits, signaled by its name change from the Government Accounting Office to the Government Accountability Office in 2004.[75] (The name change, enacted through the GAO Human Capital Reform Act of 2004, was made by the GAO itself to better reflect its workload, only 15 percent of which comprised financial auditing.[76]) Though the GAO and the IGs frequently collaborate on oversight projects, they also offer each other regular criticism (accountability through "mutuality," or peer monitoring and evaluation). In practice, the GAO serves as one of the most consistent critical monitors of, and sources of accountability for, the IG community. However, the two bodies also provide complementary forms of executive oversight with slightly different foci. Whereas the GAO takes a broad view and tackles governmentwide problems, IGs target the problems specific to an agency or an event recovery. And in comparison to the IGs, the GAO's work is largely performance based and evaluates the utility of government programs—what works and what does not—rather than wrongdoing through individual instances of fraud and waste.[77] Though the IGs moved closer to performance monitoring in the 1990s, their reviews remain slanted toward compliance with regulations. Individual IGs also have more discretion to investigate problems as they arise, unlike GAO investigators, who rely on public laws or congressional committees to direct their work. And unlike the GAO, IGs are full members of the law enforcement community.

Congressional investigations have long been the most visible and aggressive of the legislative tools of oversight—more so than appropriations, authorizations, and confirmations.[78] In theory, there is the potential for considerable overlap between congressional and IG investigations, leading either to competition or to redundancy between the two efforts. In practice, however, congressional oversight committees use IGs as part of their investigative tool kit and regularly request reviews from IGs to complement their parallel investigations. IGs feature regularly as prominent witnesses in congressional hearings, thereby contributing their work to the broader oversight effort. However, in one crucial instance, IG reviews provide a clear advantage to their legislative counterparts: they have unfettered access to agency information and, with a few exceptions, can circumvent the executive secrecy privileges that can stymie congressional probing. IGs themselves have varying philosophies about how many and which congressional requests to accept. Some accept all requests; others choose according to visibility or size; one accepts all requests from the committee chair as a matter of course, strongly considers requests from the ranking member, and dismisses most others.[79] The two types of investigations can also vary in their intent: whereas IG investigations must be nonpartisan, congressional probes frequently suffer from deep partisan biases. Despite some overlap in function, they can be seen as complementary, mutually reinforcing instruments of oversight.

In a broader perspective, however, as early as the 1990s, IG investigations began to grow in prominence in relation to IC investigations authorized by the Ethics in Government Act (coeval with the original IG Act), slowly replacing them as a method of investigation. The Clinton years were punctuated with multiple special ICs to oversee the Whitewater and Monica Lewinsky scandals, but the statute died in 1999, in part as a result of excessive partisan usage.[80] However, its demise as an instrument of executive oversight provided an opening for IG investigations to gain prominence. Although ICs were replaced with the Office of Special Counsel in 1999, by the next decade, the preferred method was to appoint an IG to oversee instances of wrongdoing.

Finally, the relationship between IGs and whistle-blowers is vexed. Rather than mutually reinforce each other, in practice, IGs have undervalued whistle-blowers as a legitimate source of information, and at times IGs have even punished them for their breaches of agency loyalty, as an analysis of the DOD OIG suggested.[81] Individual whistle-blowers also assume personal and professional risks that are far more menacing than those facing IGs, who can fall back on institutional support should their allegations provoke ire in the host agency. Whistle-blowers might call attention to the same types of misconduct that IGs seek, but their motivation to do so can be quite different from that of the IGs. Individual justice, revenge, idealism, publicity—that is, mostly personal drivers—can all color a whistle-blower's reasons for reporting wrongdoing. While this does not necessarily detract from their validity of their complaints—as one former IG inspector commented, "Where there is smoke, there is usually fire"—IGs at times find the need to separate the legitimate claims from the claims tinged with motives of personal revenge. But the suspicion, even irritation, with which some IG regard whistle-blowers also colors the whistle-blowers' own view of the possible channels through which to report wrongdoing. In an era increasingly concerned with the power and responsibility of whistle-blowers (seen, for instance, in the controversy surrounding the case of Edward Snowden), destroying legitimate options for them to come out through legal, protected channels will undermine both their goals and those of the IGs.

External groups (such as POGO) and Congress have developed some procedural and legislative reform proposals to encourage mutual support, rather than antagonism, between the IGs and whistle-blowers, and in surveys, POGO found evidence that the IG community was receptive to reforms.[82] For instance, in August 2012, the Justice Department added a further whistle-blowing protection position within its OIG, the whistle-blower ombudsman, which will "train employees about the importance of reporting potential misdeeds and monitor investigations." The decision, however, was met with skepticism by whistle-blower advocates.[83] The relationship is crucial because IGs gather many, at times the majority, of their complaints through their much-advertised hotlines. Ultimately, however, the IG's choice of strategy—that is, whether it relies on the tip of a whistle-blower, on congressional direction, or on its own intuition in pursuing a review—depends crucially on its level of independence.[84]

Challenges and Countervailing Developments

IGs continue to face a set of political challenges that affect vacancies, misconduct, and resources. These problems are not unrelated: most IG misconduct occurs by or under the watch of acting IGs. Partisans of reform over the selection process argue that carefully structured improvements in vetting minimize the chances of corrupt IGs and improve the likelihood of a speedy confirmation process.[85]

Vacancies

The phenomenon of IG vacancies has plagued the community since its inception, and despite the purported apolitical character of the IG, it has played into partisan power struggles. On the one hand, many IGs note the unavoidable length of the confirmation process, particularly for members of the IG community.[86] These often leave OIGs in limbo for many months, if not years, with no cohesive organizational direction. On the other hand, leaving an IG post unfilled offers distinct advantages for a president reluctant to have important programs inspected; it can also be a tool of congressional obstructionism (such as during the Obama administrations). The IG positions in the key national security departments of State, Homeland Security, and Defense remained unfilled for five years, three years, and two years, respectively; in the DHS, the acting IG ultimately resigned for misconduct in 2013.[87] Senator Charles Grassley observed that acting IGs "tend to function as caretakers of the office" and "are not necessarily equipped to take on an entrenched bureaucracy and challenge senior officials with the tough questions necessary to get to the bottom of a controversy."[88] OIGs headed by acting IGs often suffer from a lack of direction, and they find themselves subject to more intense political pressure because of their lack of job security. Frequently they occupy more than one position within the department and are vetted by the department's top officials, placing them in the conflicted position of having to criticize the very officials who will have

Table 3.4. Average Tenure by Department/Agency, 1978–2014

Agency or Department	Confirmed IG	Acting or Deputy IG
USAID	7 years, 7 months	7 months
CIA	5 years, 2 months	7 months
Corporation for National and Community Service	5 years	1 year, 11 months
Agriculture	4 years, 11 months	1 year, 4 months
Commerce	6 years, 4 months	1 year
Defense	2 years, 7 months	2 years, 6 months
Education	4 years, 11 months	6 months
Energy	8 years, 8 months	9 months
Health and Human Services	7 years, 3 months	1 year
Homeland Security	3 years, 3 months	1 year, 7 months
Housing and Urban Development	4 years, 4 months	1 year, 8 months
Interior	4 years, 5 months	1 year, 4 months
Justice	5 years, 4 months	1 year
Labor	3 years, 8 months	1 year, 2 months
State (and Broadcasting Board of Governors)	1 year, 3 months	1 year, 1 month
Transportation	5 years, 1 month	8 months
Treasury	3 years, 3 months	8 months
Treasury IG for Tax Administration	6 years, 4 months	1 year, 4 months
Veterans Affairs	8 years, 7 months	11 months
Environmental Protection Agency	5 years, 4 months	1 year, 5 months
Federal Deposit Insurance Corporation	7 years, 10 months	1 year, 9 months
General Services Administration	4 years, 8 months	5 months
NASA	7 years, 5 months	7 months
US Nuclear Regulatory Commission	11 years, 9 months	10 months
Office of Personnel Management	12 years, 11 months	1 year, 4 months
Railroad Retirement Board	13 years, 11 months	6 months
Small Business Administration	2 years, 9 months	1 year, 11 months
Social Security Administration	4 years, 7 months	9 months
Tennessee Valley Authority	11 years	1 year, 2 months
Total	6 years, 4 months	1 year, 3 months

influence over their employment. Finally, agency heads feel less pressure to implement the recommendations of acting IGs. A survey conducted by the House Committee on Oversight and Government Reform found that "agencies without permanent IGs have a disproportionately high number of open and unimplemented recommendations," meaning that even good quality work by acting IGs can be ineffectual.[89] IG reports led by confirmed IGs carry more weight with Congress and the press than acting or deputy

IGs. The rigorous and lengthy vetting process for confirmed IGs lends them authority in the eyes of their stakeholders because of the assurance that they are truly independent and competent. Moreover, acting IGs do not have the capacity to set OIG priorities or strategic plans, leaving the office unable to adapt to the changing needs of the host department or agency. Given that many IG investigations span multiple years, the need for direction and leadership is crucial.

IG Misconduct: Who Watches the Watchdogs?

Though government officials regularly tout the IGs' success as reason for public trust, the phenomenon of IG misconduct has repeatedly reared its head, and the IG community's strategies for addressing it have grown piecemeal. IG scandals regularly surface and weaken the IGs' overall public image. In 2007 alone, Department of Commerce IG Johnny Frazier and NASA IG Robert Cobb were both found guilty of misconduct, but neither received direct disciplinary action; Department of State IG Howard Krongard resigned amid a flood of similar accusations.[90] With neither the PCIE nor the Office of Special Counsel able to prod the president or department heads to discipline the intractable IGs, the onus fell on Congress to address the problem. The 2008 Reform Act proved partly successful in its acknowledgment and support of IG accountability. By consolidating the PCIE and ECIE into a single entity, the act streamlined IG oversight from within the community; moreover, it strengthened the Integrity Committee in place to assess IG misconduct, bolstering congressional oversight capacity of the IG community. The act replaced the executive order that established the PCIE and ECIE with a statute, which gave the council (and the Integrity Committee) permanent authority.

Political Constraints

Though the IG community has voiced a continuous refrain of budget complaints since the late 1970s, other challenges faced by the IGs have evolved. In the 1980s and early 1990s, many IGs complained about the congressional pressure for measurable outcomes—that is, immediate results in the form of numbers documenting funds recovered and saved, arrests, indictments, and convictions—that precluded more effective but less visible investigations.[91] Legislators can easily use such data for political gain—more so than the less quantifiable structural changes that have a greater long-term impact on departmental behavior. In a 2013 survey of the IG community, however, IGs expressed more concern with a new type of congressional pressure: the growing number of statutory requirements for regular IG audits, inspections, and investigations of particular programs, all of which limit the discretionary funds IGs have to pursue unexpected but serious breaches of accountability.[92] Yet the budget woes continued: the added congressional responsibilities came not with additional resources but rather with budget cuts. Despite the 2008 IG Act's support of IG independence, the fragility of the IGs' position and capacity to act can still be shaken simply by department heads unwilling to cooperate. An August 2014 letter to Congress, signed by forty-seven of the seventy-three federal IGs, wrote in defense of three IGs who experienced repeated blocks by their departments in accessing crucial documents for investigations and audits. Their grievance focused not on overt executive wrongdoing, but rather on "restrictive" and "cramped reading[s] of the IG Act" that stalled and prevented IG investigations from taking place: "The constricted interpretations of Section 6(a)(1) by these and other agencies conflict with the actual language and congressional intent. The IG Act is clear: no law restricting access to records applies to Inspectors General unless that law expressly so states, and that unrestricted access extends to all records available to the agency, regardless of location or form."[93] The IGs found their fragile authority compromised by a set of agencies eager to guard their secrecy; the agencies overrode the IG Act by having creative recourse to the legal arsenal at their command, exploiting legal ambiguities to render individual IGs powerless.

Identity and Organization in the IG Community

The history of the US federal IG community since 1978 is one of proliferation, increased capacity, and fortified independence, along with a slow expansion of the very concept of accountability and a gradual crystallization into a coordinated, institutional web. Its transition from an early monitoring function to a more positive consulting function was driven by neoliberal demands for privatization and enhanced economic performance, while a concurrent politics of emergency occasioned the invention of special, event-specific OIGs. The IG model has expanded outward—internationally in many African countries (who have mostly adopted military-style IGs), Iraq (the only American-style IG outside of the United States), and Europe—and inward, to state and local governments, which increasingly conform to the federal model.[94] This core model has strengthened as it has developed. While the majority of legislative provisions for IGs have supported their independence, Congress has also sought to expand their authority by codifying their capacities and responsibilities. Congress established a statutory requirement for OIGs in December 2007 to track the status of their recommendations, creating added pressure for departments to follow IG direction. Their mounting independence from host agencies has been accompanied by growing institutional support in the form of CIGIE, as well as standards common to IG performance and training. Despite its early twentieth-century roots in financial auditing, the IG position has developed into a tool in the investigation of civil liberties abuses and an internal check on executive prerogative.

Yet both internal and external pressures plague the IG community. A poor internal accountability structure, coupled with IGs' status as political appointees, make their integrity dependent on the goodwill of individual IGs, and this has permitted periodic but persistent IG scandals. Externally, the IGs' delicate institutional placement between the branches and their susceptibility to politically motivated budgetary reprisals ensure that their position will remain tenuous.

The IGs' history is also a story of a democratic instrument's return to the basic functions of state from a seemingly delimited administrative remit. The IG now plays a crucial role in supporting the state's security function through its deployment as a tool of emergency governance and in defending the state's function as guarantor of rights. Neither of these two functions was foreseen or written into the IG Act's original structure in 1978. Rather, political actors, as well as pioneering IGs themselves, have exploited the ambiguities of their role and transformed the model into an instrument of both administrative and democratic values. It is to these narratives that I now turn.

PART II

THE IGS AT WORK

CHAPTER FOUR

BUNGLING BUREAUCRATS

Searching for Independence at State

MAYOR: *Gentlemen, I have invited you here to convey to you some extremely unpleasant news. We are to be visited by a government inspector.*

JUDGE: *Inspector?*

WARDEN OF CHARITIES: *What inspector?*

MAYOR: *A government inspector from St. Petersburg. Incognito. And, what's more, with secret instructions.*

JUDGE: *Well there's a thing!*

WARDEN OF CHARITIES: *As if we hadn't enough on our plates already!*

—Nikolai Gogol, *The Inspector General* (1836)

Introduction

Like Gogol's government inspector, the arrival of the IG into any State Department matter was hardly a welcome affair, and at best an irritating irrelevance. But unlike Gogol's comedy of errors, the history of State OIG unfolded as a tragedy, with a succession of ineffectual and hamstrung IGs struggling to tame an unruly department. For much of its history, the OIG's success in effecting departmental change and accountability was limited, in part because of the weak institutional strategies of its IGs and in part because of the extensive bureaucratic and political constraints on the office. These constraints included not only a perennial lack of resources but also the weight of a pre-IG institutional legacy and a department culture resistant to IG work. The length of tenure of its permanent IGs shrank rapidly in the two decades after the early 1990s, leaving the office to be headed by successive career Foreign Service Officers (FSOs) with leadership stints of only a few months each.

The State Department crafts a political face for the nation. Its IG is thus poised to temper the political consequences of mismanagement and the partisan stakes of scandal. Pursing a political democracy would require the

IG to refine the way the nation instantiates abstract democratic values and to promote a healthy bureaucratic space in which to do so. But where the State IG could have forged such a democracy—one that directed its energies toward refining necessary agonistic impulses in the public sphere—its work repeatedly failed to rise above the very scandals it was tasked with managing.

Throughout its history, the OIG also suffered an acute case of audit–investigative animosity, a condition familiar throughout the IG community as a cause of compromised work. These two branches of the office maintained decades-long institutional rivalries that prevented the kind of cohesive bureaucratic culture necessary to the pooling of scarce resources and expertise. Historically, the inspection teams had taken pride of place in the OIG (in its various incarnations dating to 1906); this only served to worsen the audit–investigative tension that accompanied the 1978 act and dilute the office's capacities. State OIG's history demonstrates the precarious dependence of IGs on material resources, independence, a cohesive office culture, and a broad web of actors to effect change.

Before the IG Act

Unlike any other federal IG, the State IG traces its roots to the early twentieth century. The department conducted routine inspections of its foreign posts beginning in 1906 through the chief of the Foreign Service Inspection Corps. In 1957, this management function was formalized and renamed the Inspector General of Foreign Service.[1] Known as S/IG, this proto-IG resulted from an internal administrative decision. Periodic legislation and reorganization in 1961, 1971, and 1980 amended the position: Section 624 of the Foreign Assistance Act of 1961 gave S/IG the further responsibility of overseeing foreign assistance; amendments in 1971 merged other evaluation bodies from within the department under the OIG; and finally, in the 1980 Foreign Service Act, Congress declared the IG to be presidentially appointed, housed it in a separate OIG, and instituted a five-year cycle for foreign bureau inspections.[2]

Yet the State IG avoided the reach of the 1978 act for eight years after the act's passage. Although all cabinet departments resisted the IG Act in 1978, the departments with national security functions proved most intransigent, and State was no exception. After a negative GAO review of State's OIG in 1982, Senator Jesse Helms (R-NC) pushed the issue of State's inclusion in the 1978 framework back onto the legislative agenda. The review reported that State OIG inspectors found impartiality impossible because of a threat of professional reprisal. Only on August 16, 1985, did Congress fold the State IG into the 1978 framework, again despite the resistance of department staff, as part of the Diplomatic Assistance Act.[3] State OIG's responsibilities were further specified a year later, in the Omnibus Diplomatic Security and Antiterrorism Act of 1986.[4] The two acts combined the requirements of the 1978 framework with State OIG's previous inspections duties. The slow process of institutional change in the OIG distinguished it from the development of other federal OIGs, whose offices were often created by fiat and rapidly cobbled together. In contrast, the legacy from State OIG's precursors within the department shackled the office and restrained its capacity to gain independence. IGs contended with an entrenched culture that resisted challenges to its long-standing practices and purposes.

The State of State: The Management Context of the Department

The State Department, the first executive department to be established in 1789, directs the nation's relations with foreign states. Its foreign posts are scattered geographically and administratively, as are its satellite agencies. The State Department's internal management dynamics created an operating context more troublesome than those in other federal departments. IG Sherman Funk observed that "bureaucracy . . . is done with a particular lack of thought in the State Department," and though he made the quip in 1994, observers twenty years later echoed the same sentiments.[5] State IGs battled not only individual instances of fraud, waste, and abuse but also a culture of excessive bureaucracy, and a custom, according to Funk, of not taking care of one's own.

Funk's observations revealed one perspective on the late Cold War–era State Department, but in 2001, Colin Powell announced his strategy to address the same dysfunction, still in place a decade later. The outlook that led to the mistreatment of individual staff also led to an allergy to management officials, with "stacks of reports decrying the state of State now sit[ting] on department officials' shelves."[6] The antimanagement attitude came in part as a by-product of the department's mission, which was to focus on foreign affairs and policy rather than the practicalities of management, and "as a result of which the State Department perhaps has the worst logistical support arrangements of any federal agency."[7] The culture at State prized diplomacy and policy expertise; management acumen fell by the wayside. Different agencies within the department suffered different patterns of corruption and mismanagement. Whereas in the 1980s and 1990s the Foreign Service and consular offices had reputations for being free of corruption, Consular Affairs (CA) and the Immigration and Naturalization Service (INS) were permanent management headaches.[8] Yet according to one 2012 assessment, the only secretaries in recent history committed to solving management problems were Colin Powell and Lawrence Eagleburger.[9]

By the end of the first decade of the twenty-first century, the department's reputation for self-management sank even further. State lacked a budget office until 2005, but this office held jurisdiction only over programmatic functions, to the neglect of personnel or management.[10] The disparate, independent entities that make up the United States' foreign policy apparatus—such as United States Agency for International Development, better known as USAID, the Peace Corps, and the Export–Import Bank—pose the additional challenge to any management official of coordinating multiple functions, bureaucratic cultures, budgets, jurisdictional overlaps and gaps, and institutional allegiances.

State's management difficulties had a direct impact on its performance. Poor management led to lax security, a charge leveled at the department repeatedly in IG reports beginning in the early 1990s and continuing steadily over the next twenty years. Yet the IG reports merely echoed what a host of other reports confirmed: studies by the Overseas Presence Advisory Panel (November 1999) and the Henry Stimson Center (October 1998) both detailed the poor management and security controls of the State Department.[11] Notoriously, less than nine months before the 9/11 terrorist attacks, the Hart-Rudman Commission report of January 2001, *National Security in the 21st Century*, suggested that an attack on American soil was likely as a result of changes in the international security environment, and that the United States needed to reorganize its foreign policy and security institutions. All of these reports offered suggestions for reform of the State Department that were left unheeded by successive secretaries.

Over the preceding three decades, Congress duly lacked any faith that State could mange itself efficiently or effectively, and it accordingly limited State's resources. Partly in response to 9/11, and partly as a result of Secretary Powell's "resource for reform" management strategy, in which the department promised a more efficient use of resources in return for a larger budget, Congress increased State's budget by 50 percent (in constant dollars) between 2001 and 2005, in marked contrast to its stagnant—in some years even shrinking—budget in the previous decade. Yet even during this

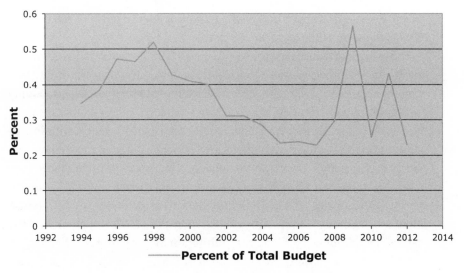

Figure 4.1. OIG Budget as Percentage of State Department Budget

period of resource expansion, and unlike the budgets of other OIGs, the IG's budget was increased a mere 1 percent (Figure 4.1).[12]

The spikes in revenue seen in 2009 and 2011 reflect supplementals related to the State OIG's oversight of SIGAR. Aside from SIGAR, the State OIG's budget as a percentage of the department's budget fell steadily from the mid-1990s.

Statutory Inspections and Expertise

Even before its establishment as a statutorily independent IG in 1985, the OIG was saddled with duties that overwhelmed the organization's meager resources. The State OIG operates under a statutory requirement to inspect all foreign bureaus and posts. This responsibility finds its roots in Theodore Roosevelt's 1906 request to Secretary of State John Hay to establish a corps of inspectors to monitor consular competence. These became known as consuls at large, and they wielded considerable power to dismiss staff of embassies and consulates abroad.[13] The inspection function thus preceded any other monitoring function in the future State OIG. This institutional legacy has had dramatic consequences for the expertise, appointment, and turnover of its staff; its apportionment of resources; and its organizational structure. Familiarity with the experience of living in foreign posts was prized as expertise above and beyond audit or investigative expertise, and led IGs to marginalize these functions.

The primary practice inherited from the OIG's pre-1986 modus operandi, and the primary impediment to its independence and impartiality, was its custom of appointing Foreign Service officials (FSOs), especially active-duty ambassadors, as the leaders of inspection teams. On the face of it, this practice clearly compromises the ability of OIG inspectors to report with impartiality; the targets of their inspections are former colleagues and friends, and perhaps future supervisors. Yet because of the history of State inspections in providing support and a line of communication between Washington and the foreign outposts, many OIG members have defended such in-house familiarity. Although in the 1985 act, Senator Jesse Helms ensured that the IG itself could not be an FSO, this prohibition did not extend to the inspection team leaders, who continue to be active-duty ambassadors. One solution to the compromised independence, developed over the 1990s and first decade of the twenty-first century, was to take only officers at the end of their careers, when they were unlikely to be recycled back into the Foreign Service, as a last assignment.[14]

As a result, the kinds of "expertise" in State OIG differed from other OIGs. Unlike inspectors in other OIGs, State inspectors brought experience of the field rather than "site-based expertise," and this made critical evaluation difficult. Inspection teams might be deployed only for short periods, with teams making rounds of multiple countries and staying in each for a few weeks at a time. FSOs brought familiarity with the challenges of living abroad in a US-diplomatic bubble; however, they lacked knowledge of the particular difficulties in the host countries (that is, of the demands related to each post's political and economic situation). Most inspectors worked for the OIG for stints of two years or less. Their expertise was that of diplomatic experience, not of a technical kind in line with governmentwide inspection or auditing standards.

In most OIGs, audits and investigations traditionally comprise the backbone of IG work, with inspections (and evaluations) a later, secondary development; in State OIG, the situation was the reverse. The inspections function has historically dominated the OIG's work. A 1982 GAO review of State's inspection practices revealed that in the OIG, "only two or three auditors and a handful of investigators" worked in the office.[15] Over time, individual IGs (including acting IGs, such as Harold Geisel) have gradually altered the balance of audits, inspections, and investigations, but even as of 2014, "investigations" still does not appear as a primary report category on the OIG's website. Nearly two decades after State OIG was folded into the 1978 act, the office still had not developed strong audit capacities. As a result, the office lacked a cohesive identity and a culture conductive to combining resources and expertise.

Lack of Independence

Two of State OIG's distinctive institutional traits—the preference for FSOs instead of external personnel and the dependence on inspections instead of audits—provoked the consistent condemnation by the GAO, Congress, and external observers in the media and civil society. Their reports highlighted both the real and perceived threat posed to State OIG's independence by the use of Foreign Service personnel. The substance of these reports hardly changed from the 1970s to the second Obama administration. A 1982 GAO letter to Jack Brooks, chairman of a subcommittee of the House Committee on Government Operations, decries the compromised independence of a FSO-run OIG and urges him to place State OIG under the 1978 act framework.[16] (The accompanying report provoked Senator Jesse Helms to put the State OIG question back on the legislative agenda, and this eventuated in the 1985 conversion to the 1978 framework.) Twenty-five years later, the GAO issued a near-identical assessment: State OIG's practice of using Foreign Service officials as acting IGs and inspection team leaders severely compromised its independence and effectiveness.[17]

The OIG's reliance on inspections over audits and investigations also troubled external observers. Within the OIG, a saying suggests that "audits are an inch wide, but a mile deep; inspections are a mile wide, but an inch deep."[18] A 2011 GAO assessment of the merit of inspections was even less positive: "GAO also reported that inspections, by design, are conducted under less in-depth requirements and do not provide the same level of assurance as audits."[19] A year earlier, an external peer review conducted by NASA of State OIG's Middle East Regional Office (MERO) identified multiple deficiencies in its auditing practices.[20] NASA OIG's assessment demonstrated that State OIG's "audits" did not even pass muster as audits, and its discoveries forced State OIG to reclassify all of its audits between 2008 and 2009 as "assessments reports."[21] A government watchdog group, POGO, pressured Congress to address State OIG's problems, and the topic was taken up in a hearing of its own in the House Committee on Foreign Affairs, *Watching the Watchers: The Need for Systemic Reforms and Independence of the State Department Inspector General.*[22]

State OIG Work

What is the nature of State OIG activity? First, the historical legacy of the Foreign Service Inspection Corps has resulted in its inspections performing a role unlike those of any other OIG inspection teams: that of psychological counselor. Second, its audits and investigations are political. Though over time, external criticisms of State OIG's performance have pointed to numerous compromised reviews and a lack of independence, the perspective from which such reports emanate often reflects ignorance of the office's unique historical functions. The inspection function, usually considered a second-rate means of oversight in other OIGs, has long formed the bread and butter of State OIG's activities since the early twentieth century. But this bias hid the ancillary functions that evolved out of State's historical inspection role. In particular, State OIG's inherited mandate to conduct consular inspections—a large drain on its resources—pushed it into the business of counseling. The original consular inspectors served as "sort of travelling psychiatrists" for FSOs and consular staff who had been working in foreign posts for decades and felt estranged from the bureau in Washington.[23]

> I found that people, if you approach [FSOs] properly in an embassy in private interviews, began to unburden themselves in a way they would perhaps to a priest or something, or to a dear, close friend. There was an assumption on their parts that it would be discreet, that we could be trusted, we weren't going to get them into trouble, and, therefore, they could pour out their hearts to us.[24]

Nowhere else in the federal IG system have IGs cultivated a soft, supportive role in their host department. Rather, the oft-cited query, "Watchdog or lap dog?," reinforced the role and disposition assumed to be characteristic of a successful IG: a tough, no-nonsense enforcement officer trained to root out fraud and waste, or at the very least a hard-nosed management consultant.

With pressure from Congress, a wave of "audit qualified inspectors" sent from the GAO dealt a blow to the office's counseling culture in the 1980s. "The new inspection thing," as one former FSO referred to the reforms pushed by the GAO and Congress, made department members "treat [OIG staff] as someone you've got to have an attorney sit with you when you go in," rather than as a counselor or friend.[25] The importance of the counseling function for OIG and department members proved difficult to convey to Congress. It also reinforced another controversial element of OIG practice—the use of FSOs as OIG staff—because field inspectors need to have knowledge and experience to provide the psychological and logistical support demanded by the counseling expectation. In contrast to the antagonistic relationship that exists between some inspection teams and their host departments in other OIGs, State office and embassy staff often viewed IG inspections as opportunities to gain leverage with Washington and obtain support for additional resources.[26] Moreover, inspection reports lack the "gotcha" language so valuable to members of Congress seeking blatant evidence for their political crusades.

If the counseling function has dominated State OIG's inspections, its political function strongly tinges its audits and investigations. State IG reviews can be political in a way that few other federal IG reviews have the potential to be. The State IG has the capability—some IGs would claim the obligation—to weigh in on ideologically driven actions by the State Department, to provide evidence for political appointments, and to assess the overall success of foreign policy initiatives. In theory, there exists a distinction between questions of management and questions of foreign policy; any IG's domain should encompass the management problems of the department. Yet in practice, such a distinction is tenuous, as former IG William "Bill" Harrop explained:

> There has always been, in the Foreign Service and in the Department of State, an odd dichotomy between administration, management, budget, and personnel questions on the one hand, and policy questions on the other. . . . [The IG] doesn't intervene in policy matters, although his inspectors do try to take a look to see that the policy being pursued is appropriate and coherent and makes sense.[27]

State OIG is the "war zone" IG, and a different standard is immediately at play: is the department's action in accordance with US foreign policy? This requires an interpretive schema very different from that of an OIG focused on accordance with rules and regulations. Unlike other departments, such as Health and Human Services or Veterans Affairs, the State Department does not operate high-budget programs at great risk of fraud. Its most immediate "constituency" comprises the many Americans living or traveling abroad, including those stuck in foreign prisons or caught in emergencies, all of whom depend on the resources and diplomatic skills of State Department officials. Bringing in the new inspectors, trained by Yellow Book standards, brought with it a demand for quantitative indicators of failure. But as Robert S. Steven, former inspector at State OIG, demanded,

If your visa rejection rate and visas were so bad, INS picking people up back here, you can measure that, but how do you measure success in foreign policy? Even in economic sections you could quantify it some-times—was the economic reporting [and] forecasting logical or not?—because you could see what happened; and with the business assistance, did they get business? The political side of it particularly was extremely difficult to measure. We still have never really found a good way to do that.[28]

How do you measure success in foreign policy? The question fits uneasily with the 1978 inspector general model's emphasis on efficiency and effec-tiveness. Successive IGs would contend with questions of how to evaluate decisions in accordance with US foreign policy, marking a set of evaluative criteria very different from those applied by OIGs concerned primarily with financial waste. While inspection teams performed the bulk of State's IG work before the 1990s and contended with dilemmas of poor policy plan-ning, investigations provided the grist for the high-profile incidents that made their way to the ears of Congress and the press. The GAO's periodic negative reviews of State OIG, though accurate in their charges of com-promised independence, have been issued from a standardized perspective on IG work that pays little attention to the distinctive history and require-ments of the State Department. The difficulty of defining success also high-lighted a problem within State regarding policy planning that was (partially) addressed by IG Bill Harrop during the transition to the 1978 framework. IG inspectors had long experienced difficulty in assessing individual embas-sies because they could not ascertain which policies were in place. No policy papers were available to inspectors, who then fumbled to ascertain, often in the space of two weeks, which country-specific goals the individual embassy was pursuing. In 1985, Harrop persuaded Secretary of State George Shultz to require a basic policy planning practice, but the process was limited in scope and ultimately overlapped with the fruits of the National Security Council's foreign policy planning.[29]

Sherman Funk: Confronting the Counseling Culture

By the early 1980s, Congress and the GAO were determined to fold State OIG into the 1978 framework. The 1982 GAO report reproving State OIG for ineffectiveness and compromised independence gave Senator Jesse Helms ammunition for his "relentless campaign against career Foreign Service professionals."[30] Bill Harrop, in the seat of the OIG, found himself waging a "defensive operation" against Helms to save the OIG as it was.[31] It was a war Harrop ultimately lost, and it cost him his job. State's model of IG—an inside source of support, a management tool, a counselor that engaged in what was affectionately termed nonconfrontational inspection—was abhorrent to Helms. Congress wanted a tough inspector general to serve as an enforcement mechanism, and through the 1985 amendments, it formally brought State OIG under the banner of the 1978 framework, ruling that State OIG's director general (the IG) could not be Foreign Service.

In the new OIG's first years, the "counseling and inspection" and "federal statutory" models of IG coexisted side by side. The new congressional system "basically wasn't even staffed; it was a theoretical organization."[32] Although the confrontation, and slow resolution, of the two models had begun in the years preceding the 1985 transition, the result in part of the cross-fertilization that took place in monthly PCIE meetings with other federal IGs, the ultimate integration of the two would take years. Just before the passage of the 1986 act that caused Harrop to lose his job, Sherman Funk, the Commerce Department IG, found himself professionally restless and submitted his name to the White House for consideration at the IG posts in State and Defense. The IG vetting process in the 1980s depended less on expertise than on political connections, as Funk, a registered Republican, well knew.[33] His time at Commerce gave him IG experience and allowed him to build a reputation that later satisfied the White House, Secretary of State Schultz, and Senator Helms. In August 1987, Funk was confirmed and succeeded his old Harvard friend Harrop as State IG. Funk and Harrop had been classmates at Harvard in the late 1940s, along with Freddie Chapin, whom Funk enlisted as one of his inspection team leaders.[34] These old college ties lent the early State OIG an "old boys" quality that mirrored the tight-knit networks of the Foreign Service.

Though nearly all IGs came with backgrounds in criminal law, investigation, or auditing, Funk brought expertise in general management. With his arrival, the OIG expanded its size and remit, growing from a single unit that combined audit and investigative functions to a five-unit office with a considerable staff increase.[35] Together, Funk and Hollingsworth built a staff of around 260, including roughly 100 auditors; this low number was a decision Funk was later to regret. Despite disapproval from the GAO, Funk did not buck State's tradition of using internal candidates as the bulk of his army of inspectors; he drew his teams almost uniformly from the Foreign Service. Other members of the OIG appreciated Funk's prudence in

Table 4.1. Academic and Professional Backgrounds of State IGs

Inspector General	Date Confirmed	Academic Background	Professional Background
Steve Linick (IG)	9 September 2013	Philosophy; law	AUSA (CA and VA); DOJ criminal division (various posts)
Harold Geisel (acting IG)	2 June 2008	Finance	Foreign service (ambassador); State Department management
William E. Todd (acting IG)	16 January 2008	Accounting	Foreign service (ambassador)
Howard J. Krongard (IG)	2 May 2005	Law	Private lawyer
Cameron R. Hume (acting/deputy IG)	23 August 2004		Foreign service (ambassador)
John E. Lange (acting deputy IG)	3 August 2004	Law	Foreign service (ambassador)
Anne W. Patterson (deputy IG)	28 September 2003		Foreign service
Anne M. Sigmund (acting/deputy IG)	4 January 2003		Foreign service (ambassador)
Clark Kent Ervin (IG)	3 August 2001	Law	Law (private practice and state attorney general)
Anne M. Sigmund (acting IG)	4 February 2001		Foreign service (ambassador)
Jacquelyn L. Williams-Bridgers (IG)	7 April 1995	Public management	GAO (managing director); accountability consultancy
Harold Geisel (acting IG)	12 June 1994	Finance	Foreign service; State Department management
Roscoe S. Suddarth (acting IG)	15 February 1994	Liberal arts; music	Foreign service (ambassador)
Sherman M. Funk (IG)	14 August 1987	Liberal arts; military	Military and federal management; Commerce IG
H. Byron Hollingsworth (acting IG)	27 August 1986		Foreign service
William C. Harrop (acting IG)	16 August 1985	Liberal arts; military	Foreign service (ambassador)

respecting long-standing organizational culture, but the sheer lack of auditing expertise in the office forced him to import auditors and accountants gradually from the GAO and other departments; he tripled the number of accountants during his tenure.[36] The clash of cultures between State OIG's cozy inspection practices and Yellow Book auditing standards proved tense and required a great deal of adjustment on both sides. Sarah Horsey-Barr, a career FSO who served as an inspector from 1989–1990, described the culture clash thus:

> One of the things that we would have endless arguments about was, first of all, what was the difference between an audit and an inspection and, secondly, whether one could apply the approaches used by financial auditors to what in the department we call substantive work like political and economic reporting. Many of them had this idea that you could set up a grid and via this grid you could evaluate the effectiveness of, say, a political section, how many contacts, how many phone calls, how many lunches, how many cocktail parties, how many cables sent. . . . [The political and economic officers] were just absolutely rabid about the idea that this was a way to measure the effectiveness of a political section.[37]

Here the practicalities of the IG Act's injunction to combat "fraud and waste" and to "promote economy, efficiency, and effectiveness" produced confusion when applied directly to the State Department's work. Accountability has little meaning outside of context; it can be, inter alia, political, legal, moral, or hierarchical. These discussions among OIG staff led to the discursive construction of a political conception of accountability by forcing them to reckon with their own organizational purpose. The challenges of implementing a standardized methodology (that is, the rules governing audits and inspections) and its attendant problems also played a decisive role in determining accountability's substance.

During Funk's tenure, external auditors learned to adapt to the exigencies and limits of two-week inspections, and the in-house State OIG staff augmented its level of professionalism. However, the tension between the two, and the doubt about their ultimate reconcilability, remained.[38] State OIG opposition to embracing the congressional IG model in its entirety came not merely from cultural resistance but also from the misfit between State's mission and the exigencies of the dominant federal IG model—a tension often not appreciated by external observers.

In the mid-1980s—even before Funk—State OIG fell into yet another hiring practice distasteful to the GAO: rehiring retired FSOs as contractors and paying them both full pensions and the hourly rate awarded to contractors. Because of their experience, the contractors often supervised actual department members, despite the regulations prohibiting such an arrangement. Former ambassador Bob Steven observed, "There are rules about contracting, what can be done by contractors and what requires regular government employees, and they were breaking every rule in the book."[39] Only in 1990, after embarrassing GAO testimony in Congress, the OIG discontinued the practice and replaced it with WAE (when actually employed), a system that regulated the amount a retiree could work and be compensated.

If Funk's strategy toward his own department was accommodating of its culture, he saved his toughness for his dealings with Congress. When resisted by members of Congress, he used a strategy of "indirect intimidation," presenting their lack of compliance with his recommendations as grounds for certain electoral failure. "Of course it was [blackmail]," Funk asserted when describing his approach.[40] Yet the power game worked in both directions. Despite his strong reputation, Funk experienced firsthand the precariousness of the IG position vis-à-vis Congress. Senator Jesse Helms, who had pushed for State's inclusion under the 1978 act, and who had personally supported Funk's appointment at State, later took umbrage at a report contradicting his concerns about a covert operation in Nicaragua. The Senate Foreign Relations Committee believed the State Department was financially supporting Nicaraguan contras who supported the candidacy of future president Violeta Barrios de Chamorro. Under the guise of a relocation program, President George H. W. Bush was suspected of attempting to manipulate the 1990 Nicaraguan elections by supporting the contras with cash payments.[41] The review had been commissioned by the unlikely pair of Helms and Senator Christopher Dodd (D-CT), but its outcome—exonerating the State Department—so infuriated the Republican senator that he drafted legislation to have Funk removed from his position and, moreover, to limit all IG positions to a maximum of six years.[42] The bill failed, but it underscored the power of Congress—in addition to the president's own power—to exercise de facto removal power when dissatisfied with IG work.

The Nicaraguan incident with Dodd and Helms also called into question Funk's own biases. Despite Funk's self-styled reputation for being a "junkyard dog" (according to the plaque on his desk), the two senators claimed that the IG had given the department a free pass in order to improve his chances of keeping his job in the Clinton administration (a strategy that worked). The committee charged that Funk limited his investigation to select members of the department accused of complicity and failed to interview any Nicaraguans involved. Funk defended his methodology, claiming that the committee's original request for the investigation asked only for an account of the State Department's role in the affair.[43] After considerable congressional pressure—and after the 1992 presidential election—Funk agreed to reopen and expand the investigation to include recipients of the payments.

Funk's strategic investigation design in the contras case may well have been motivated by personal concerns, but the impulse for IGs to restrict the scope of their investigations can stem from the practicalities of permanently inadequate resources. (Years later, State IG Clark Kent Ervin would be accused of the same offence—producing a substandard report as a result of circumscribing the investigation—by senators Susan Collins and Joseph Lieberman [D-CT], who ultimately prevented his confirmation as Homeland Security IG in 2004.) The meager resources at an IG's disposal force the IG to make hard decisions about what can be investigated. Many investigations are statutorily mandated (for instance, the requirement that the Homeland Security IG oversee parts of the Patriot Act), and much of the audit agenda is determined by risk assessments that dictate which programs are most likely to be in danger of fraud, waste, or abuse. In addition to the constraints felt by other OIGs, it must reserve part of its budget for the regular inspection of foreign posts, and because of George Schultz's decisions, it manages security oversight for the department—a situation that leaves the IG with even less scope and capacity to pursue unexpected matters.

Earlier in 1992, Funk's office undertook an equally controversial review, one that soured already strained US–Israeli relations. Originally part of a routine audit to track illicit sales of US weaponry by foreign governments, the investigation led quite clearly to Israel. Funk's classified report, whose draft version was publicized by the *Wall Street Journal*, provided evidence of Israel's fault in the matter. The investigation uncovered a host of legal violations by Israel with regard to US weapons and technology regulations dating to 1983, including the resale of American arms to China, South Africa, Ethiopia, and Chile without US approval.[44] Yet a parallel investigation by the State Department, led by a team of seventeen investigators, found no evidence that Israel had transferred a Patriot missile to China and publicly absolved Israel of wrongdoing in an effort to ease tensions relations between the two countries.[45] (This inquest, far more limited in scope than the IG's, examined a single instance of an alleged arms sale.) As the public controversy raged, Funk traced the trail of evidence back to the State Department and discovered that the department's Bureau of Politico-Military Affairs had issued instructions to exempt Israel from the standard checks on recipients of US arms and technology that all nations, in theory, must undergo.[46]

The report recommended disciplinary action against Richard Clarke, assistant secretary of state for Politico-Military Affairs, but this was never acted on. Department officials were embarrassed and furious, and they did their best to discredit Funk's conclusion. The review failed to affect US diplomatic action—the administration stood adamantly by its position in support of Israel's innocence—but it did provoke considerable public debate about the nature of the relationship between the United States and its Jewish ally. The State Department refused to accept the conclusions of the review, and Funk's work thus had no immediate effect on policy. In the early 1990s, IG reviews lacked the stature to compel departmental acceptance in response to all instances of IG criticism (especially in such high-profile incidents). Though this would change slowly over the course of the following two decades, Funk's review demonstrated that one of the collateral strengths of IG work is to provide a narrative of executive activity and present it for wider deliberation. The report provoked a vigorous public debate, bolstered with evidence from internal documents, about US foreign policy and the motivations behind it, and demanded that the State Department justify its actions publicly.

The war on drugs also provoked Funk's ire. In 1989, he began an audit of elements of the program. As he would later insist, the State Department's drug strategy was profoundly misguided. Not only was its use of the Drug Enforcement Agency to carry out paramilitary operations in Latin America inappropriate because of the agency's lack of military expertise and authority, but it was also highly ineffective in achieving its goal of reducing the flow of cocaine. Rather than reduce coca cultivation, the International Narcotics Matters programs merely placed American employees in danger. In the comments in the final report, the International Narcotics Matters countered that the OIG failed to comprehend the difficulty and complexity of their task, dismissing many of Funk's allegations as already having been dealt with, or as "currently being addressed," and agreeing only to "take the OIG comments seriously."[47] To Secretary of State Shultz, Funk said, "Scrap it. It's not working, it's not going to work, and I don't see how it can work, short of giving it vastly more resources we aren't going to get."[48] Shultz, though understanding, indicated that dismantling US drug policy was not a tenable political position, and the audit ended there. (State IG reviews of the war on drugs more than a decade later would point to the same conclusion, and with the same effect.)

In his six years at State, Funk served under four secretaries: George Shultz, James Baker, Lawrence Eagleburger, and Warren Christopher. Shultz was skeptical of the IG position and disapproved of a proposed reorganization of security duties between the IG and the director of the CIA. Security abroad had not been an IG function previously, but Shultz informed Funk that he was to take over security oversight, and provided him with an additional 350 staff from other agencies to help carry out the work.[49] Baker and Christopher shared Shultz's skepticism, but they took his recommendations seriously. In fact, in Funk's view, despite personality variations among them, all four secretaries worked well with their IG and addressed his concerns.[50]

Funk resigned in 1994 after six years at State OIG. In his view, his major accomplishment was to have countered the stereotype of the regulation-bound IG. Rather than contributing to the culture of red tape (as IGs are often accused of doing), he claimed that he had worked according to a philosophy of "easing things up" and "d[oing] away with silly recommendations" that he deemed unnecessary.[51] Funk made a first effort to bring State OIG in line with the 1978 framework by altering the composition of his staff in order to include more audit and investigative expertise, but he refrained from disrupting the long-standing inspection culture that lent unity to the office.

The Unintended Consequences of Management Reforms: Reinventing Government

Before he resigned, Funk recommended that Ambassador Harold Geisel serve as acting IG until the Senate could confirm a new, non-FSO candidate.[52] Geisel was a career diplomat, sympathetic to the particularities of the Foreign Service and personally close to many in the upper ranks of the State Department. (Later, in his second and longer stint as acting IG, he would recuse himself from investigations a number of times on the grounds of being too close to the accused.) He steered the OIG for nearly a year until Jacquelyn Williams-Bridgers arrived at State OIG on 7 April 1995, after sixteen years of accountability work at the GAO and the Housing and Urban Development Department OIG. She came with considerable academic training in formal theories of public administration, and this, coupled with her experience at the GAO, predisposed her to approach State OIG with a critical eye, suspicious of the OIG's accommodating inspection culture. When she arrived, the OIG had two parallel deputy IGs, with the audit, security, and law enforcement functions entrusted to a non-FSO professional auditor and the regular FSO overseeing the inspection function and security and intelligence functions. This separation served to minimize the friction between FSOs and career civil servants and to preserve the peace between the two internal OIG cultures, but it was managerially redundant and stifling.[53]

Williams-Bridgers countered this difficulty with a set of administratively sophisticated management reforms aimed at integrating the diverse functions, practices, and managerial threads that had failed to coalesce after the transition in 1985. She brought in the use of matrices in evaluation, and she switched from office-based assignments to job-based assignments.[54] However, for the culturally divided State OIG, such deeply cutting reforms, in conjunction with the budgetary stressors on the office, created havoc. Around this time, the OIG saw a drop-off in high-quality applicants. This resulted both from shrinking resources and the growing distance, encouraged by the GAO and the wider IG world, between the OIG and State. Both State and the OIG had suffered from the budget crunches of the mid-1990s that followed a post–Cold War downgrade in foreign policy. Between 1996 and 2003, OIG staff plummeted by nearly 10 percent; over the same period, the State Department's ranks swelled by 25 percent.[55] Fewer inspection teams made rounds, and those tours were understaffed and underresourced, creating frustrating working conditions for FSOs. Moreover, active-duty FSOs had previously viewed IG inspection positions as stepping-stones to further ambassadorial placements. Once the pressure to limit in-house recycling of staff curbed this practice, FSOs saw fewer and fewer advantages in taking IG positions, viewed them as professional dead ends, and ceased to bid for them.[56]

Williams-Bridgers's reforms led to an even greater drop in the body of inspectors and inspections carried out. State Department officials bristled at the new OIG, complaining that it failed to respect due process rights in its investigations. After receiving multiple complaints from members of the State Department, Representative Lee Hamilton (D-IN) proposed a bill curtailing State IG powers to conduct investigations. Lee cited numerous cases (dating back to the investigation of the Clinton passport files under Funk) in which "individuals will appear voluntarily for an interview with the IG staff, having no indication that there is an investigation of a criminal nature against them pending."[57] Through his proposed legislation, Hamilton responded not only to complaints about Williams-Bridgers's investigative procedures but also to complaints about her predecessors. The fault, it seemed, lay with the office's long-standing practices and not with any particular IG.

The IG community was irate. A battery of IGs testified before the House that such a curtailment of IG authority would prevent them from carrying out the very mandate that Congress had handed to them. The confrontation raised two serious questions regarding the rising salience of federal IGs. First, for Congress, it was no less a question than "watching the watchdogs"—a matter that both POGO and Congress would underline repeatedly in the next two decades. Indeed, one former IG cited the misdeeds and accountability of his own community as the most important ongoing challenge for the IG model.[58] Second, it was clear that the IGs were exploiting the ambiguity of their role to heighten their capacities, and this made parts of Congress and the executive branch uneasy. Representative Lee argued, "Inspectors General are in a grey zone. They appear to view themselves as identical to Federal law enforcement agencies, but they are not prosecutors. They are not statutory law enforcement, although incrementally, through executive branch agreements and other means, they have gained broad investigative authority in recent years."[59] Here the debate became murkier. The IGs at the hearing protested Lee's exclusion of the IGs from the law enforcement community, arguing that IGs took their role as law enforcers seriously. Representative Peter Goss (R-FL) cautioned against "creating new rights" for department members, lest this weaken the system of accountability upheld, in theory, by the IGs.[60] The bill never passed, but the question of the IGs' role and authority stayed open. And the internal resistance at the State Department to its OIG—the original impetus for the bill—continued. Notable in this debate was the lack of partisanship at play: Williams-Bridgers was a Clinton appointee, challenged by a Democratic congressman and some Clinton-appointed diplomats, supported by both Democratic and Republican legislators, and still yet defended by IGs of both Republican and Democratic persuasions. Though lawmakers frequently used the substance of IG reviews as a partisan tool, the concept of the IG itself had begun to enjoy exceptional bipartisan support.

Troublesome Agency Heads

One prominent Democrat with little reverence for the State IG was its department head. Secretary of State Madeleine Albright showed only modest interest in the work issued by her OIG, and this limited the effect that Williams-Bridgers's reviews could have. Indeed, Albright rarely sided with her IG. After accusations that a senior diplomat, James F. Dobbins, had lied to Congress about his knowledge of a Haitian death squad, Williams-Bridgers conducted an investigation that concluded that he had "acted with reckless disregard" in testimony that was "incomplete, misleading and possibly perjurious."[61] The report was not made public, and Dobbins was subsequently appointed to lead the American delegation to the Kosovo peace talks. Despite the gravity of the IG's findings, Albright refused to take disciplinary action and continued her support for Dobbins. Williams-Bridgers's attempt to have the Justice Department review the matter for prosecution was met with similar reluctance, and the matter was sent back to the State Department for internal resolution.

The lack of secretarial support frustrated Williams-Bridgers's efforts. Albright's impulse to defend her staff may not have been unusual among department heads, but the secretary was similarly dismissive of less personal criticisms. OIG audits and investigations during her tenure repeatedly reported lax security protocol in embassies, as well as the alarming phenomenon of foreign spies entering the department with press passes. OIG investigators discovered that surveillance of US embassies was far more common than expected. Despite repeated warnings about weak security in embassies and in the Washington bureau, from vanished laptops to negligent airport security, the department failed to heed the IG's warnings or adopt its recommendations.

Despite the internal turmoil, Williams-Bridgers's OIG produced a number of consequential reviews with notable effects, though some were more symbolic than others. In 1996, she issued the fruits of a yearlong investigation into the conduct of the ambassador to Ireland, Jean Kennedy Smith. The scathing report faulted Kennedy Smith for punishing two staff members who protested the grant of a visa to Sinn Fein leader Gerry Adams.[62] The report was challenged by Senator Christopher Dodd, who appeared in a less than flattering light in Williams-Bridgers's account. But it resulted in a formal reprimand by Warren Christopher. Although Kennedy Smith's punishment was modest—Clinton refused to dismiss her—the review stood for a protection of free speech and dissent within the ranks of the government. Calling for a revision of the department's guidelines for disclosures of embassy information, the review described the ambassador's action as having "at a minimum violated the spirit of the department's regulations."[63] In its framing, the review thus challenged the "compliance monitoring" philosophy and implicitly articulated standards for political behavior befitting of a diplomat. But it remained classified and garnered limited attention—a mere thirty-three media citations in four years. Because of the hostile departmental environment in which the report was received and its classified status,

Table 4.2. Number of Media Citations for Selected IG Reviews

Review	Date of Issue	Citations	Date Range for Citations
Clinton passport files[a]	November 1992	430	1 October 1992–1 October 1996
Israeli weapons sales[b]	March 1992	116	1 February 1992–1 February 1996
Bush appointee personnel files[c]	January 1994	55	1 July 1993–1 July 1997
Jean Kennedy Smith visa[d]	March 1996	33	1 March 1996–1 March 2000
Ambassador Richard Holbrooke finances[e]	May 1999	105	1 September 1998–1 September 2002
Chavez coup d'état[f]	July 2002	56	1 April 2002–1 April 2006
Obama passport files[g]	July 2008	224	1 January 2008–1 January 2012

[a]Search terms: "inspector general" AND ("state department" OR "department of state") AND "passport" AND "clinton." A spate of references to this report appeared again in 2008 when the IG began to investigate the alleged breach of Obama's passport files, with another 171 citations making reference to the precedent with Clinton.

[b]Search terms: "inspector general" AND ("state department" OR "department of state") AND "israel" AND "weapons."

[c]Search terms: "state department" AND "inspector general" AND ("personnel files" OR "appointee files").

[d]Search terms: "inspector general" AND ("state department" OR "department of state") AND ("jean kennedy smith" OR "ambassador smith" OR "ambassador kennedy").

[e]Search terms: "inspector general" AND ("state department" OR "department of state") AND "holbrooke."

[f]Search terms: ("state department" OR "department of state") AND "inspector general" AND "Chavez" AND ("coup" OR "ouster").

[g]Search terms: "inspector general" AND ("state department" OR "department of state") AND "passport" AND "Obama."

which shielded its conclusions from the media, the accountability effected by the investigation, at least in terms of direct punishment, visibility, and departmental change, was minimal.

Table 4.2 displays the media citations for selected reviews. Although the two passport violation reviews garnered a few hundred citations each, the others rarely surpassed 100; in comparison, a number of high-profile Justice and Homeland Security OIG reviews surpassed 1,000 citations.

The OIG also pursued a variety of reviews that demonstrated the scope of IG accountability. Even when the direct consequences of the reviews were limited, their wider effect penetrated deeper waters: in addition to addressing the operational functionality of the department, the reviews weighed in on the protection of free speech within the government; the role of ideology in compromising US foreign policy; the State Department's preparation for the Y2K problem (that is, the fear that outdated computer systems would shut down on 1 January 2000, thus provoking an international technological meltdown); and the finances and conduct of Richard Holbrooke, nominee for the position of ambassador to the UN.[64]

Williams-Bridgers's legacy proved controversial. She had come under fire both from Congress and from her department, but her office left its mark on the department in the form of innovative structural changes, such as the invention of miniembassies with a single American with a staff of one or two, to replace large, costly embassies at risk of being shut down.[65] Though the department was initially loath to alter its embassy structure, the new format proved highly successful. But though she came with excellent credentials in public management, her top-down reforms seemed too radical and too rapid to many career FSOs, in part because the reforms imposed an external model of inspections antithetical to the long-standing bureaucratic culture and practices that Funk had tacitly permitted to continue. Some FSOs recognized the cultural sclerosis of their institution and refrained from blaming Williams-Bridgers directly. Said one former inspector, "She reorganized the OIG with some of the very latest management concepts. . . . For whatever reason, it hasn't worked. A large part of that, of course, is just resistance."[66] Regardless of their success, the reforms provoked considerable internal debate about the nature and purpose of OIG work, in particular of inspections.[67] The struggle over the meaning of this basic IG function translated to a definition of the very nature of accountability as well as the IG's role in preserving it: Was it rule-book conformity? Integrity? Innovation? The question remained unresolved.

Williams-Bridgers left the office in 2000 to take a job in the private sector. She was only the second but would be the last permanent State IG to stay in the position for longer than two years. Only Harold Geisel would stay longer, later having a four-year stint as acting/deputy IG from 2009 to 2013—much to the distress of onlookers demanding that a permanent Senate-confirmed IG take the helm. The ensuing instability proved damaging for the OIG's morale and reputation, and by the middle of the decade, State OIG began to receive the kinds of scathing reviews from the GAO and Congress that it had not seen since the early 1980s. After Williams-Bridgers's departure, Clark Kent Ervin was sworn in as acting IG on 3 August 2001. A Republican and personal friend of the Bush family, Ervin was the first IG to bring legal expertise to State. However, under Powell's direction, he focused first on information technology (IT), quickly establishing a separate IT unit within the OIG. Though respectful of his predecessor's work, Ervin made some efforts to return to the traditional State inspection practices, thereby partially undoing her reforms.[68]

In 2002, Ervin was asked by Senator Christopher Dodd to undertake a review of the Bush administration's role in the coup that briefly ousted Venezuelan president Hugo Chávez.[69] Allegedly, the Bush administration had met secretly with members of the Venezuelan opposition in the months preceding the ouster, and by certain accounts had encouraged his overthrow. The IG review cleared the administration of any wrongdoing. Though Ervin later called the Chávez-ousting case one of his most important achievements as State IG, the results of the investigation left many external observers dissatisfied with its methodology and conclusion.[70] Critics argued that Ervin's investigation missed the mark and that Ervin's failure to interview any Venezuelans made its conclusions suspect.[71] Though the report asserted that the administration had not "planned, participated in, aided, or encouraged the brief ouster," it documented copious evidence of indirect or subtle American support for the coup. The report stated, "It is clear that NED [National Endowment for Democracy], Department of Defense (DOD), and other US assistance programs provided training, institution building, and other support to individuals and organizations understood to be actively involved in the brief ouster of the Chávez government, we found no evidence that this support directly contributed, or was intended to contribute, to that event."[72] A parallel investigation by the New York Times found that administration officials' accounts of the meetings in Venezuela were not consistent.[73]

But because the final conclusion exonerated the State Department, the IG review went no further. It was not released to the public until a Freedom of Information Act (FOIA) request prompted a redacted, unclassified version four months later. The incident itself, however, proved far more difficult to play down. Subsequently, the Pentagon would begin an informal review of its own role, and international pressure soon led the administration to backtrack on its enthusiasm after the ouster and to make statements in support of the reinstated Chávez government.[74] Two years later, further challenges to the report's conclusion emerged. A FOIA request by a New York attorney uncovered a host of CIA documents that demonstrated the government's knowledge of an impending coup in the weeks leading up to the ousting—a topic mentioned in only a single sentence in the IG review.[75]

The review's diagnosis exonerated the administration's actions and thus brought no immediate sanctions or meaningful recommendations for departmental modification. In the IG's view, this did not necessarily mean a weak review. Rather, it was a valuable statement of the department's innocence. In the eyes of critics, the exoneration was the result of weak methodology resulting from a political bias. Whether or not the review effected the accountability that was warranted, Ervin's choice of topic signaled an important commitment to a particular vision of government propriety and of an IG's role. As he would later comment, he saw the Venezuela review as emblematic of the types of reviews the State IG ought to pursue, above and beyond routine audits for fraud and waste.[76] This vision of accountability did indeed differ from the conception implied in the 1978 act. Rather than solely checking accounting and searching for corrupt bureaucrats, Ervin saw the role of the IG—and the aim of accountability—as passing judgment on US adherence to particular democratic values. Did the administration live up to its commitment to supporting democratic governments? Ervin used diplomatic and democratic norms, rather than performance measures, as the standards by which the department's actions should be assessed. Another Ervin review that impacted the conduct of foreign policy brought practical, rather than ideological, considerations to bear on the State Department's decision making. After auditing the leading Iraqi opposition group, which had been receiving US funding, the IG concluded that its accounting practices were too shoddy and haphazard for the United States to risk continued financial support.[77] Though the opposition groups had not broken any laws, their financial accountability structure did not conform to US stipulations.

After just over a year at State, Ervin was called by the Bush administration to head the OIG of the newly formed Department of Homeland Security, and he accepted. After his departure, State OIG was led by a series of short-term acting and deputy IGs. These acting IGs—Anne M. Sigmund,

Anne W. Patterson, John E. Lange, and Cameron R. Hume, all career Foreign Service—successively oversaw State OIG over a period of twenty-eight months. The office immediately garnered criticism. For instance, a review of the State Department's democracy-promoting Arabic-language radio station, Radio Sawa, was originally planned for release in August 2004 but was delayed indefinitely. Officials familiar with the review reported "intense political pressure to make the report more palatable," but it was never ultimately released on the grounds that the quality of the audit was too poor.[78]

When the eventual permanent IG, Howard Krongard, took over on 2 May 2005, he found, in his words, an OIG that "had fallen into disrepair, and that was known to have dissension and rivalries."[79] This organizational instability within the OIG occurred at arguably one of the department's most sensitive and precarious periods in its post–Cold War history: during the onset of the wars in Iraq and Afghanistan. In theory, the department of State and Defense OIGs might have been responsible for overseeing the US role in reconstructing the war-ravaged countries, but State OIG's shaky reputation and its lack of audit experience encouraged onlookers to cede responsibility for Iraq and Afghanistan reconstruction to independent special IGs—SIGIR and SIGAR—giving State OIG only a supervisory role.[80] The model of creating special webs of IGs was new—it was used for the first time after 9/11—and the PCIE's experience in establishing and coordinating them was limited.

The Curse of Partisanship

After Hume, Bush nominated private lawyer Howard J. "Cookie" Krongard to be the permanent State IG. With him came a wave of scandals that would destroy State OIG's already weak reputation. Like Ervin, Krongard was a registered Republican, believed to one of Bush's many "political" nonpolitical IG appointees, although he himself denied any association with the Bush administration.[81] Colleagues recognized him to be intelligent but an inept leader, and even a Republican-drafted House report meant to exonerate him conceded that his was an "extraordinarily abusive management style."[82] Repeatedly, according to critics, Krongard protected his partisan and personal interests to the detriment of the department and of broader democratic considerations. Aside from his own contentious decisions, there was little doubt that Krongard had inherited an office in disarray. Such was the dysfunction that Krongard sent to all staff, on the second anniversary of his appointment, a letter imploring them to seek reconciliation with one another. "I also ask you, frankly, to make an effort to reduce some of the static that interferes with the harmony we would like to achieve. We have enough challenges to focus on without spending energy in rivalries between functional offices, SA-3 [the Office of Investigation] and SA-39 [the Offices of Audits and of Inspections], and Foreign Service and Civil Service, or in rumoring, backbiting, and complaining," he wrote.[83] The tension between audit and investigative staff in OIGs had their roots in the 1978 act's awkward unification of the two disparate functions, and it was a well-known hindrance to OIG success across the federal government. Offices with the greatest success in issuing consequential reviews were those (such as the Justice and Homeland Security departments) that had managed to integrate the two functions formally through institutional structures designed to pool resources and expertise. Often an OIG is faced with violations that require both audit and investigative components. OIG structures that enable collaboration within the office give ready access to investigative teams in need of multidisciplinary skills. Such refining institutions define and clarify the office's goals and purpose, foster trust, and help give substance to the concepts of fraud, waste, and abuse as well as of accountability more generally. However, State OIG lacked any kind of formal, unifying unit or strategy, and it consequently continued to be riven by internal cultural competition.

Krongard had surely walked into a bureaucratic mess, but staff accused him of exacerbating the situation with his management style and his own abuse of power. In the scandal that would ultimately be the grounds for his resignation, Krongard blocked investigations into his role in protecting corrupt contractors for political reasons. The State Department had contracted a Kuwaiti company to build its sprawling new embassy in Baghdad, and the company was accused of human trafficking to bring cheap forced labor from Southeast Asia to complete the building. Other State Department officials later complained that the foreign workers' labor conditions violated American standards and that the embassy was so shoddily built that it was not safe for use. When the IG was brought in to investigate, Krongard allegedly performed the investigation himself, and, according to Representative Henry Waxman, he allowed the contractor to dictate the terms of the investigation and followed their suggestions regarding whom to interview.[84] The IG absolved the company of any wrongdoing.

Unlike some less high-profile IG reviews, the Iraqi contracting investigation also caught the attention of the departments of Defense and Justice. IG Krongard's pass on the contractor's performance was implicitly challenged when DOD auditors found evidence of misconduct where Krongard had found none. The Justice Department was asked to investigate to provide a third opinion.[85] But once scrutiny of Krongard's role in the matter was underway, he threateningly ordered staff not to cooperate with the congressional investigators.[86] Finally, CIGIE's Integrity Committee was called in to adjudicate. State Department OIG staff and other anonymous complainants submitted myriad allegations about the contracting investigation, but also about other investigations and Krongard's general management style, which included controlling investigations by withholding funds, interfering with the investigative process, or failing to report all findings, and basing his decisions on loyalty to political and family connections.[87] The oversight body elected to conduct an administrative investigation but was blocked by the FBI until the FBI's own criminal investigation was complete.

The Krongard controversy added fuel to the fire in a partisan dispute over the use of contractors in Iraq. In the House, Waxman crusaded against Krongard and provoked Republicans on the House Oversight Committee with his own tactics, leading Representative Tom Davis (R-VA) to accuse Waxman of "making 'grossly exaggerated and inflammatory charges.'"[88] However, in December 2007, before the months of political mudslinging could attain resolution, and before the FBI completed its investigation, Krongard stepped down. In his resignation letter to President Bush, Krongard cited his "concerns regarding inherent structural and conceptual defects in the inspector general position" at the State Department, and he blamed the polarized political environment for his difficulties in carrying out public service.[89] In 2007, the GAO also pointed out that the State OIG's budget had increased a mere 1 percent between 2001 and 2005, while its host department had seen a budget increase of 50 percent.[90] Moreover, because SIGIR could, by statute, only oversee funds for "relief and reconstruction," State OIG was assigned responsibility for overseeing a new block of "foreign operations" funding for Iraq authorized by Congress in 2006. Congress had offered the OIG $1.7 million the previous year for Iraq oversight, but Congress reduced it to $1.3 million in this bill; by comparison, SIGIR operated with a budget of $24 million.[91] As Krongard protested, the OIG at the time hardly had sufficient resources for its routine duties, much less for a further project on such a scale.[92]

For all the personal and professional allegations that plagued his stint as IG, Krongard contended with major, long-standing structural and organizational obstacles to providing oversight, and these were compounded by considerable resource constraints. The attention he called to the OIG's crippling lack of resources, as well as the toxic political and bureaucratic environment in which he operated, may not have been the only factors behind his controversial decisions at State, but his claim that it lacked the structural conditions for successful oversight could not be gainsaid.

Limbo

For less than a year, William E. Todd filled Krongard's position before Secretary of State Condoleezza Rice recruited former acting IG and ambassador Harold Geisel to head the office until a permanent IG could be confirmed. Bush nominated a former counterintelligence official, Thomas Betro, in June of 2008, but he was never confirmed. No more nominees were put forward until June 2013. This five-year period was the longest any OIG had gone without a permanent head.[93] State Department officials themselves preferred that the disempowered leader stay in charge and did not press for a new appointee.[94] Meanwhile, Geisel found himself without the permanent status to engage in far-reaching bureaucratic reform—sorely needed—but with the task of restoring the reputation of a badly battered office and healing the internal rifts that had been aggravated by Krongard's tenure. Previously he had worked under Funk as deputy IG and considered Funk a mentor.[95]

Geisel's office produced a variety of reviews that evaluated policy by applying principles other than those of efficiency and effectiveness. Just as Ervin's 2003 audit of Iraqi opposition groups led the United States to suspend their funding, Geisel's reviews of the embassies in Iraq and Afghanistan presented a sharp critique of the president's overall strategies. A routine inspection of the embassy in Kabul found that the "unprecedented pace and scope of the civilian build-up," in addition to a host of contextual factors, "will constrain the ability of these new officers in the short-term to promote stability, good governance, and rule of law . . . in Afghanistan."[96] The OIG framed its judgment in terms of pursuing the success demanded by the administration, but implicit was a critique of the administration's values. "There is tension among the US Government's lofty goals, the Embassy's ability to advance them, and the capacity and commitment of elements of the Afghan Government to implement them."[97] Other reviews did target efficiency but failed to recommend rigorous solutions. A 2011 review of the US embassy in Baghdad implied that the embassy was bloated and could be rightsized by eliminating more than a third of its positions; it estimated that this mismanagement cost the department over $100 million each year. Yet aside from this vague diagnosis, the report failed to identify any department members with responsibility and thus provoked no individual accountability.[98]

Geisel regularly attracted criticism for the rigor of individual reviews produced by his office, and the OIG continued to receive external criticism. In April 2011, the House Foreign Affairs Committee held a hearing in which Geisel was taken to task for his personal ties to former Foreign Service colleagues. The hearing was motivated by a GAO report from 2011 that followed up on compliance with and changes resulting from its evaluation in 2007. The GAO charged that State OIG's use of career Foreign Service officials "creates at a minimum an appearance of a conflict of interest at the very top."[99] External reviews lent credence to the GAO's concerns. At the behest of CIGIE, NASA's OIG conducted a review of State OIG's MERO and discovered that none of the audits performed by MERO followed the guidelines required by the governmentwide Yellow Book standards. Consequently, all of the "audits" were downgraded to inspections, meaning that MERO had failed to complete a single audit during its first year of existence. The GAO's 2011 report found that in the intervening five years, the OIG had taken steps toward acting on only two of the five main recommendations.[100] The GAO and Congress were unimpressed.

While State OIG continued to be the target of attacks from the GAO and external watchdog groups such as POGO, OIG staff insisted that the lack of a permanent IG did not necessarily hamper the rigor of reviews.[101] Geisel defended his office in his testimony, pointing to the substantial gains the OIG had made between 2007 and 2010: it had increased its number of annual reports from 107 to 157; its open investigations from 36 to 101; subpoenas issued from 0 to 25; and its contractor suspension and debarment actions from 0 to 5.[102] Moreover, he had expanded the OIG's staff twofold. But Geisel received more criticism for the circumstances of his position—unconfirmed—than for his personal behavior. This raised the perennial question of independence, what CIGIE executive director Phyllis Fong identified as the crux of the political debate over IGs.[103] How important is the independence of the IG to accountability? Can an acting IG lead an office that produces consequential reports? In essence, how important is leadership in an OIG? Throughout his term, staff and department members would complain that his lifelong career in the department led him to be too close to senior management, and private e-mails demonstrating his deference to them lent credence to the staff's claims.[104] Although the routine work of the OIG continued—the mandated audits and inspections—Geisel could veto or limit larger-scale projects that would prove embarrassing or costly to the department.

During Geisel's tenure, members of both the House and Senate joined forces to demand that President Obama move to fill the State IG position, but not until September 2013 did lawyer Steve Linick take the helm.[105] Linick had previously served as the Federal Finance Housing Agency IG and thus had IG experience, as well as investigative skills from his legal training. Even within his first few months, Linick attempted management reforms to steer the office in a new direction, such as management updates, which elevate certain recurring departmental problems to higher visibility. The OIG also developed a system of online crowd sourcing within its own offices to share best practices among embassies and foreign posts, and presented the model to other OIGs through CIGIE.[106]

A Lackluster Political Democracy

Much State OIG work was geared toward the maintenance of the department's political face and attempted to umpire the scandals that diminished the department's legitimacy in the public eye. Reviews analyzing the department's failure to provide accurate statistics for the public—such as in the 2005 review of incorrect terrorism data released to the public—forced transparency on the department, and though it fostered partisan wrangling, it also provoked wider public debate.[107] As OIG staff in the 1990s would complain, this type of accountability is not easily quantified; it touches directly on the difference between political and ideological commitments, on US defense of human rights and its commitments to democracy, on the government's tolerance of free speech and protection of privacy, and on the transparency of its actions and reports.

But there is a difference between defining accountability and effecting accountability. If some State IGs interpreted "effectiveness" as a question of diplomacy and democratic values, then they tacitly allowed the management pathologies and ineffective practices rooted in departmental culture to continue, thus undermining the department's ability to defend these values. The distrust that existed between the dysfunctional OIG and the dysfunctional department rendered the IG impotent in effecting accountability and underscored the highly relational and precarious authority wielded by the IGs.

The criticism leveled at the State OIG by Congress and the GAO has been warranted as well. Its mottled history is tied to decades-long constraints that have hampered the ability of individual IGs to produce consequential reviews. Some IGs, such as Funk, departed from the compliance model, but in the early days, they lacked the political clout and legitimacy to make their reviews carry weight. Though the OIG received persistent external criticism for the lack of rigor, consistency, and impartiality of its reviews, the obstacles preventing the OIG's success were rooted deeply in the organization's past and in its host department's recalcitrance. The GAO–congressional model of the IG was designed to look for malfeasance, waste, and inefficiency. The State IG model, in contrast, had long been a soft management support tool, an arbiter of turf wars, a therapist, and a line of communication between the bureau in Washington and far-flung posts with disparate needs and unheeded complaints. The clash of cultures endured long after the OIG's institutional conversion in the 1980s.

These failures prevented the OIG from contributing to a political democracy. If the State IGs could have prevented partisanship and ideology from playing an undue role in the nation's public international face, or in guarding the department from the ravages of political scandal, then they floundered consistently. The office either fell prey to the very scandal it was tasked with eradicating, or it was ignored when its judgments clashed with the politically expedient preferences of ambassadors and secretaries of state. In its capacity as a narrative provider, it failed as well: its reviews wallowed in the events qua scandal.

In 2001, former ambassador and OIG inspector Robert Steven reflected on State OIG's early history:

> I don't really think myself that the Inspector General's office, in the many, many years since 1980 that I've been associated, has made that much of a contribution. The department has resisted. We were pretty good at finding the fraud, you know. If somebody's embezzling the money, you'll find that, or something really wrong or if the ambassador is pinching the behinds of the secretaries, that will get reported, but the overall ability of our Inspector General system to influence the department positively, I think, has been minimal. It's pretty sad.[108]

In the decade after Steven's disillusioned reflection, the OIG endured further scandal, instability, and its own empty-chair policy.

CHAPTER FIVE

A POLITICAL DEMOCRACY AT STATE

Protecting Passport Privacy, 1992–2008

Everyone has three lives: a public life, a private life, and a secret life.
—Gabriel Garcia Marquez, *Gabriel Garcia Marquez: A Life* (2008)

Introduction

The private lives of public figures pique the curiosity of state officials as well as citizens, and protecting that privacy—controlling who has access to the details—has political as well as constitutional stakes. The two reviews analyzed below investigate the passport violations of two presidential candidates in the months before an election. At stake in both cases were the credibility of the administration in power and the integrity of the opposing campaign. In neither case was the IG able to protect administrative practice from partisan and ideological wrangling. The first case occurred in 1992, under the IG leadership of Sherman Funk, and the second in 2008 under newly installed acting IG Harold Geisel. Though these reviews cannot be taken as necessarily emblematic of all State OIG projects, they form part of a series of similar, related reviews of privacy violations (including a 1993 investigation of an unauthorized search of Bush administration officials' personal files). Both reviews were limited in their direct effects on the department and on democratic integrity, in the first instance because of external pressure to produce a report and in the second as a result of weak recommendations that were limited to compliance. Notable in both cases was the absence of language of rights: fundamental questions of the right to privacy were at stake, yet the IGs framed the events as scandals of individual or partisan origin. In this sense, the IGs' work was geared toward a political mode of democratic practice, but because in both cases the IG's institutional strategy targeted only the immediate source of the breach, neither review left long-lasting effects on the department.

"A Tempest in a Teapot": Clinton Passport File
Violations Reviews, 1992

In late September 1992, George H. W. Bush's reelection campaign found itself floundering. In a last-minute attempt to discredit his opponent, Bush's campaign stepped up its accusations of Democratic presidential candidate Bill Clinton's draft dodging during the Vietnam War and raised suspicions about his 1969 trip to Moscow as a student—what kind of relationships had he been forging? A FOIA request from the media triggered an expedited search for Clinton's passport files within the State Department.

By early October, the press reported suspicions that Clinton's files had been tampered with. Congressional Democrats—led by Senator John Kerry (D-MA) and Representative Howard Berman (D-CA)—initially enlisted the GAO to assess whether any laws had been broken and to determine who was responsible for the security lapses. Within the department, acting secretary of state Lawrence Eagleburger demanded an expedited investigation from IG Sherman Funk.[1] In media interviews, Funk insisted that he was pursuing "tough political questions" and not limiting the enquiry to procedural concerns.[2] Funk was among the first, and also among the most vocal, IGs to declare that IG reviews should go beyond compliance monitoring in their approach. In light of the stakes riding on the outcome of the investigation—the result of the imminent presidential election, with echoes of Watergate—he deemed the affair to be "a matter of national moment" and ceded the criminal investigation to the FBI, while he himself continued to pursue the administrative offense.[3]

According to Funk's account, the investigation began when Elizabeth Tamposi, head of CA and a Bush appointee, came to see him urgently and informed him that State had received a FOIA request for Clinton's passport file. While researching it, Tamposi said, State Department personnel discovered a file that appeared to have been tampered with. Numerous suspicious clues pointed to tampering: a tear at the corner of the documents, suggesting that a formerly stapled paper had been removed, and an odd placement in the file cabinet, with the Clinton file standing straight up as though recently consulted. The document that remained, however, appeared to be a normal passport application from 1968. She claimed that she was alerting Funk to the potential problem and asked him to investigate. Tamposi had brought the situation to the attention of a number of high-ranking officials, and moreover had (without telling Funk) taken the files in question home with her before their meeting. From Funk's perspective, the situation as it could unfold was win–win for the Republicans. Whether or not it was true, the mere charge that the files had been tampered with would weaken the Clinton campaign's credibility.

But the Bush administration had overstepped in its haste. In violation of its own regulations, the State Department had quickened the response to the requests. At first the Department maintained that all procedures had been followed correctly in checking the files, but Democrats protested vociferously. Vice presidential candidate Al Gore argued that "this goes way beyond a freedom of information request. The White House is politically using the State Department in a blatant attempt to politicize the entire bureaucracy in a failed effort to try to discredit Bill Clinton."[4]

Though on the surface the affair seemed to be an instance of an isolated violation of privacy—a single politically motivated act—the story behind the scenes suggested that the department's culture played a role in enabling the breach to occur. According to Funk and other department members, the Consular Affairs Bureau had long suffered from dysfunction, and Tamposi's leadership was a mixed bag. CA fostered a culture of blame dodging where "nobody wanted to be naked" in front of Congress.[5] Indeed, when accused, Tamposi would shift the blame to her superior, Undersecretary of State for Management John F. W. Rogers. One of Tamposi's staff members, FSO Elizabeth Ann Swift, recalled that under Bush's leadership, political appointees were taught "don't trust the bureaucracy." She observed, "The people who came in at high levels to the State Department, with a few exceptions, tended to be exceptionally arrogant and very, very suspicious of us."[6] Their loyalty remained with the administration, and so when Tamposi received a request to expedite the search from the White House, she launched an urgent search. The call came from John H. Sununu, Bush's chief of staff, and a friend and neighbor of Tamposi's back in their home state of New Hampshire.[7] The view from below—that of the career FSOs under Tamposi's watch in CA—was that Tamposi's appointee attitude got the better of her. In short, the wrongdoing, from the perspective of some fellow State Department members, had its source not only in dubious ethics but also in poor leadership and bad management. If the bureaucracy could, in theory, have served as a check on executive overreach, in this case, it was overridden by the administration's philosophy of keeping appointees aloof and mistrustful of their agencies.

The FBI quickly concluded that there had been no tampering by anyone.[8] So Eagleburger tasked Funk with new questions: how and why had the files been searched? A new wrinkle emerged: the State Department had broken its own regulations in monitoring Tamposi—potentially a criminal offence. The department's Operations Center, known as the Watch, through which intradepartmental telephone calls were routed, had monitored calls between the main suspects in the passport case. In late September and early October, Tamposi and Stephen K. Berry, assistant secretary of state for legislative affairs, shared a number of telephone calls about the details of the case. In one of the conversations, Tamposi asked for recommendations of other Bush appointees who might assist in the file searches at the embassies in London and Oslo.[9] Unbeknownst to Tamposi and Berry, their calls were not only intercepted but also broadcast live to the entire call center, in direct violation of the center's manual, which stipulates that calls between officials "should not be monitored unless they so request."[10] This discovery by the IG investigation opened the door to an entirely new set of concerns that extended far beyond the initial charge of violating privacy laws (an administrative misdemeanor).

The IG Review

The OIG refused to investigate the center's actions until it finished the passport files case. This was highly unusual and in conflict with the OIG's standard practice of pursuing criminal misconduct before administrative misdeeds. The OIG finally released its report on the passport files, *Special Inquiry into the Search and Retrieval of William Clinton's Passport Files*, on 18 November 1992. It was damning of Berry's role in the affair and suggested that his actions had political motives, and "were inappropriate and probably a violation of the Hatch Act." Accordingly, it recommended disciplinary action. Tamposi was the primary political casualty of the affair even though she had not personally rifled through the files and the request to expedite the search had come from Sununu, who was above her. Her dismissal on 10 November 1992 came as a direct result of the anticipated findings of the IG report. She claimed that she was being made the scapegoat for a much larger, White House–orchestrated incident. Her special assistant, political appointee Steven M. Moheban, resigned voluntarily in mid-November, similarly in anticipation of the IG report.[11]

Though Berry left his post, he was merely reassigned to another office within the department with the same salary.[12] The IG report pinned the blame squarely on the two appointees but exonerated the White House, suggesting that while it may have had knowledge of the probes, it was not an active player.[13] However, the report did not satisfy Congress. For Representative Howard Berman (D-CA), there were too many inconsistencies and unanswered questions about the White House's role in the matter.[14]

The IG's sparing of the White House made congressional Democrats call foul, and so the report's release prompted another round of parallel oversight. Eagleburger requested the appointment of an IC to investigate. A Republican, Joseph diGenova, was appointed special prosecutor. Although diGenova declared the Bush administration aides had done "stupid, dumb and indeed partisan things" during the passport searches, he cleared them of criminal wrongdoing.[15] He also sharply disapproved of the IG investigation, describing it as "incompetent" and suggesting that Funk's staff had conducted their interviews poorly and misinterpreted evidence.[16] Moreover, the special prosecutor declared that Funk had pressured his investigators to submit a review too quickly and thus produced a substandard report.[17] The pressure, however, resulted from the hastening sunset of the Investigative Counsel Act, which was due to expire in early December 1992. Had the IG report not been released by then, no special counsel investigation would have been possible. In 1995, after a three-year, $2.2 million special investigation, Tamposi and her colleagues were exonerated.[18]

Immediate Effects

The reviews had a greater impact outside the department than inside. Though two staff members were terminated (one was fired and the other resigned in anticipation of being released), no higher-level personnel were disciplined for knowledge or involvement. Because the review focused on an individual act, assumed to be politically motivated, the IG's conclusions related to the culpability of the individuals involved rather than to the procedural problems that may have enabled the transgression in the first place. Despite its inaccuracies and inadequate methodology, outside the department, the report led to considerable publicity, generating 430 media citations between October 1992 and October 1996—a larger than usual number for an IG report in the early 1990s (see Table 4.2). It also led to the immediate launch of an IC investigation.

The IG in the Web of Accountability

Despite its failure to provoke positive, long-lasting effects on either the department or the protection of privacy, the IG review played a pivotal role in influencing the way other actors in the web of accountability conducted their own business. The GAO and the IC both shaped their respective investigations in reaction to the IG's, and the IC's conclusion would later contribute to the retirement of the Independent Counsel Act in 1999.

The GAO—The Senate Foreign Relations Committee, the House Foreign Affairs Committee, and the House Committee on Post Office and Civil Service together requested an investigation by the GAO; indeed, in the early 1990s, Congress preferred this mode of investigation to the IG review. Congress's decision to ask the GAO for an investigation was based on its lack of trust in Funk, a political appointee, to conduct a rigorous independent investigation. There were good reasons for Congress's suspicions of the IG. Funk was a registered Republican who had recently traveled for two weeks with one of the primary suspects in the case, Undersecretary for Management John F. W. Rogers. But the GAO, part of the legislative branch, was cautious about following leads that took it to Representative Gerald B. H. Solomon (R-NY), ranking member of the House Rules Committee.[19]

Even in this early period in its history, the IG already wielded more investigative authority than the GAO (even though the GAO was preferred by many members of Congress). Like the OIG, the GAO also broadened its investigation beyond the passport file search to include the department's eavesdropping on itself. But the GAO's investigation proceeded at a much slower pace than the IG's; it was still underway when Congress appointed a special investigator under the Independent Counsel Act in December.[20] Over a year later, when the GAO had still not completed its investigation, the State Department found itself embroiled in yet another passport file breach scandal. This time the tables had turned: Clinton administration officials had illegally searched the files of outgoing Bush appointees. The GAO folded the old investigation into the new one. It finally released a pair of reports in July 1994, nearly two years after the initial breach. These reports surveyed the privacy controls that various agencies had over political appointees' personal files and found them still deficient.[21] Like most of the GAO's reports, they were written from a broad perspective that focused on the governmentwide problem rather than the specific manifestations of it. In the case of the second incident, the GAO initiated its investigation after State OIG had begun its own. To avoid repetition and overlap in oversight, the two bodies met, and the GAO discovered that twenty-one of twenty-two questions that they had been assigned to investigate were already being investigated by the OIG. (The final question concerned privacy controls outside of the State Department, and thus fell outside the OIG's remit.) Rather than duplicate the OIG's work, the GAO effectively ceded the authoritative narrative to the OIG, declaring, "Based on our review of OIG's report and supporting evidence, we concluded that OIG's work had answered almost all of the questions that had originally been posed to us by congressional requesters. We did not attempt to reinvestigate the same issues that OIG had covered."[22]

Because the GAO lacked the statutory authority to demand interviews with department members, the main actors in State's White House Liaison Office declined to be interviewed by the GAO. In short, the GAO's contribution to the oversight effort consisted in little more than a partial reproduction of the IG's investigation and a summary review of its conclusions.

Independent counsel—Special prosecutor Joseph diGenova spent three years conducting an investigation in response to the IG's conclusion. Although the IG's role in the matter was complete once his review was released in November, Funk stayed entangled in the case as the IC investigation proceeded. In February 1993, Funk took the unusual step of publicly challenging the court testimony of a senior administration member, Frank M. Machak, saying that his testimony contradicted earlier statements he had made to the OIG interviewers.[23] But the IC's investigation ultimately won the battle for narrative legitimacy, nullifying the claims of the IG report. In addition to discrediting the IG's authority, diGenova's report and public statements all put the role of the IC investigation in question. He insisted that the affair should never have been referred to the Justice Department and should never have had a special prosecutor assigned to it, implying that the cost of the special investigation was a waste and the investigative work redundant, in light of what should have been accomplished by the IG. DiGenova's criticism played an important role in spurring wide discontent with the special counsel framework, which was finally retired in 1999.[24] Arguably, the elimination of the IC as an instrument of accountability had the effect of encouraging Congress to resort to the IGs as their primary executive oversight tool in the next decade. Ultimately, the IG's failures may have had the paradoxical consequence of generating congressional support for the IG model in the long term.

Other processes—The IG report and the subsequent special investigation provoked three parallel court cases.[25] First, the disgraced former appointee, Steven Berry, refused to cooperate with the special prosecutor's subpoena for documents on the grounds that the entire special investigation was premised on information that was gathered illegally. He later brought an unsuccessful suit against Funk for having used illegal information.[26] US district judge Charles Richey brought a second civil suit against administration staff for not adhering to data storage regulations; some of the unpreserved data in question was potential evidence in diGenova's investigation. Finally, on the basis of the evidence provided in the IG report, *Nation* magazine sued the State Department for politically manipulating the FOIA process. All of these cases interfered with the special investigation and delayed its outcome.

Pursuing a Political Democracy: A Failed Investigation

Though his investigation was loud—reaching the ears of the media and of Congress—Funk's report had limited long-term effects on the department and no effect on administrative procedure, norms, or departmental infrastructure. Funk's staff still lacked highly qualified, experienced auditors and investigators, lending credence to diGenova's later assessment that the investigative team had misinterpreted their own interview notes. Its conclusion was responsible for direct accountability in the sense of sanctions, with the immediate dismissal of two public officials, but this was based on a poorly conducted analysis that proved to be in error. The IG's institutional strategy of only targeting the individual circumstances of the case rather than evaluating the existing procedures for privacy protection, coupled with the time constraints imposed by the impending expiration of the Independent Counsel Act, led the IG to conduct a substandard investigation that vexed the overall process of accountability and discredited the department's reputation.

However, the incident proved to have unintended and indirect but lasting effects on the web of accountability. An IG investigation as a process of accountability must be separated analytically from the validity of the report's results. The Clinton passport review produced an analysis later deemed to be incorrect. Despite this, it provoked, interacted with, and complemented other processes of accountability.

Obama Passport Files, 2008

In March 2008, a headline in the *Washington Times* announced that presidential candidate Barack Obama's passport files had been accessed three times without authorization. Although the department's automated security system alerted officials to the breaches in January 2008, department officials kept mum until approached by journalists. Calls for accountability came from many corners: acting IG Geisel initiated a review immediately after the first news report, and simultaneously, senators Patrick Leahy and Arlen Specter (R-PA) sent a letter to Attorney General Michael Mukasey requesting a Justice Department investigation, but Mukasey declined to launch one until the IG report had been released.[27]

No echoes were heard of the Clinton file scandal fifteen years earlier, and any privacy protections the department had put in place as a result had long since eroded. The passport breaches were partly enabled by two parallel phenomena: the post-9/11 movement to expand data collection and sharing within the government (the pressures of emergency governance), and the government's expanding use of contractors.[28] In October 2007, President Bush had implemented the National Strategy for Information Sharing, which encouraged specific modes of expanding data collection and sharing, such as fusion centers and the Homeland Security Information Network.[29] The plan did not, however, update or strengthen existing privacy protections. Across the board, the statutory framework for privacy protections had not evolved at the same pace as national security demands and technological innovations. To compound the problem of loosened privacy protections, 40 to 45 percent of the State Department's visa personnel were private contractors between 2001 and 2008.[30] Although, according to the Privacy Act, contractors must be treated as agency employees in their standards of conduct and in corresponding disciplinary actions, the IG found that the "CA management does not believe it has the authority to discipline department employees outside CA" and that "contract supervisors, rather than CA management, [should] discipline contract employees."[31]

The State of the OIG

To compound matters, the OIG was emerging from its own set of scandals, with its independence acutely in question. The OIG's resources had fallen in real terms since 2001, while the department's staff and responsibilities had grown. Moreover, when the Obama passport file scandal began to unfold, Geisel had just been elevated to the position of acting IG after a mere six-month stint of leadership by Ambassador William Todd. Only a year earlier, the GAO had issued a negative assessment of the OIG, questioning its independence and effectiveness as a result of its long-standing practice of using career FSOs to lead the office when lacking a confirmed IG.[32] A peer review performed by the NASA OIG found other problems in Geisel's OIG, including a lack of rigor in MERO audits.[33] The OIG's critics feared that it lacked the protection from political influence that organizational security affords. The OIG had suffered many years of instability, and its reputation on the Hill and in the media—and the legitimacy of its judgments—was in tatters. The independence of the acting IG himself was equally tenuous. In addition to his lacking the blessing of the Senate, Geisel's professional background was entirely at the State Department; he had a degree in finance and experience as a manager, but he had no credentials as an auditor or investigator.[34] Some anonymous State Department members sent letters to watchdog groups claiming that Geisel had excessively close ties to management, and e-mails between Geisel and top department officials in Iraq demonstrated Geisel's deference to departmental prerogative.[35] The OIG lacked sufficient resources, reputation, cohesive bureaucratic culture, and an individual independent IG at the head of the organization. In short, it was not poised to issue a consequential report.

The IG Review

The IG report, *Reviews of Controls and Notification for Access to Passport Records in the Department of State's Passport Electronic Records System (PIERS)—AUD/IP-08-29*, was released in July 2008. However, it was heavily redacted, with only six of the twenty-two total recommendations released. Nearly the entire results section and all of the substantive appendices, which include the discussion of recommendations between the State Department subcomponents and the OIG, were redacted. In addition to the executive summary and occasional isolated paragraphs throughout the report, only the broad assessment and methodology were accessible, and each of these suggested considerable systemic problems with the security system linked to PIERS and with the associated disciplinary processes.

Given that the monitoring system had detected the accessing of the passports, the breach was not in question and was not the subject of the IG's audit. Rather, the audit probed the context in which the violations took place to determine whether the department's current system prevented unauthorized access and whether the department took appropriate action after breaches of the system.[36] In the review, the OIG censured the efficacy of the privacy protection framework. The review was critical of the department's monitoring system, reporting that "it was very limited in the number and types of individuals captured," that "the list contained the names of thirty-eight of about 127 million passport holders," and that no mechanisms were in place for detecting the illicit search of less famous, or ordinary, citizens. As a way of testing the frequency of searches on less prominent individuals, the OIG investigators produced a list of 150 high-profile individuals not already registered in the system and checked to see the number of times their passport records had been checked, if at all, between September 2002 and March 2008. One hundred twenty-seven, or 85 percent, of a total of 150 individuals' passport files had been accessed during this period. But though the report hints that these statistics might be anomalous, it refrains from declaring an unequivocal judgment, stating, "Although an 85 percent hit rate appears to be excessive, the department currently lacks criteria to determine whether this is actually an inordinately high rate."[37] The review also acknowledges that it relied on the State Department itself (the CA) to produce the data, and that even between two data sets produced by the CA, there were important discrepancies—factors that put the accuracy of the data in question.

Moreover, although the monitoring system alerted authorities that a breach had occurred, the perpetrators had been able to access the files successfully. The review highlighted two troubling aspects of the overall system. First, the State Department could not identify either the number or the identity of government staff and contractors with access to the database; and second, the system itself had no protocols to protect the information. Because the database was shared with other agencies and departments, such as the FBI, DHS, and the Office of Personnel Management, each with entirely different procedures for security, State effectively lost control of the information's security.[38]

Effects of the Review

The incident resulted in an apology from Secretary of State Condoleezza Rice to the three candidates whose passport files had been breached. All three demanded a congressional investigation in addition to Rice's apology, but the oversight committees were not forthcoming. As a result of the IG audit, the department fired two contractors and disciplined a third.[39] Over the course of the next eighteen months, eight further contractors were found guilty of a misdemeanor in the Justice Department's criminal investigations of personnel referred by the IG. This ongoing criminal investigation, which began at the behest of the IG in December 2008 and which continued for over year, found a number of State Department employees guilty of accessing the passport files of celebrities, and the culpable persons were placed on probation.

Although the department indicated in the immediate aftermath of the original report's release that it would implement all of the IG's recommendations, the partially unredacted review released in 2010 under court orders revealed that the CA had still failed to implement the suggested reforms. Because investigators feared that releasing the entire review, which described the privacy system in detail, would enable further abuse, much of it was left redacted (even after a court case by a civil liberties watchdog group). Although this in theory protected the integrity of the system, it did little to increase the transparency of the government's actions and commitment to protecting citizens' rights. The report did have the effect of prodding the department to expand the size of the watch list from thirty-eight high-profile individuals to over 1,000; however, most of these people were members of Congress, the Supreme Court, and the upper echelons of the administration, as well as some media and sports celebrities.[40] The department's response, in short, was egocentric self-protection.

Limits of the Review

Like many State IG reviews, the Obama passport review concentrated narrowly on the case at hand, without linking it explicitly to the broader phenomenon of passport breaches and lax data security in the State Department or to governmentwide data protection more generally. As in many IG reviews, a breach of rights was framed as the result of a procedural deficiency. The lack of procedural safeguards led to lax security, which in turn led to a violation of privacy rights. This general topic had been on the IG's agenda since the early 1990s and resurfaced multiple times later in that decade when foreign spies posing as journalists were able to gain access to the department, and again when computers with sensitive information were lost in the late 1990s. However, the IG report left the wider implications to political actors—a task that Leahy took up in his congressional testimony by urging further criminal investigations and concrete legislation.

At least in the unredacted portion of the review, the IG did not address the lack of governmentwide standards for privacy protection or the absence of any sort of data breach law on the federal level. Moreover, despite the White House's suggestion in 2007 that federal agencies establish notification policies after breaches occur, no such policy existed at the State Department when the candidates' files were improperly accessed.[41] Of the six unredacted recommendations, the CA concurred with all but one. However, the recommendations were couched in weak language, suggesting, for instance, that the CA "consider the types of controls" that other government agencies had put in place, that it "ensure the accuracy of its Privacy Impact Assessments . . . for PIERS," and that the CA "review its Memoranda of Agreement and Memoranda of Understanding with all other federal agencies and other entities to ensure that they are revised to adequately and specifically address issues related to PIERS and the passport data it contains."[42] Rather than propose robust reforms, the review merely urged the bureau to review its existing framework.

Not only did the review fail to provoke any kind of reckoning with privacy policy wholesale but it also failed to make effective changes in the immediate object of investigation: the PIERS database. Within two years of the review, another breach occurred. In 2010, a department employee was found improperly accessing the PIERS system to investigate the passports of certain celebrities and was given a fourteen-day suspension. The OIG contextualized the breach by explaining that "it should be noted that this employee's improper PIERS accesses occurred after the initial PIERS inquiry began in 2008 and notice had been sent to all department of State employees with PIERS access regarding the consequences of improper use of the PIERS system."[43] This commentary suggested that the OIG's primary defense against privacy breaches after the 2008 affair was a single notice sent to department staff. In the long term, the IG's recommendations did little to stem the tide of privacy breaches; a 2014 GAO report revealed that governmentwide, the number of personal data violations had climbed steadily from 10,481 breaches in 2008 to 25,566 in 2013.[44] Though not limited to the State Department, these figures suggest that privacy protection frameworks had not kept pace with technological advances in data storage and access.

The IG in the Web of Accountability

As in 1992, the IG report's role in triggering external accountability processes was stronger than its direct effects in terms of reforms and immediate accountability within the department.

Congress—Unlike the 1992 event, the 2008 passport file breaches did not generate a series of congressional movements for further investigations (i.e., through the GAO or a congressional investigation). Congress's attitude toward the IG had shifted since 1992. Though senators Leahy and Specter were suspicious of a purely internal investigation conducted by the IG, they were appeased when, at their behest, DOJ agreed to assist the IG in its work.[45] Rather than defer to the GAO's judgment, the oversight committees waited for the IG to complete its report before making any decisions about further action. A spokesperson for Senator Joe Biden (D-DE), the chairman of the Senate Foreign Relations committee, declared that the "committee is sort of yielding to IG and the DOJ," and the DOJ itself awaited the IG's report before getting involved.[46]

Senator Leahy used the report as the basis for his testimony in a hearing on the affair, and he also used it as evidence for the privacy protection bill he coauthored with Specter (the Personal Data Privacy and Security Act, S.495), though it never passed. The immediate concern of senators Leahy and Specter was that the IG urge the development and adoption of common standards for civil servants and contractors. In other words, they pushed the IG to adopt an institutional strategy that built procedural infrastructure rather than simply suggest that the department consider reform.

The GAO—While the GAO was asked to produce a general review of the then-current status of privacy protection laws (a review it released in May 2008), its report made no mention of the candidates' passport breaches.[47] Rather, it surveyed possible solutions to emerging privacy protection issues and recommended appropriate congressional action. However, no action was taken.

Civil society—A FOIA request in July 2008 by a watchdog group, the Electronic Privacy Information Center, failed to produce an unredacted version.[48] The government's refusal to release the full report prompted the Electronic Privacy Information Center to take the State Department to court, forcing the department at last to issue a partly unredacted version in June 2010. It remained partly redacted on the grounds that many of the review's recommendations had yet to be implemented by the department—two years after their issuance. The newly revealed portions of the report exposed the department's weaknesses and provided more specific criticisms. The report faulted the department's ability to detect unauthorized access to the database and blamed this on the design of the monitoring system, which required proactive checks by administrators (not usually forthcoming) to function properly.[49]

PIERS Controls Review: Limited Scope, Limited Effects

The review produced little individual accountability in the form of sanctions, aside from a small number of low-level suspensions, and little procedural reform. In its framing of the problem, there was no reckoning with the broader legal context of privacy protection or with the ambiguities of responsibility and challenges associated with contractors. The department's attention to the report was dilatory and partial, with the rereleased version of the report in 2010 indicating that the Bureau of Consular Affairs had yet to implement some of the recommendations even two years later. Of the unredacted recommendations, all were couched in weak language, and none provided clear, forceful guidance for building the procedural framework or for developing clear disciplinary practices. Moreover, the OIG's two stated goals of determining whether the department's protections were "adequate" and whether it "responds effectively,"[50] gave the audit a narrow interpretive focus and led the OIG to neglect the department's parallel efforts through its "Working Group to Mitigate Vulnerabilities to Unauthorized Access to Passport Data" in its investigation. Finally, the review itself attracted little attention, eliciting a mere 220 media citations—half the number of citations of Funk's 1992 review (see Table 4.2).

Privacy in a Political Democracy

State OIG consistently found itself as the defender of privacy rights through the monitoring of passport searches, but its reviews transposed questions of constitutional right into the register of political expedience, thus engaging in a political mode of democratic practice. Yet neither review surveyed above was ultimately consequential in its effects on departmental policy or in refining the system in place to prevent future abuses. The reviews also failed to provide a rigorous and trusted narrative for the public. Whereas the Funk review was forceful in the blame it laid on the accused, its methodology, and thus ultimately its conclusions, were judged by subsequent investigators to be sloppy and incorrect. Both reviews stumbled into the very scandal under investigation and managed to provoke internal scandals in the OIG.

Though the challenges faced by each were distinct, both reviews contended with contextual difficulties. Funk's review suffered from the pressure to complete a review in time to invoke the Independent Counsel Act— pressure that led him to rush and bungle a delicate operation. Like most OIGs at the time, Funk's office lacked the budgetary resources to conduct rigorous analyses. The review uncovered an unexpected additional breach of privacy by the State Department, which both complicated and compromised the integrity of Funk's investigation. He also made strategic mistakes, privileging the administrative side of the affair over the criminal dimension (potentially for political reasons). With his characteristic zeal, he publicized his review even before the results were complete, and he kept the media abreast of developments. This stoked public ire and put pressure on the administration to act quickly.

Geisel's challenges were different. Although the IG community as a whole enjoyed bipartisan support in 2008, with Congress actively debating the most sweeping amendment to the 1978 IG Act in twenty years, State OIG was the emblem of a troubled office. Observers on the Hill and beyond attested to this in GAO assessments, congressional hearings, and complaints from watchdog groups. If IG effectiveness—or any kind of bureaucratic success—depends on reputation-based legitimacy, State OIG's credibility and latitude were at a nadir. Geisel struggled with an office in turmoil, one that was underfunded and riven by internal rivalries. Because of his unconfirmed status, he himself lacked the independence to issue a strongly critical review. This partly explains the weakness of the report's recommendations.

The differences between the two cases illustrate the changes seen in State OIG and in the role of the IGs over time. The first review investigated the circumstances of a particular case, assigning blame to individuals; the second targeted the privacy protection framework and faulted the inadequacy of the systems in place. The difference in congressional attitudes between the earlier investigation and a similar one sixteen years later could not have been starker. Whereas in 1992 Congress did not even have sufficient confidence in the IGs to commission an investigation, by 2008 it was the IG report that sparked an urgent Senate hearing. In his testimony before the Senate Oversight Committee, Arlen Specter remarked on how unusual it was for an oversight hearing to be called only three days after an evaluative report, yet he justified the decision by referring to the weight of the IG's review.[51] The differences between the two cases also highlight changes in the nature of oversight: by 2008, a computerized monitoring system was in place to detect when any department official accesses the passport files of a high-profile individual. It was this automated system, rather than an individual, that instigated the investigation, creating an entirely new security framework with which to contend.

However, certain processes remained the same. In both cases, the IG was responsible for provoking a second mode of accountability by referring the matter to the criminal division of the Justice Department for a criminal investigation. The reviews demonstrate the IG's fragility on account of its material resources and organizational capacities, as well as its reliance on a web of accountability to effect immediate, direct change in its host department. The IGs' task in both investigations was to manage the political impact of privacy breaches and to restore the department's integrity through structural and procedural change. Where they could have safeguarded the reputation and legitimacy of the department, their weak institutional strategies and material handicaps caused them to fall radically short.

CHAPTER SIX

LAWYERS OUT OF COURT

Guarding the Guardians at Justice

It is not what a lawyer tells me I may do; but what humanity,
reason, and justice tell me I ought to do.
—Edmund Burke, *Second Speech on Conciliation with America*
(1775)

Introduction

In the muddled separation of powers provoked by the administrative state, IGs often find themselves in the position of a judge, forced to hold bureaucratic actors to standards of constitutional right. In its first twenty-five years, the Justice Department OIG pursued many high-profile reviews that identified executive activity violating civil and human rights, and that promulgated norms of the appropriate scope of executive behavior beyond those codified in law. These reviews went beyond mere compliance monitoring and questioned the propriety of government action, whether through individual behavior or through agencywide decisions about the implementation of policy. The Justice IGs' ability to forge a constitutional democracy was underpinned by a special organizational capacity oriented toward issues of misconduct, overreach, and rights violation. Discursively, this direction depended on the IG's interpretation of his role and what constitutes government wrongdoing; materially, it required a fusion of the OIG's audit and investigation functions, and led to the cultivation of a specific bureaucratic organization and culture oriented toward investigating abuses of a constitutional nature.

The OIG's strong reviews were made possible in part because of successive IGs' high level of independence, which in turn contributed to its reputation and thus its legitimacy. This independence had its source in three interlinked places: a culture (in the form of a distinctive mission); structural capacity (in the form of specific expertise); and statute. It was cultivated over time and was grounded in an OIG identity that rested on a specific skill set (i.e., investigative legal experience embodied in the Special

Investigations and Review Unit); later it was buttressed with national security expertise. Most important, the perception of independence on the part of congressional and other public actors resulted from its reputation. The main institutional innovation of IG Michael Bromwich, the creation of a special unit staffed primarily with people with investigative legal expertise, unified the OIG with its combined audit–investigative capacities, and in so doing overcame the audit–investigative division that hampers many OIGs from issuing consequential reviews. This unit was the embodiment of a capacity whose exercise proved to be the long-term basis for the IG's strong reputation in Congress and in its host department, and led to both the perception and fact of independence.

Finally, the Justice IG's independence also resulted from a Congress eager to curb the excesses—both actual and potential—of the executive in times of emergency. Although the IG's work was not limited to executive emergency action, it was the mandate that it gained as a result of emergency-related legislation that permitted it to expand its scope and undertake the robust reviews that appeared in its second decade of existence. In short, Congress's reaction to executive emergency action, coupled with the vision and aggressive management of particular IGs, led to a broad expansion of the IG's capacities and the scope of its activity, and deepened its independence. As the OIG developed a reputation for neutrality, rigor, and independence, its legitimacy grew, and the reviews were used in conjunction with other internal and external mechanisms of accountability.

Modest Beginnings, 1990–1994

At the time of the 1978 IG Act, the Justice Department was loath to host an IG within its ranks, arguing that Congress's attempt to monitor the executive branch with IGs was an improper violation of the separation of powers.[1] With the help of congressional Republicans, it successfully resisted a statutory IG on grounds of sensitive information and national security concerns, and the Reagan administration maintained this line by holding to the notion that it would be impossible to have an IG in the cabinet agency that is headed by the nation's chief law enforcement officer. In the debates leading to the 1988 amendments to the act, Senator John Glenn (D-OH) and Representative Jack Brooks (D-TX) successfully fought for the act to include Justice and Treasury against a bevy of Republican congressmen reluctant to submit the national security apparatus to further internal oversight. In 1989, Congress established an IG in the DOJ.

The Justice Department IG was not identical to the other OIGs. In addition to the national security exemption with which its host agency may block its investigations, it was the only office to have its jurisdiction curtailed by a parallel body within the DOJ, the Office of Professional Responsibility (OPR). The amended 1978 act also permitted the attorney general to block IG investigations about any ongoing department cases.[2] Finally, the DOJ OIG was required to obtain attorney general permission for any criminal case involving the FBI or the Drug Enforcement Administration (DEA). When it was established, the OIG emerged as a unique patchwork of administrative centers from within the department, fusing offices with vastly different purposes and bureaucratic cultures, including the Audit Office in the Justice Management division, the Policy Development of the DEA, and the INS's Internal Affairs Office.

The first Justice IG thus contended with a number of institutional and political obstacles to its oversight. In its first years, the OIG lacked critical bureaucratic unity and identity. It took over a year for the position to be filled by the Bush administration, but beginning in 1990, the job was held by Richard Hankinson, who had previously served as a Secret Service agent and special agent in numerous federal entities.[3] Hankinson's first challenge was to unify the patchwork of bodies from which the OIG was culled, and he found himself intertwined in a series of resources battles that stemmed from OPR–OIG rivalry. Some of his staff—highly qualified auditors and inspectors—were automatically transferred to the OIG from other parts of Justice, but Hankinson was able to choose his own chief counsel and executive assistant. He hired former colleagues from the Secret Service.[4] He also struggled with the definitional limits of his office: given the restrictions placed on it by the 1988 act, it was unclear what kind of issues the OIG could and should pursue. He was criticized for not pursuing criminal FBI investigations, but Hankinson was deterred by the law prohibiting such investigations without attorney general approval. Although the majority of issues followed by the OIG came from requests within the department, the IG also investigated sensitive or large programs and congressional requests.[5] Despite the IG's institutional struggles, the department proved responsive to the reports, especially the audits, which helped to streamline department management.

Building an OIG Identity, 1994–1999

The second IG, Michael Bromwich, whose tenure lasted until the end of the decade, established a precedent for strong reports within this hostile institutional context, particularly by putting consistent pressure on a troubled FBI. Bromwich, a Clinton nominee, was originally slated to head a joint OPR–OIG pending the resignation of Hankinson. He had been a prosecutor in the Iran-Contra investigations. At the time, he had been accused of prosecutorial misconduct by Oliver North's defense attorneys, but the judge dismissed the motion for a mistrial. Bromwich came with Harvard credentials, a string of prosecutorial successes, and a reputation for being "an able and vigorous prosecutor" and a "consummate professional."[6] Though his adversaries characterized him as being "mean" and as having a "nasty demeanor," Senator Orrin Hatch (R-UT) noted in the press that these were ideal characteristics for an IG.[7]

Bromwich came to the job with a dubious view of the IG profession, having been unimpressed with how "shoddy" and "unbalanced" the IG work had been that he encountered earlier in the 1980s in his capacity as a lawyer.[8] When he asked Bromwich to take the job, Assistant Attorney General Philip Heymann promised that the OPR would be fused with the OIG so that the IG's jurisdiction would extend to the DOJ's legal activity. From the beginning of their custody battle in 1990, the OPR and the OIG saw jurisdictional tension limit their cooperation, and the Justice Department often privileged the OPR in delegating responsibility.[9] In addition to the jurisdictional struggle, Heymann had been highly critical of the OPR for its lack of strength and transparency in holding DOJ attorneys to account, and he advocated a new department policy of disclosing the wrongdoing of department attorneys in a larger number of cases.[10] Heymann's next move (before his own resignation) was to push for the OPR–OIG merger. With some reluctance and skepticism toward the IG profession, the prospect of working with a cadre of lawyers tempted Bromwich, and Heymann's promise to merge the two bodies lured him to take the job.

But the merger never materialized. There had been early recognition that the two bodies would have overlapping jurisdictions, but OPR head Michael Shaheen resisted the proposal.[11] Bromwich's past as a prosecutor in Iran-Contra opened him to charges of partisanship. In response to the proposed merger, in March 1994, Republicans on the Senate Judiciary Committee—with the exception of William Cohen (R-ME)—wrote a series of letters to the attorney general to voice their opposition.[12] In them, they suggested that the conduct of lawyers should stay out of the hands of a political appointee (the IG) and rather be entrusted to the career Justice Department officials. Faced with the threat of a blocked IG nomination, potentially for months, Attorney General Janet Reno obliged.[13]

Over the better part of the next two decades, this institutional separation would significantly hamper the IG's capacity to investigate DOJ legal actions, including certain national security policies, because it precludes the IG from investigating the DOJ's own attorneys' actions, such as the written justification of enhanced interrogation methods; the role of DOJ lawyers in the NSA's warrantless surveillance program; and the use of material witness warrants to detain immigrants after 9/11.[14] The arrangement creates a conflict of interest within the OPR, which is not independent of the attorney general yet must evaluate the attorney general's actions.[15] It would also provide an escape clause for the attorney general when faced with allegations embarrassing to the department—allegations that could be steered toward the OPR, which does not publish the majority of its reviews.[16] Heymann also tasked the new IG with building a strong internal review capacity within the department. This came on the back of two embarrassing scandals for the DOJ in the early 1990s: the Ruby Ridge incident, in which the child of tax resisters was shot by an FBI SWAT team, and the Branch Davidian disaster in Waco, Texas. Both of these cases revealed the DOJ's lack of self-investigative capacity, and Heymann believed that the IG could serve as the solution.

Once at the helm, Bromwich pursued a two-pronged strategy for building an OIG identity: recruit investigative lawyers with good writing skills, and initiate special investigations above and beyond the semiannual reports. Bromwich's background as a lawyer biased him toward legal expertise and led him to prioritize hiring prosecutors for their investigative skills over and above candidates with auditing or criminal law backgrounds. Bromwich's recruits had a particular skill set: the ability to lead an investigation and to write the results in a coherent narrative. Attracting these skills took time. At the beginning of his tenure, the IG did not have the budget authority to hire a large permanent staff. When he found himself short-staffed for a particular investigation, he used the strategy of asking then-US attorney Eric Holder to lend him prosecutors "on detail."

To pursue his mandate from Heymann, Bromwich embodied his two principles in the Special Investigations and Review Unit (SIRU) office (later called the Oversight and Investigations Division), established in 1995 and unique to the Justice OIG. Like all other OIGs, the DOJ OIG was initially organized around an audit–investigative split, with auditors conducting routine audits of programs and investigators pursuing instances of specific wrongdoing, fraud, or abuse. A third division inspected programs for compliance (known as Inspections, and from 2001, Evaluations and Inspections). The SIRU unit was unique in the way that it bridged the methodolog-

Table 6.1. Academic and Professional Backgrounds of DOJ Inspectors General

IG	Date	Academic Background	Professional Experience
Michael Horowitz	March 2012–present	Law	DOJ criminal division (various posts); deputy assistant attorney general; AUSA (Southern District of NY)[a]
Cynthia Schnedar (acting)	January 2010–March 2012	Law	AUSA (Washington, DC)
Glenn Fine	December 2000–January 2010	Law	Private law; AUSA (Washington, DC); DOJ OIG special counsel
Glenn Fine (acting)	August 2000–December 2000	Law	Private law; AUSA (Washington, DC); DOJ OIG special counsel
Robert L. Ashbaugh (acting)	August 1999–August 2000	Law	Justice OIG; Justice Department trial lawyer
Michael R. Bromwich	June 1994–August 1999	Law	AUSA (Southern District of NY); associate counsel in Office of Independent Counsel for Iran-Contra
Richard J. Hankinson	June 1990–June 1994	Liberal arts	US Secret Service; federal government investigator (multiple agencies)
Anthony C. Moscato (acting)	April 1989–June 1990	Law	Law; Justice Department

[a] Assistant US attorney.

ical divides between these divisions to expand the OIG's remit. It was clearly lawyer led (lawyers composed half the unit) but included teams of analysts, auditors, and special agents.

Bromwich hired attorney Glenn Fine to head the new division. This was an office that Fine would continue to cultivate when he succeeded Bromwich as IG, and that proved to be a source of strength of the OIG's work. The unit gave birth to the category of special investigations (or "specials") within the IG community. The fruits of the special investigations issued from this office became the hallmark of DOJ IG work and helped it establish its reputation both within the IG community and in the broader federal bureaucracy as a rigorous source of internal review. Special investigations were not meant to be given primacy over other types of IG work (audits, inspections, and regular investigations). Rather, they were so named because of their length, the complication of the issue, the resources they demanded, and the public attention with which the issue was associated.[17] For each special investigation, the IG initially assigned a team leader (usually a lawyer), a special investigative counsel from the SIRU or an assistant US attorney, and senior personnel from the other component parts of the OIG (audit, inspection, and investigation).

Bromwich pushed for this particular organizational configuration and set of skills. He then funneled the OIG's limited resources into the SIRU. Despite the unit's legal investigatory bent, it also had an audit component that worked in conjunction with the investigators. The process of completing special reviews in many ways bridged the long-standing divide between audit and investigative capacities, but Bromwich's bias led to a sidelining of the audit function. Other members of the OIG staff were initially reluctant to accept an influx of lawyers into the organization: it required changing their professional patterns and overcoming a bias against the legal profession.[18] Moreover, such investigations proved costly for the OIG because they sapped limited resources from the OIG as a whole; special investigations were often longer and more resource intensive than other investigations. Ultimately, however, the SIRU grew to become the backbone of the OIG's special reviews.

Forging a Constitutional Democracy

Bromwich's vision of the types of issues to pursue—special investigations that demanded complex legal judgments—led to the forging of a new category of investigation, a new methodology, and a specific bureaucratic capacity anchored in the SIRU. However, his desire to pursue his two-pronged strategy had roots in a specific conception of accountability. In a 1997 article in the IG journal, *Journal of Public Inquiry*, Bromwich distinguished between specific breaches of the law and more general wrongdoing. Describing the OIG's June 1995 review of the "Good Ol' Boy Roundup," in which FBI officers engaged in racist and other kinds of misconduct at annual agency gatherings, he stated,

> It was clear that the likelihood that any Justice Department personnel committed any crimes in connection with attending the event was slim. The primary concern of the Attorney General and the Senate Judiciary Committee [who requested the review] was whether Justice Department employees engaged in any incidents of racial and other misconduct. Our lengthy report told the story of the Good Ol' Boy Roundup over sixteen years, a narrative of historical reconstruction that no criminal prosecution could have accomplished.[19]

The distinction between the object of his office's attention and that of a criminal investigation underpinned a conception of government accountability as one of propriety of action. Regardless of legal status or efficiency, what is the nature of proper government action? At stake as well was the role of IG investigations: they were, on this account, to play a distinct role, fusing quotidian oversight with the power of investigative counsels. Between 1995, when it was formed, and 2013, the SIRU completed ninety-nine special reviews. Of these reviews, seventy pursued issues of government impropriety and overreach, while the remaining twenty-nine evaluated the management and performance of various DOJ components.[20]

Bromwich's Reviews

Over the next five years, Bromwich repeatedly clashed with FBI chiefs, but he also struggled with a number of limitations to his work—limits on the initiation of investigations, control over his completed reports, and the protection of whistle-blowers. At the behest of Congress, in 1996, he opened a review of the CIA's involvement in a crack cocaine scandal in which a number of federal agencies channeled drug profits to the Nicaraguan contras in the 1980s.[21] Senator Dianne Feinstein and Representative Maxine Waters of California initiated this review after a series of articles in the San Jose *Mercury News* appeared in August 1996; they referred the problem to Attorney General Janet Reno, and the task was then passed onto Bromwich.[22] But once the report was complete, Reno withheld it from public release on the grounds of sensitive information—the first time the attorney general had invoked this privilege under the 1978 IG Act.[23] Bromwich publicly stated his opposition to Reno's decision but did not challenge it. Without Reno's blessing, he spoke with a disgruntled Maxine Waters, who protested the review's delay, and reassured her that the report would be released, delayed but unredacted. Reno's move thus did not ultimately undermine the IG's work, but it demonstrated the latent power that an agency head could hold over an IG and threaten his independence.

Despite the need to receive attorney general permission to investigate the FBI, Bromwich repeatedly held the agency up to the microscope of inspection. He focused on the constitutionality of the mistakes, even when this threatened to undermine the FBI's performance. Following tips from FBI scientist Frederic Whitehurst, the IG began a series of investigations that would prove to be one of his most visible—and with the most significant effects. The timing of this report was also noteworthy: it was not a post hoc but rather a concurrent investigation. Concurrent investigations were rare in the IG community, but Bromwich saw the investigation as a kind of preemptive action that would be protective of the department's ongoing cases. Beginning in the late 1980s, Whitehurst had alleged that many of his colleagues had performed sloppy forensic work and fabricated testimony that compromised hundreds of criminal investigations; Whitehurst was then sacked as a result of his complaints. In April 1997, the IG review found FBI director Louis Freeh guilty of misleading Congress about Whitehurst's dismissal and suggested that the incident was part of a "damage control operation" to cover up wider problems in the FBI.[24] Underlying the deceit was a seriously malfunctioning crime lab that led to over fifty criminal cases being interrupted as a result of Bromwich's investigation.[25] The legacy of the reports was mixed. On the one hand, the FBI was placed under public and congressional pressure to clean up its act, and the FBI did initiate some reforms, such as outside accreditation of its labs. But a follow-up report a year later found only modest improvements; most importantly, no attempt had been made to establish systematic reviews of FBI court testimony.[26] Of the thirteen guilty parties, none was fired and only two were reprimanded.[27]

The limited consequences of this review—a review that would be one of Bromwich's largest and best known—reflected the weaknesses of the broader IG community in the 1990s. Though strong in the rigor of its recommendations, it lacked consequence externally. Despite their good reputation (as reflected in congressional statements), IGs did not always command the legitimacy to pressure their departments into formulating a consequential response, and the reviews were not used instrumentally by other actors to pursue greater accountability: no public or congressional pressure to implement the recommendations resulted from it.[28] From a legal perspective, however, the FBI review highlighted the latent power of IG reviews in addressing the propriety of executive action: this was one of the first times that Congress carried the interpretation of a review beyond the IG's stated conclusions. Significantly, the review found no evidence of overt criminal activity but rather of mishandling of evidence, deficiencies, management failures, poor and incomplete reports, and substandard performance. The errors, in other words, were procedural at base.[29] Taken together, however, the narrative suggested broader, more serious impropriety. The problem lay in the fact that the FBI's procedural sloppiness was uniformly skewed toward prosecutorial success. While Bromwich maintained the FBI's innocence in his public statements (insofar as there was no obvious intent to commit perjury), Congress questioned this interpretation. In a hearing, Representative Robert Wexler (D-FL) demanded of Bromwich, "What is improperly supplementing reports, what are omissions, what are alterations if they do not amount to fabricating evidence?"[30] The distinction between mistakes and abuse of executive power was a fine one. The report's recommendations focused on procedural reforms that would in theory prevent the FBI from repeating such abuses.

Walking the line between mistakes and wrongdoing created ambiguities in much IG work and stemmed from the original act's structure. From its inception, IG work—shaped by the compliance paradigm of oversight—lent itself to defining problems in terms of rule following, and thus to offering recommendations in the form of new regulations and devoting additional resources to monitoring bodies. This structure of problem definition and solution seemingly limited the immediate effect of the IG's work by leaving the systemic sources of many problems aside and frustrated the IGs' congressional supporters. For instance, the ambiguous nature of Bromwich's FBI investigation led to demands in the Senate for further investigation. Although Bromwich insisted that his office had searched for evidence of criminal misconduct ("a hybrid criminal–administrative investigation"), Senator Grassley maintained that the investigation was only a management review and was insufficient. Despite Grassley's request for further criminal investigations of the thirteen FBI staff implicated in the report, Bromwich refused. This interpretive split was indicative of a more profound difference over the diagnosis of the problem. Whereas Grassley viewed the report's focus on procedural reforms as neglecting the wider constitutional issue of impropriety, Bromwich's insistence that the investigation had been criminal–administrative suggests that although it was not expressed in constitutional terms, his narrative recognized the inherent impropriety of the FBI's modus operandi. Bromwich's background as a lawyer led him to be sensitive to the exigencies of the law: standards for establishing intent, for instance, are higher in the courts than in common parlance. This led his team of lawyers to exercise caution in formulating their narratives.[31] The review pointed at constitutional wrongdoing, but Bromwich's circumscribed understanding of the IG's authority left the conclusion to be made by Congress.

Bromwich thus insisted on his independence from Congress. His independence from his own agency head, Attorney General Janet Reno, was less clear. His failure to investigate two Democrats involved in a campaign finance scandal in 1996 prompted conservative critic William Safire to accuse Bromwich of being part of "Reno's see-no-evil network."[32] But the IG and attorney general did not always see eye to eye. Unlike Bromwich, Reno placed a premium on the audit function of the OIG rather than on investigation, in part because this helped her to manage the department.[33] Whereas investigations seek out individual wrongdoing in exceptional cases, audits and program reviews address quotidian management challenges: two conceptions of accountability and the IG's role were at stake. The OIG did, in 1998, begin to compile a list of *Top Ten Management Challenges*, a public document that served as a kind of strategic plan and explanation of the IG's choice of issues to investigate. (This became a statutory requirement of all OIGs in 2000.) Nonetheless, Reno did not use the IG for her own designs; she gave him the latitude to pursue the issues that he deemed the most important—issues that ultimately led him to sideline the OIG's auditing capacity. This strategic choice provided the institutional basis for its orientation toward a constitutional mode of democratic practice.

In addition to building the OIG's investigative capacity through the Special Investigative Unit, Bromwich spearheaded other significant institutional innovations. His experience with the FBI crime lab probe also spurred him to challenge the limits of his position—limits unique to the Justice Department OIG. In order to undertake investigations in certain sensitive units within the DOJ, such as the FBI and the DEA, the IG needed to receive approval from the deputy attorney general.[34] This lack of approval had been the factor preventing Whitehurst's claims from being investigated for eleven years after the fact. After a series of hearings, Robert Wexler began legislation to grant the IG precisely this capacity, but not until 2001 was the IG's jurisdiction expanded to include the FBI and the DEA.[35]

The OIG under Bromwich issued a number of hard-hitting reviews that kept the FBI in check, but there were significant limitations on the scope of the IG's activity and the effects that resulted from his reports. As with the CIA cocaine case, many of the investigations were initiated by Congress and tacitly approved by the attorney general. Beyond the political limits, the IG had difficulty protecting the whistle-blowers who brought abuses to his attention. However, the reports were able to effect some change; for instance, Whitehurst's initial ousting provoked President Clinton to extend a whistle-blowing protection law to cover the (previously exempt) FBI.[36]

Guided by a particular vision of accountability and the role of the IG in effecting it, Bromwich effectively cultivated the institutional prerequisites for the strong special reviews that the OIG would produce in the future and for its growing reputation as a rigorous and independent source of internal review: a coterie of investigative lawyers and a special unit in which to organize and funnel resources with a constitutional conception of accountability as a guiding principle.

Glenn Fine and the Post-9/11 Mandate: National Security and Rights Monitoring, 2000–2011

The special reviews of Bromwich's OIG framed many of the department's activities as improper, irrespective of the legal status of the actions, and set a precedent for the types of issues the future IGs would pursue. In July 2000, Clinton named Glenn Fine as acting inspector general to replace Bromwich, who had resigned in 1999. Also a Harvard lawyer by training, Fine had extensive experience in the OIG, having served as special counsel to the inspector general from 1995 to 1996 and later as director of the SIRU. He had also served as an assistant US attorney from 1986 to 1989, which greatly added to his legitimacy as a Justice IG. He began by continuing the largest internal security investigation in the history of the Justice Department, and his first report—while still only the acting IG—shocked Congress with its damning indictment of top Justice officials. The report failed to lead to any immediate accountability in the form of sanctions: none of the accused was either prosecuted or fired. What it did provide, however, was transparency, and both the media and Congress used it as the basis for further scrutiny. The report was described as detailing "serious, substantial and egregious misconduct" and "general moral turpitude" within the upper ranks of the DOJ.[37] The investigation, begun by Bromwich and completed by Fine, overcame numerous internal obstacles, including the efforts on the part of Justice officials to discourage cooperation with the IG and pleas with the OIG to temper its conclusions. The immediate effect of the report was to spur Congress to hold full committee hearings on the department's international law enforcement programs.

Like Bromwich, Fine followed a distinctive vision for his office. He operated under eight principles, the first two of which were "independence" and "transparency."[38] Transparency was not merely an abstract goal but dictated the OIG's activities and was integral to maintaining the OIG's reputation for independence and to drawing in other actors. In testimony to Congress, Fine emphasized that "we believe it is important to release publicly as much information about our activities as possible."[39] This mission of the IG complemented Bromwich's desire to create an organization of narrative builders—storytellers—in order to publicize and disseminate facts. The IG's narrative-building function placed it in a paradoxical position. On the one hand, the IG played the role of neutral arbiter and remained aloof from political processes. On the other hand, the legitimacy of the narrative stemming from the IG's neutrality enabled the politicization of the actions under review and invited their use by Congress and others. This simultaneously apolitical and politicizing role implicitly bolstered the political processes of accountability by legitimizing the narratives on which they were based.

Fine also continued to build Bromwich's SIRU unit (changing its name to the Office of Oversight and Review, or O&R). His first project was to build a permanent core of OIG lawyers within it, giving lawyer and policy analyst Carol Ochoa the task. Ochoa crafted a flat body with a structure very different from the hierarchy of the other divisions within the OIG.[40] The lack of permanent teams gave the SIRU flexibility in the kinds of issues it could pursue, and its interdisciplinary skills permitted analysis on multiple levels. When Bromwich left the position in 2000, the unit had comprised six permanent staff and received many on detail, but Fine rearranged the OIG as a whole to concentrate more staff and resources in the office. By the time of his departure in 2011, there were over thirty permanent members of staff. O&R's flexibility ultimately gave it the leeway to define different types of issues to investigate: whereas the audit division identified much of its work using a "bottom-up approach" in which it generated a list of problems to be reviewed by the IG, O&R chose its investigations through conversations with the IG.[41] If the IG identified an issue that was "bigger than it looks," or if there was legal analysis needed (as would be the case in the office's reviews of Patriot Act– or FISA-related matters), the issue was given to O&R.[42]

The office that Fine inherited continued to be pitted against significant institutional obstacles. From the mid-1990s, the ranks of the DOJ had grown without a concomitant growth in OIG personnel or capacity.[43] As a result, the percentage of complaints that were investigated fell nationally from 14 percent in 1996 to 7 percent in 2000.[44] And within the first year of Fine's appointment, the Justice Department circumstances transformed radically. The first change was the growth of a highly politicized department that led to political hirings and firings, many instances of which would later be investigated by the OIG in a 2008 report. Second, the department sustained a deep restructuring after the 9/11 attacks, and its strategic plan began to focus first and foremost on counterterrorism.[45]

The Patriot Act of 2001 ushered in a new era for the DOJ OIG. The legal landscape changed, not only because of the effect of war (the war on terror, and later, in Iraq and Afghanistan), but also because of the Bush administration's legal strategies to avoid court review for executive actions.[46] In the midst of fear over the potential threats to liberties from the act, Congress inserted Section 1001 into the Patriot Act. This clause mandated the IG to monitor potential civil rights and liberties abuses. In addition to its regular semiannual reviews of departmental activity, the act stipulated that the OIG was in addition to produce semiannual reports on the implementation of Section 1001.[47] Moreover, the act created a new deputy IG for civil rights within the department, with requirements for an IG oversight plan for the FBI. Supported by House Democrats such as Barney Frank, this was an attempt to "increase the negative incentives" for leaking surveillance information.[48] However, support for the DOJ IG's work was not limited by partisanship. By 9/11, the IG commanded enough legitimacy to muster support from both sides of the congressional aisle. Despite their early resistance to a DOJ IG, congressional Republicans gradually became strong champions of the IG's work over the 1990s and first decade of the twenty-first century. Republicans Orren Hatch, Charles Grassley, and Arlen Specter of the Senate Judiciary Committee, and Darrell Issa (R-CA) of the House Oversight and Government Reform Committee used IG reports as the basis for calling hearings and supported legislation strengthening the IGs' independence. For both sides of the congressional aisle, the IGs provided a crucial political instrument of investigation.[49]

Congress's recourse to the IG as an integral mechanism of accountability in the war on terror reflected the IGs' wider reputation as an effective,

Table 6.2. Number of Media Citations for Selected IG Reviews

Review	Review Date	Media Citations	Date Range
CIA-Contra–crack cocaine controversy[a]	December 1997	105	1 January 1996–1 January 2000
FBI laboratory[b]	April 1997	457	1 January 1996–1 January 2000[c]
Good Ol' Boy Roundup[d]	March 1996	20	1 January 1996–1 January 2000
11 September detainees (three reviews)[e]	June 2003–March 2004	1,012	1 May 2003–1 May 2007
NSLs (three reviews)[f]	March 2007–January 2010	945	1 January 2007–1 January 2014
Attorney firings[g]	September 2008	387	1 June 2008–1 June 2012
Fast and Furious[h]	September 2012 (November 2012, partially unredacted version)	1,073	1 January 2011–1 October 2014

[a] *The CIA-CONTRA–Crack Cocaine Controversy: A Review of the Justice Department's Investigations and Prosecutions.* Search terms: "inspector general" AND ("justice department" OR "department of justice") AND "cia" AND "crack cocaine."

[b] *The FBI Laboratory: An Investigation into Laboratory Practices and Alleged Misconduct in Explosives-Related and Other Cases.* Search terms: "inspector general" AND "justice" AND "whitehurst."

[c] Although I have used a general parameter of four years following the final review in question to trace media hits, if the date range of the search is expanded to the present, then there is a total yield of 591 media hits. The findings of the IG review were revived in 2012 when further evidence of FBI mishandling arose.

[d] Search terms: "inspector general" AND ("justice department" OR "department of justice") AND "good ol' boys roundup" AND ("justice department" OR "department of justice").

[e] Search terms: "inspector general" AND "detainees" AND ("justice department" OR "department of justice").

[f] Search terms: "inspector general" AND ("justice department" OR "department of justice") AND ("nsls" OR "national security letters" OR "exigent letters").

[g] *An Investigation into the Removal of Nine US Attorneys in 2006.* Search terms: "inspector general" AND ("justice department" OR "department of justice") AND ("us attorneys" AND ("dismissal" OR "fired" OR "firings" OR "scandal").

[h] *A Review of ATF's Operation Fast and Furious and Related Matters.* Search terms: "inspector general" AND ("justice department" OR "department of justice") AND "fast and furious."

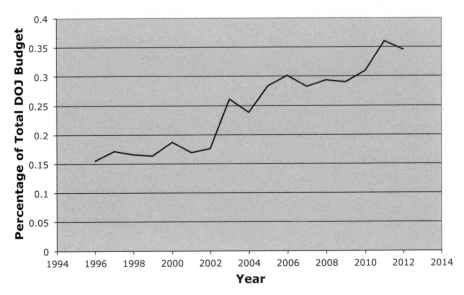

Figure 6.1. OIG Budget as Percentage of DOJ Total Budget. *Sources:* OIG Semiannual Reports, 1997–2012; DOJ Annual Budget, 1997–2012.

legitimate check on executive behavior (Table 6.2). Despite the IGs' earlier reputation for compliance monitoring, Congress placed the IGs in positions to reframe their missions. (The newly minted Department of Homeland Security would similarly receive a rights-monitoring mandate when it was established a year later.) However, the act provided no additional resources for the new responsibilities.[50] Ironically, although the Patriot Act increased the IG's investigative scope specifically to include violations of civil rights and liberties, it was not directly within this framework that the IG moved into the domain of rights protection. Notably, in none of the Section 1001 reviews between 2002 and 2005 did the IG find significant abuses of civil rights and liberties.[51] However, the Patriot Act Reauthorization Act of 2005 included a mandate for the OIG to look at specific provisions of the Patriot Act, including the use of NSLs. It was this congressional provision that prompted and reinforced the IG's capacity to hold the executive to account on a constitutional level.

From the early 2000s, the OIG began to receive more resources, modestly increasing the ratio of its personnel to the department personnel (Figures 6.1 and 6.2). This permitted it to expand significantly the number of reports that it completed (Figure 6.3). The focus of its work remained the FBI, reflecting a long-standing tension between FBI heads and the attorney general, but the OIG also targeted the Bureau of Prisons (BOP) and

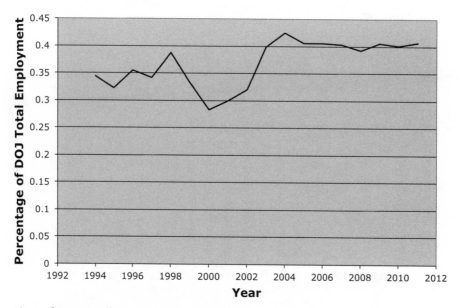

Figure 6.2. OIG Full-Time Equivalent (FTE) Personnel as Percentage of Total DOJ Personnel. *Sources:* FedScope database; US Federal Budget FY 2003, Historical Tables. The drop in overall DOJ FTE between 2002 and 2003 reflects the transfer of the Immigration and Naturalization Service to the Department of Homeland Security. The number of DOJ total FTEs for 1994–1997 were gathered from the US Federal Budget FY 2003, issued before the transfer to the DHS. Total FTE for 1998–2013 were gathered from the OPM's FedScope database. Though it risks some inconsistencies, this methodological choice was made because the number of Justice Department FTEs reported in the historical tables published after 2004 were revised to show only the personnel in agencies in the current DOJ (i.e., not including the INS). However, this would provide an inaccurate estimation of the ratio of OIG to DOJ personnel because the OIG was responsible for overseeing a much larger staff than it would appear from the post-2003 revised numbers.

completed a large number of special reviews that reflected a constitutional conception of accountability.

The post-9/11 period also saw a protracted struggle between Attorney General John Ashcroft and the IG for the upper hand in checking the war on terror; the Patriot Act granted both the department and the OIG new tools. This was a dynamic that contrasted with the close relationship between Bromwich and Reno. The battle between Ashcroft and the IG also mapped onto a partisan struggle between congressional Republicans and Democrats regarding the strength of Patriot Act tools. While Ashcroft and the Republicans pushed for stronger provisions in the war on terror, the Democrats pointed to the OIG's early reports as reason to exercise caution.[52] But the

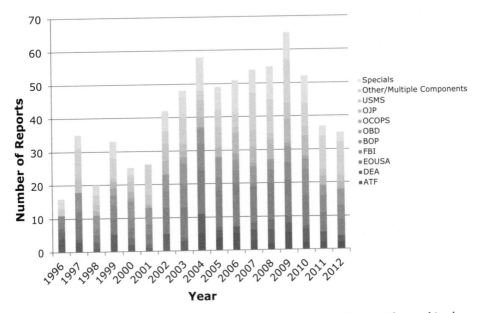

Figure 6.3. Number of DOJ IG Reports by Component, 1996–2012. The combined number of reports is greater than the actual total because of overlap in the classification of reports that covered more than one DOJ component.

IG did not directly enter the partisan fray. In fact, IG Fine maintained that despite vocal public opposition to the IG's work from Ashcroft,[53] the attorney general refrained from interfering with OIG reviews.[54]

As a result, the question of the IG's powers became entangled with the state's response to emergencies and was cultivated as a primary check on executive action. Fine had a wide reputation for his even-handedness and nonpartisanship, but his efforts were often used to partisan ends in shaping the war on terror. Democrats used the reviews documenting FBI misconduct as proof of executive overreach, but partisans of Bush's counterterrorism strategy claimed that the IG's work provided a sufficient review of executive power. In testimony to Congress, Office of Management and Budget and CIGIE head Clay Johnson III used the IGs' legitimacy as a way of reassuring Congress of the built-in checks in the executive branch, thus justifying expanded executive power. In short, he used the IGs' legitimacy politically to shore up the legitimacy of executive action.[55]

The OIG disseminated its broad evaluation of the department's performance annually through its list of *Top Ten Management Challenges*. Although the nature of the document led it to focus on management problems and matters of performance-based accountability, in 2006, the Justice OIG began to devote substantial discussion to violations of civil rights and liberties. The discussion reviewed the OIG's ongoing civil rights– and liberties-related reviews but notably passed broad, preemptive judgment on the Patriot Act renewal and its potential for abuse. It cautioned, "Investigative and intelligence authorities enacted or expanded in the Patriot Act and the Patriot Improvement and Reauthorization Act of 2005 invest broad new information-gathering powers in FBI agents and their supervisors, often permitting these tools to be approved at the field office level on a minimal evidentiary predicate."[56] The discussion centering on civil rights and liberties in subsequent years retained this detailed and critical stance and reflected a broad range of reviews conducted by the OIG in checking the war on terror: reviews of the uses of Section 215 orders to obtain business records; of the terrorist surveillance program operated by the NSA; of the management of the consolidated terrorist watchlist; of the FBI's targeting of domestic advocacy groups; of the use of material witness warrants; of its compliance with FISA regulations, in particular the use of its pen register and trap-and-trace authorities; and of the use of new technologies such as drones. In each of these discussions, the OIG framed the challenge as one of balancing liberty and security, but cautioned overwhelmingly that the onus lay on the department to develop appropriate procedures for protecting liberties. In so doing, it held the department to a constitutional standard of accountability.

Continuing the Constitutional Tradition: Michael Horowitz, 2011–2014

In January 2011, Glenn Fine resigned after eleven years of service, and the post remained empty until March 2012. He left the office billed as "the most powerful law enforcement agent you've never heard of," having established a strong reputation within Congress for rigorous and independent reviews, though his reputation was still limited in the wider public.[57] The department's temporary release from rigorous oversight made room for the FBI to push back against the limitations the OIG had previously levied on it. In June 2011, with the helm of the OIG still empty, the FBI planned to release a new field manual with relaxed standards for privacy.[58] But in July, President Obama nominated Michael Horowitz, a DC-based lawyer with extensive experience in the Justice Department under both the Clinton and Bush administrations. Like his predecessors, his nomination languished in the hands of Congress for nine months, between July 2011 and March 2012, before a confirmation hearing took place. Both as a lawyer and a bureaucrat, he specialized in white-collar crime, and he was esteemed by both Senate Republicans and Democrats.[59] Horowitz inherited a large investigation begun by Fine's OIG on the Justice Department gun-running program known as Fast and Furious. The program, run by the Arizona field office of the DOJ's Bureau of Alcohol, Tobacco, Firearms, and Explosives (ATF) between 2009 and 2010, was designed to track gun smugglers by selling firearms to suspected smugglers. The untracked guns were later discovered at crime scenes and were connected with the death of at least one US Border Patrol agent.[60]

On the one hand, the ATF's actions were the actions of an agency in over its head—one that made missteps and misjudgments, with fatal consequences. On the other hand, the mistakes came in part because of relaxed oversight, including an expansion of executive power and wide discretion in getting wiretaps. At stake in the IG report was not only the cause of the fatality but also the use of executive privilege, contempt of Congress, and the violation of Fourth Amendment protections in illegal wiretaps. The IG found itself faced with administrative "mistakes" that went far beyond "limited and necessary invasions of privacy" and that amounted to significant breaches of the constitutional limits of executive action.[61] As with previous IG investigations, there was a fine line between mistakes and oversights on the one hand, and executive overreach through the violation of rights on the other. Although he noted that the mistakes were oversights, Horowitz was adamant that the unchecked authorizations of electronic wiretapping by the ATF were a violation of Fourth Amendment rights.

In its report, the OIG recommended the standardization of law enforcement policies and procedures across the DOJ and the systematic comparison of the various law enforcement units "to ensure broad uniformity."[62] Beyond its interaction with a host of parallel accountability mechanisms, what was significant about the IG's recommendations was the attempt to standardize national security state procedures on the micro, law-enforcement level—that is, it reflected the recognition that the origin of executive overreach is often located in micro-level administrative discretion rather than macro claims of executive privilege. The Fast and Furious review also had institutional consequences within the OIG. Because the whistle-blowers responsible for sparking the investigation had faced retaliation from federal prosecutors, the OIG established a new ombudsperson in July 2012 to protect and inform all DOJ employees of their right to report misdeeds.[63] The establishment of this post was strongly supported by Grassley, who championed such a position in all federal OIGs.[64]

Like his predecessors, Horowitz took on reviews whose subject matter scraped against highly partisan and ideologically charged issues. And like his predecessors, he stopped just short of making his reviews political. A 2014 review of the FBI's use of forensic evidence—the topic of some of Bromwich's reviews nearly twenty years earlier—unveiled that the evidence on which sixty-four death row cases had been decided rested on "flawed forensic evidence and overstated testimony."[65] Yet the IG's monitoring over time had tangible effects. The department set up a task force between 1996 and 2004 to review previous FBI cases and to inform the relevant parties. The task force itself provided little accountability, excluding many categories of cases and not reporting findings that incriminated the FBI. But when the IG released a review of the task force's findings in 2014, it discovered evidence that three men had been sentenced using faulty work, leading to the exoneration of all three men.[66] From a broader perspective, the reviews provided significant data to support anti–death penalty advocates and were quickly cited in national news outlets.

Shaping the IG's Role: The Nature of IG Investigations

The limits of the IG—as they were conceived by individual IGs in the DOJ—also played a role in shaping the bureaucratic contours of the OIG and in the nature of the reviews' effects. In a 1997 article published in the *Georgetown Law Journal*, Bromwich laid out a distinctive conception of the IG: "We conduct investigations primarily to determine what happened rather than to bring prosecutions. . . . Because of the impetus behind special [IG] investigations—the interest in finding out what happened—this explanatory purpose may, in many cases, rival, or even exceed, the imperative to hold individuals accountable, either through the criminal process or through administrative discipline."[67] Although Bromwich contrasted this narrative-building vision with accountability (understood in the vernacular sense of sanctions), he in fact described a key moment in the broader process of accountability: the gathering of information and the subsequent construction of an explanatory narrative. This narrative-building function of the DOJ IG, explicitly cultivated by Bromwich and his successors, was the focal point of the OIG's identity, but it is also what permitted the instrumental use of IG work by external actors.

It was a precedent followed by subsequent Justice IGs. In Congress's interrogation of Glenn Fine after the first 9/11 detainee review, Senator Arlen

Specter raised the issue of the IG's scope of responsibility and stressed the ambiguity of its role:

> SPECTER: Does your department, the Inspector General, get involved at all with a case like Padilla on raising a question as to whether there is a justifiable basis for denying access to court-appointed counsel?
>
> FINE: No, we have not and we do not. I believe that it is a Presidential decision to make the determination that someone is an enemy combatant and that they are held by the Department of Defense.
>
> SPECTER: Well, there is a pretty fine line as to where the Department of Justice ends and the Department of Defense begins. . . . You have the case of Yasir Hamdi where the District Court for the Eastern District of Virginia questioned the Government's affidavit as to whether there was a justification for designating Hamdi as an enemy combatant. The court said it fell far short, and that case is now on appeal. Does your role as Inspector General have anything to do with that?
>
> FINE: No, it really does not. We do not get involved with court processes or the litigation decision. . . .
>
> SPECTER: Well, Mr. Fine, the Department of Justice is the entity which is fighting to preserve the President's enemy combatant regime, that is, including the denial of access to counsel. Doesn't that implicate the Inspector General where the Department of Justice is taking that position?
>
> FINE: . . . I do note that litigation decisions by department attorneys are actually not subject to the Inspector General's authority. They are subject to the authority of the Office of Professional Responsibility.

Fine's reluctance to adopt a more expansive vision was again countered by Specter:

> SPECTER: It also seems to me, Mr. Fine, that you ought to take a close look at where the Department of Justice is acting, and the internal decision to make it to the Office of Professional Responsibility I would suggest does not bind you, that you have very broad powers as Inspector General. And the Congress has been very active in giving those broad powers. . . . I would urge you to move into those gray areas and to cross those dotted lines.

In responding to these questions, Fine articulated a circumscribed conception of the IG's role, and in particular the scope of the Justice Department's IG. The court's activity was outside the IG's remit, as were legal matters more generally—matters that were legally the responsibility of the OPR. Though Fine had repeatedly championed giving the OIG full jurisdiction within the department, he was constrained by the limits of the original institutional arrangement. Yet Fine's adherence to this arrangement, and his restrained conception of his role, did not limit the thrust of the review in question; this particular review implicitly challenged the law by simultaneously finding serious fault with actions that were technically within the boundaries of the law. He also ceded a role to other mechanisms of accountability. When pressed as to why the OIG had not taken up a review of September 11 detainees under the Material Witness Statute, he noted that he did not "want to interfere with the ongoing criminal investigations" and that "many of these are subject to oversight by courts and we try not to interfere with the courts' processes."[68]

Michael Horowitz encountered similar congressional pressure in the hearing on Fast and Furious. Once again, Congress pushed the limits of the IG's position. In his questioning, Representative Darrell Issa demanded of the IG, "Will you be looking into or doing any potential criminal referrals, which is within your authority?" In his response to Issa's questioning, Horowitz echoed Bromwich's statement of ten years earlier in asserting that the IG's task was to lay out the facts in a narrative and to leave the interpretation of that narrative to Congress. Horowitz explained the IG's role thus: "In doing this review, our standard was whether we could draw a decision, a judgment based on the evidence . . . and what we decided was we needed to put out the facts of what we found; others can draw conclusions. . . . I didn't speculate as to what I might do as a prosecutor."[69] Fine and Horowitz's self-distancing from judicial processes highlighted the different natures of the two mechanisms of accountability. Whereas courts take as authoritative judicial precedent or legislative history, the IG measured the agency's actions against a range of internal policies and statutes.[70] Moreover, even when a review addressed an issue of constitutional import, the IG did not use constitutional language of rights or separation of powers. Its diagnoses were often framed in terms of procedural mistakes and wider problems, yet by choosing problems that led to rights abuses or executive overreach, the IGs were able to address such issues without adopting the terms as such and thus pursued violations of a constitutional nature. Paradoxically, the IG's differences from the courts afforded it certain comparative advantages that contributed to the overall strength of many of its reviews. Its proximity to the department permitted it to provide specific recommendations of a highly technical nature and to enter into a discussion with the department about the precise contours of the reforms. By refusing to offer a political interpretation of the topic, the narratives drew legitimacy from their neutrality and thus invited their further use in political processes of accountability.

The DOJ IG's work also differed from IC investigations, another congressional tool of accountability that issued from the Ethics in Government Act of 1978. The remit of the IG is more expansive than that of a special counsel, which is limited to circumstances in which specific allegations are levied against certain members of the government and when the Justice Department cannot investigate such allegations because of conflict of interest. The presence of an IG in the Justice Department thus filled a gap in the fabric of the national security state accountability. IGs, however, are fundamentally limited in their inability to prosecute; they must refer their cases to US attorney's offices or to the DOJ's criminal or civil rights divisions.[71]

Reputation-Based Legitimacy and Constitutional Democracy

The DOJ IG grew from a glaring omission in the first class of 1978 IGs to an OIG of tremendous repute. All of the DOJ IGs adhered to a philosophy of laying out the facts and building narratives rather than passing direct judgment. Yet this restrained vision of the IG's role permitted wide-ranging reckoning with the propriety of the department's behavior. The legitimacy that such a conception afforded invited external actors to use the narratives to hold the executive to account on multiple fronts. The reviews often detailed procedural infractions, but the force of many of the reviews lay in their implicit challenge to the scope of executive action through standards, administrative reform, and legal challenges. Without an overt judgment about the propriety of a given action, the diagnosis that a wrong had been committed—albeit without recourse to the language of rights or executive abuse—was often enough to prompt congressional interpretations of executive misdeeds, attract media attention, and influence concurrent litigation. Through a much wider form of compliance monitoring—that is, compliance with IG's own standards for agency propriety—the IGs were able to effect reforms that shaped the norms and the institutional framework in which accountability structures operate. The process of accountability relied on a mutually reinforcing set of actors who used the legitimacy of the IG's narratives as the basis for congressional oversight and independent litigation. The Justice IGs' success in practicing a constitutional mode of democracy thus was rooted in institutional capacity and strategy, as well as an orientation to particular types of rights violations and government decisions.

CHAPTER SEVEN

A CONSTITUTIONAL DEMOCRACY AT JUSTICE

Forging Democratic Norms in the War on Terror, 2002–2010

JULIET: What man art thou that, thus bescreened in night,
So stumblest on my counsel?
—William Shakespeare, *Romeo and Juliet* (1595)

Introduction

The war on terror created a public arena in which liberty and security declared war on each other. George W. Bush's Justice Department took sides in the clash, and the question of constitutional rights was sidelined as the department sought above all to prevent future terrorist attacks. It was in this context that the Justice IG rose to prominence. Over this period, the OIG produced multiple reviews that monitored various aspects of the war on terror, partly stemming from the office's mandate to assess compliance with Section 1001 of the Patriot Act, which protects civil rights and liberties in relation to Patriot Act activity. Alongside these reviews, many standard audits and investigations took place to patrol the department's management challenges and evaluated its efficiency and effectiveness. However, the reviews analyzed below demonstrate the Justice OIG's doggedness in promoting a constitutional mode of democracy, in which the IGs reinforced constitutional norms through their framing and strategies. They highlight how institutional strategies that target the legal and institutional infrastructure can shape administrative norms and implicate a broader set of actors in the process of accountability.

The individual reviews did not always lead to direct accountability, understood in the vernacular sense of punishment or compensation for victims.[1] The force of the reviews lay in their broader effect on law, standards, and administrative procedure, all of which comprise the institutional framework for delimiting executive action, and finally in the way these reviews were used by a broader web of political actors. Moreover, these reviews pulled in and reinforced the actions of a variety of other actors in Congress and civil society in bringing the executive's behavior under scrutiny. In this sense, the IG contributed directly to a broader web of accountability by shaping the norms of accountability on the one hand and by providing a narrative link between the internal workings of government and the broader public on the other.

The September 11 Detainees Reviews

In response to a number of allegations of abuse, including an Amnesty International report that alleged the denial of human rights under international law, the OIG undertook an investigation of the treatment of September 11 detainees.[2] This series of investigative reports and subsequent follow-up analyses—a body of work that Fine later claimed was his office's most significant achievement—documented significant "problems" in the FBI and INS's handling of aliens detained after September 11, 2001.[3]

Four reviews between June 2003 and March 2004 evaluated the treatment of September 11 detainees. The first report, *The September 11 Detainees: A Review of the Treatment of Aliens Held on Immigration Charges in Connection with the Investigation of the September 11 Attacks*, retains neutral language, avoiding the term "abuse" and preferring "problems."[4] Nonetheless, it was damning in what it unveiled. Crucially, the report distinguished between the letter of the law and spirit of the law. Senator Orrin Hatch (who would later criticize the FBI) initially commended the FBI's actions by citing the report: "Like the recent court decisions upholding actions by the DOJ, the inspector general's report validates that despite partisan attacks, the department is fully within the law in seeking to protect the American people."[5] But the OIG's conception of accountability extended beyond this and emphasized the "significant problems" with the implementation of the law.

The report cited infractions in multiple areas.[6] First, the FBI failed to differentiate between terrorist suspects and aliens found incidentally to the investigation of terrorism. Second, the INS failed to issue a notice to appear (the document with the notice of charges) for over a month, which then stymied the detainees' capacity to seek legal counsel. Third, the FBI maintained an informal "hold until cleared" policy, based on the flawed assumption of a speedy clearance process. This resulted in a host of detainees being confined over a period of months (an average of eighty days) without a simultaneous clearance investigation. Fourth, the Justice Department followed a "no bond" policy to hold detainees for the duration of the clearance investigations, despite concerns raised by the INS about the legality of this policy, a conflict of interpretation unaddressed by the department. The department, moreover, altered its own policy with respect to the INS's detention authority in January 2002 when it began to permit the INS to remove aliens without FBI permission. Finally, the report disclosed numerous instances of substandard conditions of confinement, including differential treatment between prisons, patterns of physical and verbal abuse, and inability to access legal counsel. The report issued twenty-one recommendations that focused on the need for creating clear and consistent policies, sharing information, streamlining the clearance procedures, and improving the confinement conditions of aliens.

The initial report became "the talk of the law enforcement and civil rights communities," partly because so many groups had failed obtain information about the immigrants detained after 9/11.[7] The report—and the subsequent reviews of the department's implementation of its recommendations— garnered tremendous public attention, a fact that Fine himself attributed to the OIG's unparalleled legal access to DOJ information (Table 6.2). The attorney general refused to admit wrongdoing in response, stating that "we make no apologies" for detaining the illegal immigrants after September 11 and also requested that Fine make modest alterations to the report. Fine declined.[8]

Three months after the first report was issued, the OIG issued a second report analyzing the steps the DOJ and DHS had taken to implement the reforms. While it acknowledged what the department had done, this follow-up report was similarly critical of the Justice Department's handling of the emergency. The vast majority of the twenty-one recommendations were left open by the OIG, indicating that the DOJ's response did not fulfill the OIG's criteria for successful resolution (and thus for accountability). In response to the DOJ's efforts to create objective criteria in alien classification decisions, the OIG argued, "While we agree with the statement in the DOJ response that the specific criteria to be used during an emergency will depend, to some extent, on the nature of the emergency, we continue to believe that the FBI should develop general criteria and guidance to assist its field offices in making more consistent and uniform assessments."[9] This rebuttal to the DOJ's response negated the notion that the executive branch is entitled to free reign in times of emergencies, and it articulated a conception of how the Justice Department should act in times of emergency by stressing the need for clear and uniform guidelines.

In December of 2003, the OIG issued its *Supplemental Report on September 11 Detainees' Allegations of Abuse at the Metropolitan Detention Center in Brooklyn, New York*, an in-depth analysis of the prison with the worst record of the detainee abuses, and similarly followed this with an analysis of the implementation of its recommendations in March 2004. The OIG's analysis in January 2004, *Analysis of the Second Response by the Department of Justice to Recommendations in the Office of the Inspector General's June 2003 Report on the Treatment of September 11 Detainees*, continued to point to the need for specific policies to rein in executive behavior in times of emergencies. The OIG analysis stated, "We continue to believe that the DOJ should develop a process—outside its normal processes—that would require a rigorous re-evaluation of policies and operations implemented during a national crisis."[10] In response, the DOJ countered that such reforms were "not necessary and that it might be counterproductive to establish a new and separate bureaucratic process to evaluate policy decisions during a period of national crisis."[11] The report documents a written conversation between the department and the OIG regarding the specific development of such procedures and information sharing systems (including the Terrorist Threat Integration Center, the Terrorist Screening Center, and the National Name Check Unit).

Effects

By 2006, all of the twenty-eight recommendations had been resolved with one exception. This outstanding recommendation called for a memorandum of understanding to be finalized between DOJ and DHS regarding the system for managing emergencies that involve alien detainees.[12] The OIG's continuing oversight of the FBI's implementation of its recommendations, detailed in its follow-up reports and semiannual reviews, pressured the FBI into compliance. The review detailed the FBI and BOP's failure to comply with existing regulations for prisoner treatment, but it also highlighted the lack of uniform procedure that had given rise to abuses. For example, the review "encountered a significant variance of opinion among Metropolitan Detention Center staff members regarding what restraint and escorting techniques were appropriate for compliant and noncompliant inmates"—in short, it criticized not only the use of administrative discretion but also its very existence.[13] But the review's primary diagnosis was one that identified a series of rights abuses. Many of the recommendations pointed to abuses such as the illegal recording of detainees' conversations with their attorneys, the use of abusive language and behavior toward the detainees, and the excessive and inappropriate use of strip searches. Through the construction of the narrative, it contributed to traditional compliance monitoring as well as to a deeper and more wide-ranging form of constitutional accountability that evaluated the FBI and BOP's actions against a measure of rights abuse.

Standards

The reviews articulated a set of standards for the confinement conditions of aliens and their treatment. Although the effect of the September 11 detainee review was to advance a standard of rights protection, it did so without using the language of rights as such. Rather, it established an administrative framework limiting agency discretion. Many of the recommendations demanded the creation of specific definitions. These included the establishment of a detainee classification system, the definition of "what constitutes extraordinary circumstances and the reasonable period of time when circumstances prevent the charging determination from being made within 48 hours," and the formalization of a national emergency management system.[14] The import of such a recommendation should not be understated. The injunction to create a separate, legally bounded emergency regime to curtail administrative discretion maps onto the theoretical debate over the best way for liberal democracies to circumscribe or prevent "constitutional dictatorships" in times of perpetual emergency. This standard, as articulated by the IG review, directly supports a vision of emergency governance as needing to be inscribed and limited in law, a view described by legal scholars Eric Posner and Adrian Vermuele as the liberal legalist stance.

The reviews also prompted the FBI to define a "subject of interest" who would meet the criteria for detention as "those individuals whose name and identifying information appear in the Terrorist Screening Center (Identities Tracking Database), or the circumstances surrounding the subject's detention would indicate a pending act of terrorism."[15] A further definitional recommendation was for the creation of a "unique Special Management Category" for "aliens arrested on immigration charges who are suspected of having ties to terrorism" and attendant procedures to process and handle such detainees. This led the BOP to develop a new policy that both institutionalized this category and developed procedures and training guidelines.[16] Taken together, the reviews spurred numerous definitional innovations that contributed to the legal fabric of the war on terror: the development of new categories and criteria to correct the ambiguities that gave rise to rights abuses seen in the detainees (and in similarly underspecified categories such as "illegal enemy combatant").

While recognizing both the extraordinary circumstances and pressures under which the FBI operated, the reviews interpreted the violations in much wider terms, stating that "the FBI's initial classification decisions and the untimely clearance process had enormous ramifications for the September 11 detainees" and that "the classification of the detainees and the slow clearance process also had important ramifications on their conditions of confinement."[17] In this way, the reviews held the department's agencies to an implicit standard of rights without needing to use the term as such; the IG's overall diagnosis of wrongdoing went above and beyond the systemic problems and procedural violations that comprised the bulk of the report.

Procedural Reform and Administrative Law

Given that many of the egregious problems stemmed from a failure to follow procedure or from a lack of procedural guidelines, procedural reform formed the backbone of the IG's recommendations. They led to reforms regarding sharing information, creating clearance procedures, and formulating clear and consistent policies. The BOP also developed a policy of a two-day time frame in which a detainee's detention conditions must be normalized.[18] And in response to the OIG's recommendations that the FBI devote appropriate resources to conduct timely clearance investigations and to develop clearer classification guidelines, the FBI developed priority criteria for investigations. The procedural reforms suggested by the reviews were not merely isolated reforms. Together, they represented a coherent vision of an emergency response framework embedded in agency policy. For instance, the reviews documented a protracted conversation between the BOP and the OIG regarding its procedures for high-security inmates.[19] Once again, this reinforced the OIG's insistence on developing an emergency-specific regime of policies despite the FBI's reluctance.

Legal Implications

Most significant in the September 11 reviews were the implicit challenge to existing law and the preemptive challenges to future legal justifications.[20] As Fine stated in a hearing,

We did not find that anyone intentionally violated the law or the legal rights of detainees. We did find—and we point out—that there was some concern and some dispute within the department about the legality of holding detainees for more than ninety days beyond the removal period. The Office of Legal Counsel subsequently opined that this was permissible. I note that that is still an ongoing legal issue in the courts.[21]

In this way, Fine recognized the continuing legal ambiguity of the issue without overstepping his role as neutral arbiter. The OIG's 2003 analysis of the INS's corrective actions not only condemned the INS and the department for failing to address the issue of prolonged detention without review but also implicitly challenged the concurrent OLC opinion clearing the INS of some responsibility:

> In the aftermath of the September 11 attacks, whether the INS legally could hold September 11 detainees after they had received final orders of removal or voluntary departure orders to conduct FBI clearance investigations was the subject of differing opinions. A February 2003 OLC opinion concludes, however, that the INS can do so if the delay is related to the proper implementation of immigration laws, including investigating whether the alien has terrorist or criminal connections. A pending lawsuit also is addressing this issue. *Regardless of the outcome of that lawsuit,* our review found that the INS and the department did not address this issue in a timely or considered fashion.[22]

The IG verdict suggested that the INS and the department had engaged in wrongdoing despite post hoc legal justification by the OLC and (possible) clearance by the courts.

The IG Reviews in the Web of Accountability

The force of the reviews was extended by their instrumental use by other actors. Congress called three separate hearings based directly on the reviews.[23] In these hearings, Congress adopted the IG's analysis of the main problems and supported the IG's solution. Taking the IG's recommendations as the starting point for his own proposal, Senator Orrin Hatch argued, "The DOJ and DHS need to develop a crisis management plan that clearly identifies their respective duties should another national emergency occur. Specific standards should be adopted . . . to classify subjects of terrorism investigations appropriately, and to process and complete clearance investigations expeditiously."[24] The authority of the IG review was thus used as the basis for drafting legislation that aimed to institute an emergency governance regime despite the FBI's resistance to developing such a regime.[25]

Concurrent with the IG investigation, a number of the detainees filed lawsuits to challenge their status. In *Turkmen v. Ashcroft*,[26] filed by the Center for Constitutional Rights in April 2002, seven detainees in the Metropolitan Detention Center challenged then–attorney general John Ashcroft on the grounds that their First, Fourth, and Fifth Amendment rights had been violated in their detention. Although the defendants initially moved to dismiss the claims, the information in the IG reviews was subsequently used as the basis for two amendments to the original claims.[27] Ultimately, five of the seven were awarded a $1.26 million settlement.

Limits of the Reviews

As consequential as the September 11 reviews were in forging norms of accountability, there remained important limitations to the accountability they were able to effect. The narrative function of the reviews prevented it from passing direct judgment on a variety of related concerns. As stated in the reviews themselves, their scope was limited: they addressed the very particular circumstances of the detainees held in two detention centers, and they left aside the broader phenomenon of detainees in the war on terror (i.e., those held under the material witness statute, those held for non–terror-related charges within a terror investigation, and those held in facilities outside the United States). They also only lightly challenged the legality of some of the policies in place, such as the "hold until cleared" policy that is arguably at odds with the principle of "innocent until proven guilty."[28] Finally, the recommendations did not curtail executive authority to detain aliens, and some of the definitional recommendations suggested by the reviews, such as defining the "extraordinary circumstances," led to the agencies adopting standards "so broad as to permit future mass detentions with delayed notice under circumstances even less exceptional than the September 11 attacks."[29]

The narrative provided in the September 11 review formed the basis of various processes of accountability on multiple fronts by multiple actors. The reviews had many direct effects on the department and contributed to the development of an emergency regime as well as a set of categories specific to the conduct of the war on terror. But just as important was its interactive role in other processes of accountability: its instrumental use by Congress, in parallel litigation, and as a source of public information.

The National Security Letters Reviews

The second major assault on the administration's handling of the war on terror by the OIG came with Fine's investigation into the use of NSLs. Between 2007 and 2010, the OIG produced a series of three reports on the use of NSLs since the September 11 attacks. NSLs are requests for three different types of business records: subscriber and transactional information for phone and Internet usage; full credit reports; and financial records.[30] They were invented in the 1970s for terrorism and espionage investigations, but under the Patriot Act, they were expanded to cover individuals not directly linked to either of these categories.[31] Sections 358 and 505 of the Patriot Act widely expanded the FBI's capacity to issue them by removing the previous requirement of a court approval for the issuance of an order, but it did stipulate that it must be signed by a supervisory official. Moreover, the act relaxed the standards of issuance from the materials of individuals suspected of terrorist activities to those records that are "sought for" or "relevant to" an authorized intelligence investigation.[32] The OIG had a mandate to evaluate the proper implementation of the Patriot Act, but it was not required to investigate specific tools. By 2007, there were five years of semiannual IG reports asserting the DOJ's responsible use of Patriot Act provisions.

Fine's office, like most OIGs, usually depended on external complaints to launch an investigation. In the case of NSLs, however, this was an impossible situation: people whose phone records had been requested by the FBI would have no way of knowing that they were the subject of an FBI search, and thus they would have no way of challenging such an action. Fine was aware of this but even as of 2005 had not begun an independent investigation of the use of NSLs (or of any specific provisions of the Patriot Act).[33] Nor did calls from the media for an IG review of the practice, including a number of investigative pieces[34] and a subsequent editorial[35] in the *Washington Post*, prompt Fine and deputy IG Paul K. Martin to undertake a special investigation. However, Congress caught wind of the media storm, and in the renewed Patriot Act, it included new requirements for the Justice IG to report specifically on NSLs.[36]

The use of NSLs was initially difficult to track from the perspective of the IG. The Patriot Act permitted their use and had widened the criteria with which they could be legally issued from an individual under suspicion to anyone "relevant" to a terrorist investigation.[37] Their use was thus legal, and in the semiannual reports on the implementation of the Patriot Act, the IG initially found no violations resulting specifically from internally generated complaints. However, the first mandated review of NSLs unearthed a slew of breaches of the law, both in their use and in the parallel record keeping. The review suggested that the FBI lacked effective controls on their use and that it vastly underreported to Congress the number of NSLs it had issued. Its criticisms were also leveled at the failure of the FBI to report a number of possible violations to the Intelligence Oversight Board; the failure to "cross check the approval ECs [electronic communications] with the text of the proposed NSLs; . . . to issue comprehensive guidance describing the types of NSL-related infractions that needed to be reported"; and at the general confusion regarding the extent of available authority within the NSL statutes.[38] According to the review, the violations were not, strictly speaking, criminal misconduct or of illegal intent, but rather questions of procedure, clarity, reporting, and conformity with existing statues and policies.[39] They were, essentially, mistakes. The DOJ emphasized this conclusion repeatedly in its press releases.

But this was not how the actions were interpreted by Congress. Senator Patrick Leahy's response was, "The point is that it was not honest. . . . [The FBI], of all people, have to follow the law. . . . So I want to make clear that it is not a matter of technical violation."[40] This conclusion, shared by many of Leahy's Democratic colleagues, raised the question of the proper remedy: better guidelines or statutory reform? The issue came into sharper focus with the most contentious violation revealed by the IG report: the Communications Analysis Unit's use of so-called exigent letters, which can be signed by counterterrorism personnel not authorized to grant NSLs. The IG report concluded that the use of exigent letters "without first issuing NSLs or grand jury subpoenas . . . circumvented the requirements of the . . . NSL statute and violated the NSI [National Security Investigation] Guidelines and internal FBI policies."[41]

The report offered ten recommendations, ranging from the specific and targeted (specifying the type of guidance that should be issued to field offices regarding NSL use) to the vague ("take steps to ensure that the FBI does not improperly issue exigent letters").[42] The DOJ response was to announce a series of actions for increasing accountability that included implementing further internal review; putting into place new procedures for handling NSL records; coordinating bodies within the DOJ to implement accountability procedures; initiating ongoing audits and reviews of the practice of using NSLs; publicizing the IG's report; and establishing the Integrity and Compliance Program "to identify and mitigate legal compliance risks within the FBI."[43] Finally, the FBI's use of exigent letters was formally terminated in a directive from 5 March 2007.[44]

Congress responded strongly to the report and held multiple hearings.[45] In addition to prodding the FBI to undertake internal reforms, it spurred Congress to revisit the question of the scope of the Patriot Act, including the National Security Letter Reform bill of 2007, introduced by Senator Russell Feingold (D-WI), which proposed limiting the scope of information that could be acquired by NSLs and tighten the standards for granting them.[46] Although the bill died, it prompted even Republican senators to challenge the extent of executive overreach in the context of the war on terror. Senator Charles Grassley was also concerned with how FBI officials would be held to account, suggesting that an independent review of the letters was necessary. Fine countered that the FBI's accountability was an internal matter; he argued that "as a result of the report, the Attorney General has asked the department to look at the conduct of attorneys, as well as the FBI is looking at the conduct and the performance of its employees to determine accountability."[47] He further suggested that the FBI conduct an internal review first, that it "should look at what happened, and we ought to see what the results are and then see whether it was aggressive and thorough or not."[48] Despite skepticism that the FBI could effectively self-monitor, Grassley conceded that nonetheless the FBI had responded to the report almost immediately by releasing new guidelines for the use of emergency letters and ensuring an audit trail for each letter.

The conclusion that no intentional wrong had been committed brought to the surface the underlying question of whether the real problem lay with the Patriot Act or merely with compliance with its procedures. Aside from noting that "it was a lack of guidance, a lack of training, a lack of oversight, [and] inadequate internal controls," Fine was agnostic on this question, stating later only that "the problem was the implementation over time."[49] When pressed on Congress's role in amending legislation, Fine insisted that he was "not prepared to recommend a specific legislative piece."[50]

Yet the OIG ultimately provided greater accountability than the numerous parallel bodies established to check civil liberties violations. Significantly, the OIG measured the FBI's compliance with federal regulation, department policy, the Electronic Communication Privacy Act (ECPA) NSL statute, the attorney general's National Security Investigation guidelines, and FBI policy.[51] Whereas in the related investigation into the warrantless wiretap program the OPR was denied the security clearances necessary to carry out the investigation, Fine's office was granted access. In addition, part of the review's success stemmed from the willing cooperation of the FBI and the Justice Department, who did not, according to the report, impede access to documents and databases. The Privacy and Civil Liberties Oversight Board was ignorant of the NSL abuses until it was briefed by the OIG itself, but it took the findings into account.[52] Moreover, the review was "thorough and careful" and rigorous in its methodology, using interviews with more than 100 members of the FBI staff, including top-level officials.[53] And importantly, the report put previously unknown information within the reach of Congress and the public.

In March 2008 the OIG released its second NSLs report, *A Review of the FBI's Use of National Security Letters: Assessment of Corrective Actions and Examination of NSL Usage in 2006.* As with the first report, the methodology was rigorous, including analysis of the FBI's memoranda, top-level interviews, field office inspections, and reviewing random samples of most of the NSLs issued in 2006.[54] It detailed the steps taken by the FBI to correct its behavior, such as issuing guidance, training, introducing a new data system, and creating a new Office of Integrity and Compliance to check compliance with existing laws and regulations. Despite finding commitment on the part of the FBI to address the problems found in the first report, the second OIG report remained cautious in lauding the bureau and issued seventeen further recommendations (such as staffing the new Office of Integrity and Compliance with more permanent members, and requirements to submit reports of intelligence violations).

The third National Security Letters Report, issued in January 2010, focused directly on the exigent letters, one of the most controversial elements of the two preceding reports. Moreover, it assessed the measures taken by the FBI to hold its own staff to account and provided a long-term view of the FBI's use of NSLs. The final report uncovered not only a set of individual abuses but also a wider culture of casual requests for information without the appropriate authorization, which included sneak peeks at communications services' databases. The FBI developed a cozy relationship with the communications services, which led to the OIG's finding that "the FBI's use of exigent letters became so casual, routine, and unsupervised that employees of all three communications service providers sometimes generated exigent letters for the FBI personnel to sign and return to them."[55] The violations were not limited to exigent letters but extended to a host of informal methods for requesting information, and Fine testified that "the scope and variety of these informal requests was startling."[56]

Fine also raised the issue of an undisclosed (classified) legal authority with which the FBI could have secured certain telephone records without the use of exigent letters.[57] It was this authority that the FBI claimed when first confronted with the 2007 NSL report, and in response, they sought an opinion from the DOJ OLC, who supported the FBI's claims. Fine asserted in his testimony: "The OIG Report noted that the FBI's possible use of this authority had important legal and policy implications, and that the FBI, the Department, and Congress should consider how the FBI would use this legal authority when seeking telephone records. We further recommend that the department inform Congress of the FBI's potential use of this legal authority and of the OLC opinion interpreting the scope of this authority."[58] In this review, Fine was willing to challenge both the FBI's and the OLC's opinions and to prod congressional action by appealing to the contentious legal implications of the FBI's legal authority. At stake in both the immigrant detention and NSL cases was whether and how the DOJ should establish a parallel emergency regime to control administrative discretion and thus reign in the possibility of executive abuse of power.

Effects

The immediate effect of the reviews was the termination of the use of NSLs after the first report.[59] The first review also spurred the creation of an Office of Integrity and Compliance inside the FBI, an internal review body to check compliance with laws and regulations.[60] It provided an unprecedented level of transparency. Before the release of the IG review, the American Civil Liberties Union (ACLU) had attempted to sue the Justice Department for failing to disclose the extent of the government's use of surveillance tools.[61] Like the FOIA requests on which the suit was based, their efforts were unsuccessful. The IG review, however, placed this information in the public sphere and led to renewed and more specific FOIA requests by the ACLU, many of which were granted.[62] The publicity also led to public action on the part of the FBI. Beyond public apologies to newspapers by the FBI, the review also led to numerous FBI officials resigning.[63] And in the investigation leading to the third review (Exigent Letters), the OIG discovered that the FBI deleted some of the records from the databases that had been illegally gathered (but retained many on national security grounds).[64]

The OIG continued to monitor the FBI's compliance in implementing the reforms. In August 2014, it issued a review of the FBI's progress and revealed that of the total forty-one recommendations, the FBI had implemented only thirty-one. In the new report, the OIG issued ten additional recommendations that addressed problems found during the periodic compliance reviews.[65] Among other issues raised, the report underscored the vagueness of relevant legislation and the potential for this to lead to abuses of NSLs. Assessing the parameters of the ECPA NSL statute, the report cautions, "The term is undefined, and our review found that it is unclear whether all of the information the FBI receives in response to NSL requests for toll billing records falls within the scope of the statute," and it recommended that the department propose legislation to clarify the ambiguity.[66]

Standards

As with the September 11 reviews, the NSL reports' recommendations contributed toward the definition of "emergency" and emergency regimes. The ambiguous and imprecise use of "emergency" and the lack of procedure governing data collection had, in the diagnosis of the IG, led to the improper use of NSLs. After its first review, the FBI responded to the IG's recommendations by clarifying the circumstances under which the FBI could demand ECPA-protected documents or emergency voluntary disclosures; the definition of these circumstances hinged on the definition of "emergency."[67] The reviews also uncovered inconsistencies in reporting standards to the Intelligence Oversight Board and recommended that such standards be specified and issued to all personnel.[68] More generally, the reviews held the FBI to a standard of appropriate behavior beyond that expressed by law. The reviews diagnosed the FBI's practice as wrong "even if the letters are approved by management, sanctioned by FBI attorneys, part of an established practice, or accepted by the recipients."[69]

Administrative Procedure

One of the primary contributions of the reviews was to instigate the agency's creation of procedures for the use of data collection under the Patriot Act. In the first instance, they suggested instituting a system for tracking use of NSLs and recommended a series of reviews checking compliance with procedure by the Office of General Counsel.[70] But many passages in the reviews' recommendations were redacted, so precise analysis of the provisions in question is impossible. Nonetheless, the IG's intention to specify such procedures in administrative policy was clear.

Although the specific action was redacted, one of the IG's recommendations concerned the policies dictating FBI–media relations; the reports found the NSLs issued in media-leak cases to contain the most egregious abuses.[71] It recommended that the FBI coordinate with the National Security Division and other parts of the department to develop policies and procedures regarding this relationship, defining the circumstances under which the redacted provision might be used, and "specifically whether approval by senior FBI officials at the level of an Assistant Director or higher should be required," thus curtailing administrative discretion at the lowest rungs.[72] The review also addressed circumstantial factors. The convenience of the fact that communications providers had been on FBI premises had facilitated the issuance of NSLs through methods as informal as Post-It notes. The OIG demanded of the FBI that it develop procedures with this specific contingency written in.[73]

Legal Effects

The NSL reviews challenged the legal structure surrounding the Patriot Act and the FBI's information-gathering procedures. First, the IG reviews identified illegality where courts could not have been involved for lack of knowledge of the exigent letters. Second, the reviews went far beyond mere compliance monitoring by offering judgment on the validity of existing law. In the 2007 NSL review, the FBI general counsel defended its actions by claiming that voluntary disclosure of records by telecommunications companies in emergencies provided sufficient support for the use of exigent letters; this assertion was based on a provision in the Electronic Communications Privacy Act.[74] However, the IG rejected this argument on the grounds that the FBI had not used the provision at the time of its actions.[75] Once the FBI received the IG's admonishment in the first review, it formulated an alternative, retroactive legal justification for their issuance and asked the department's OLC to offer an opinion about the new provision. (The specific legal provisions were redacted in the third review.)

As in the September 11 reviews, the OIG challenged the OLC's opinion by questioning the legality regarding the FBI's prospective argument for "voluntary disclosure."[76] A further unnamed legal provision regarding data collection (seeking telephone records) prompted the IG to recommend that the "department notify Congress of this issue and of the OLC opinion interpreting the scope of the FBI's authority under it, so that Congress can consider the [redacted provision] and the implications of its potential use."[77]

The IG also stressed that the FBI advanced the unspecified provision only after the OIG found repeated misuses of its statutory authority to obtain telephone records through NSLs or the ECPA's emergency voluntary disclosure provisions and recommended that both the department and Congress formulate controls over the new provision.[78] The reviews not only contributed to the construction of a data collection regime but also challenged its proposed legal underpinnings and referred the matter to Congress.

IG Reviews in the Web of Accountability

One of the reviews' greatest strengths was the transparency it brought to national security instruments. Multiple public interest organizations had attempted to access information relating to the FBI's information gathering, but numerous legal obstacles, such as the gag order on recipients of NSLs, made these attempts unsuccessful. The OIG had been privy to documents and information that had been denied and misrepresented to Congress. By placing this information in narrative form, the OIG provided the raw material for further challenges and was cited as evidence in multiple court cases. On the back of the IG review, a federal appellate court declared the gag order provisions related to NSLs unconstitutional in a case brought against the FBI by the ACLU.[79] On 14 March 2013, a district court declared the underlying NSL statute unconstitutional.[80] Justice Susan Illston cited the IG reviews in her opinion as evidence of the extent of the problem in comparison with the evidence provided in previous court cases.[81]

Limits to the Reviews

In testimony, Fine held to the limits of his position in holding officials to account. When asked about the role of the IG in the oversight process and whether the statutory requirements regarding NSLs needed to be tightened, Fine replied, "That is a question for Congress and the administration, and my job here is to provide the facts and to show what happened and show the problems and to let the process work itself out."[82] Thus, despite the rigor of the investigation in terms of methodology, the first report's conclusion was in some ways limited by Fine's discretion in interpreting his role. Not only was the review mandated by Congress rather than initiated by the OIG, but Fine also restricted the scope of the report to providing a description of the problems that it found, limiting recommendations to nonpartisan, procedural reforms that fit within the confines of existing law.

Although the reviews recommended that the FBI adopt more definitional standards, they did not suggest more rigorous constraints to prevent future abuses. The IG also refrained from passing final judgment on the liberty versus security trade-off: despite the constitutional accountability pursued in the reviews, the IG wavered in its first review between condemning the FBI for its illegal practices and recognizing the exigencies of national security that led to the breaches. As with all of the reviews, one of the main limitations on its effects was its reliance on external actors to implement its reforms. While the FBI itself largely adhered to the OIG's recommendations, Congress did not take up the recommendation to regulate the FBI's voluntary disclosure policy.[83]

The War on Terror Reviews: Building Legal Infrastructure to Protect Rights

Fine's skill in extracting and synthesizing sensitive documents from the Justice Department under Ashcroft was remarkable in an administration known for stonewalling congressional requests for information; members of Congress on both sides of the political spectrum joined forces in condemning Ashcroft's secrecy regarding antiterrorism activity.[84] But more than his doggedness in finagling information, the restrained criticism he levied on the department attracted visibility without elevating the position of the IG to one of bureaucratic dictator. The guidance provided by his recommendations ultimately provided a concrete set of standards for appropriate action in times of emergency to which other political actors could hold the FBI to account. His strategy was both constructive, in contributing to the legal and procedural framework, and enabling, in providing the external mechanisms of accountability with the synthesized information necessary to pursue parallel processes of accountability.

The reviews were also demonstrative of an IG's capacity to engage in a constitutional mode of democratic practice. They supported the courts' individual protections against administrative wrongdoing, and they unearthed the constitutional stakes of the FBI's rule infractions. The narratives available to the public were framed in these terms and set out norms for administrative decision making and the protection of rights.

CHAPTER EIGHT

FROM TERROR TO HURRICANES
Crafting Emergency Governance at Homeland Security

The more destruction there is everywhere, the more it shows the activity of town authorities.
—Nikolai Gogol, *The Inspector General* (1836)

Introduction

In late 2001, faced with the ashes of the September 11 attacks and confronted with the threat of further terror, policy makers sought not only to find concrete measures with which to defend the nation but also to create a governing paradigm to guide their efforts. What governing vision would befit a post-9/11 *Americana anno zero*? In early 2001, the Hart-Rudman report had tentatively put forth "homeland security" as an organizational concept, and given the report's perspicacious anticipation of a terrorist act, the Bush administration adopted the term. Yet homeland security remained sufficiently novel and ill-defined to permit wide and differing interpretations of its scope. The breadth of the concept permitted any number of policies, strategies, and government actions to fall under its umbrella.

Nowhere was this ambiguity as evident as in the construction of the DHS itself. Few government entities so large have been born in such haste, and bearing the adrenaline-fueled scars of a national trauma, as the DHS. And as with any urgent political decision, the DHS's creation set in motion a host of conflicts both moral and institutional that plagued its rocky growth for its first decade. The DHS's OIG, its purpose as vague as that of its host department, was placed to be an arbiter of these tensions, but it was left to the vision and strength of each IG to guide the new department to functionality as it trundled along like a wounded animal. The bureaucratic disarray surrounding the new department reflected the activity of the town authorities.

In the DHS OIG's first decade, the strategies to tame this administrative leviathan varied but were ultimately unified by a managerial mode of democratic practice. The inaugural IG, Clark Kent Ervin, defined his outlook through the lens of 9/11: he freely acknowledged his political and ideological commitment to the war on terror, and he directed resources and bureaucratic capital toward maximizing the department's performance in that framework. However, he bequeathed his successor an unsteady office, still starved of resources. Faced with trouble from within the OIG and from without—the mounting war on terror, and then the United States' largest natural disaster in recent history—Richard Skinner, the hard-nosed second IG, expanded the office's focus from counterterror oversight to include natural disasters (a result of his prior experience at FEMA) and continued his predecessor's emphasis on performance and management. But for the gem that DHS OIG had become by the end of Skinner's tenure, its glory was quickly lost: the third IG's mismanagement and corruption sent the office into disarray, underscoring the fragility of an OIG's capacity in the absence of strong and permanent leadership.

Congress crafted the Patriot Act with the DHS IG's role as a protector of civil rights keenly in mind. Yet the vision of its first IGs pushed it firmly toward practicing managerial democracy rather than fostering a constitutional democracy. It developed strong capacities to evaluate and improve the performance of its host department rather than assessing its adherence to constitutional norms, and it framed its reviews in terms of maximizing performance and efficiency, encouraging a businesslike operation in the department. Because of this bias, the IG's relationship with Congress waxed and waned, and its success in delivering consequential reviews varied over time.

The Institutional Context: A New Department for a Novel Concept

Uniting the DHS's disparate functions was the notion of emergency. Beyond the ambiguity of DHS's structure and focus lay the question of the state's role in emergency governance. Superficially a mere bureaucratic reorganization (and an extensive one at that), DHS's creation helped to entrench "emergency" as a governing paradigm. Though its long-term effects were unclear, in this experimental model of bureaucratic organization, emergency as a mode of governmental operation trumped a functional distribution of authority and capacity. The concept of homeland security, as vaguely defined as it was, served as a new paradigm through which to comprehend state activity, and it altered the terms on which government funds were disbursed. IG Clark Kent Ervin later commented,

> It's critical, it seems to me, that we increase markedly our overall home-land security spending. You know, one of the things I was struck by earlier was there was a bipartisan consensus earlier, Senator Biden and Senator Kyl saying—both ends of the political spectrum—we've really under-funded homeland security. And I think Katrina shows the importance of greatly increasing our spending. And I say that as a conservative who understands that government spending by itself isn't always the answer.[1]

Even before it had a definite meaning, the concept marshaled action that tran-scended partisanship. Emergency governance (in its particularly American iteration of antiterrorism), overrode the traditional conservative–progressive split over government size and spending.

Similarly, not only was the partisan spending divide complicated by the homeland security concept but also was the question of the scope of exec-utive power (as wielded by DHS). DHS's very creation placed liberals and conservatives on unfamiliar sides of the size-of-government debate. In con-gressional debates (as well as in the wider public), the question of executive power was reframed in terms of the liberty–security balance. Proponents of the hypothetical DHS within the administration argued that the need for security and the "emergency" orientation of the new bureaucracy jus-tified the suspension of usual checks and balances. Senator Patrick Leahy described the debate thus:

> In writing the charter for this new department, we must be careful not to generate new management problems and accountability issues. Yet the Administration's proposal would have exempted the new department from many legal requirements that apply to other agencies. The Freedom of Information Act would not apply; the conflicts of interest and account-ability rules for agency advisors would not apply. The new department head would have the power to suspend the Whistleblower Protection Act, the normal procurement rules, and to intervene in Inspector General investigations. In these respects, the Administration asked us to put this new department above the law and outside the checks and balances these laws are put there to ensure.[2]

Far more than a mere bureaucratic reorganization, the creation of the DHS afforded its designers the opportunity to circumvent the checks and bal-ances common to most (even national security) departments in the federal government. Senator Daniel Akaka (D-HI) cautioned that "the threat of a 'Big Brother' new department cannot be overemphasized."[3] In opposing the creation of the DHS, Akaka was in the minority among Democrats, but he voiced the primary concern on both sides of the partisan spectrum. Congressional discussions around the construction of the DHS focused on the precise form, specification, and measurement of its internal checks and accountability mechanisms. The president pushed repeatedly for a department secretary with unprecedented power, but a series of corrective amendments in both the House and the Senate provided for a parallel civil rights officer and privacy officer. The debate culminated in a unique constellation of checks within DHS in the final act.[4] The OIG fell under a rubric similar to that of other national security departments and had an exemption through which the department head could prevent investigations on national security grounds. Moreover, OIG agents were given the authority to "carry a firearm, make arrests without warrants, and seek and execute warrants"—a privilege given only to select OIGs.[5]

This messy compromise gave birth to an OIG uncertain of its remit and with a distinctive configuration of institutional features. It inherited staff and responsibilities from the OIGs of FEMA and the Treasury, Justice, and Transportation departments, as well as twenty-two field installations. Because the DHS was not yet in existence at the time of the Patriot Act, the Justice Department OIG had been given responsibility for civil rights abuses relating to the Patriot Act; this clouded the new OIG's jurisdiction and its focus. To further complicate the lines of responsibility, the DHS OIG also contended with an overlap with the DHS's own civil rights unit. Similarly, the jurisdictional lines between the OIG and the DHS privacy office were imprecise and proved to be a source of friction over the OIG's first decade in the allocation of investigative resources.

The priorities of the new OIG were also uncertain. IGs should, in theory, focus on the priorities of the host department. In the case of the DHS, however, the department's own raison d'être was fuzzy at best; defining the object of homeland security was proving as difficult as hastily cobbling together the department's constituent agencies. This meant that the OIG's focus was largely up to the IG's own interpretation. It also meant that management, organization, and basic competencies presented an obvious initial focus above and beyond questions of rights. Before the IG could consider the actions of its host department, it contended with integrating four payroll systems, travel management, accounting systems, budget processes, and procurement processes.[6] While the establishment of any OIG involves bringing diverse offices together, the DHS OIG contended with the additional challenge of monitoring its host department's own rocky birth by patchwork. Moreover, the new OIG inherited a number of preexisting IG investigations from its legacy departments, including a Justice IG report on Border Patrol fraud, and it consequently found itself with the administratively complex task of tracking the implementation of previous recommendations issued by the prior OIG. Before it could even address management and reporting concerns, it tasked itself with basic operational matters. In its first year, it only managed to complete timely audit and inspection reports (completed within six months of the project start date) only 44 percent of the time. In the first two years of its existence, the OIG saw the number of its open investigations rise by 209 percent.[7]

Although the establishment of DHS was reactive in nature (insofar as it was a direct response to the terrorist attacks), the near consensus in Congress and in the Bush administration favored a proactive and preventative approach to homeland security policy. For the department, part of the shift to emergency governance involved contending with a bureaucratic reordering and switching from purely reactive to largely preventative action that required planning, prediction, and calculation. The OIG's own twofold approach to its audits and investigations, which combined a mixture of "fire alarm" and "police patrol" methods of accountability, mirrored this reactive and proactive strategy.[8] This provoked exigencies with institutional consequences in the form of permanent suboffices within the OIG and in the cultivation of a web of oversight with other OIGs.

The DHS IG had an effect on the organization and direction of its host department in a way that few IGs have been able to achieve in more established departments. The ambiguity and breadth of the DHS's mission lent it malleability, and the first two IGs, Clark Kent Ervin and Richard Skinner, targeted this uncertainty in their reviews. Because of 9/11, and in particular the manner in which the hijackers carried out their deadly objective, the OIG's first years were spent concentrating on border and transportation security, and terrorist watch lists. Despite his broad support for Bush administration policies, Ervin regularly issued harsh condemnations of how the DHS enacted its policies.[9] A December 2003 report attacked the entire organization of the counterterror intelligence system and suggested that the Bush administration's establishment of parallel antiterror organizations, such as the Terrorist Threat Integration Center, merely confused the DHS's mission and created inefficient functional overlap between many centers of authority.[10] Indeed, one of the IGs' primary de facto roles was in

Table 8.1. Academic and Professional Backgrounds of DHS Inspectors General

IG	Date	Academic Background	Professional Experience
Clark Kent Ervin (acting)	March 2003– December 2004	Law	Law (private practice and state attorney general); inspector general of State Department
Richard Skinner	August 2005–January 2011	Public and business administration	Federal administration and multiple OIGs (FEMA and Agriculture, Justice, Commerce, and State departments)
Charles K. Edwards (acting)	February 2011–December 2013	Electrical engineering	Federal administration (USPS, USPS OIG, and TSA)
Carleton Mann	December 2013–March 2014	Unknown	Unknown
John Roth	March 2014–present	Law	Law (public practice, as US attorney and Department of Justice section chief)

clarifying the lines of authority muddled by the ad hoc nature of the DHS's construction.

Steering Counterterror Policy: Clark Kent Ervin, 2003–2004

In March 2003, Clark Kent Ervin, a former Rhodes scholar at Oxford and lawyer by training, was plucked from the State Department OIG and placed at the helm of the newly minted DHS OIG. His first appointment was as acting IG until he was to be confirmed. However, Senator Joseph Lieberman (D-CT) and Senator Susan Collins of the Governmental Affairs Committee both objected to his confirmation on the grounds that he had failed to undertake an important investigation during his time as State Department IG. During his tenure at State, Ervin had refused to investigate a sexual harassment claim. On Ervin's account, he had refused because the alleged harassment took place outside of the State Department proper. Frustrated after a series of briefings and interrogations by the committee, Ervin sought support from President Bush, who gave him a recess appointment as DHS IG in December 2003.

A Republican and friend of President Bush's from his days working as deputy attorney general of Texas, Ervin had served as State Department IG under Colin Powell since April 2001. Ervin understood his mission at DHS to be inspired by the 9/11 attacks. Indeed, his Republican orientation led him to believe in and support the Bush administration's counterterror strategy. His priority was thus to ensure the successful performance of the department as a part of the overall strategy of protecting the homeland (especially preventing terrorist attacks). Ervin brought with him a number of members of the State Department OIG, but the largest staff inheritance came from FEMA's OIG, which donated 200 staff members to the new OIG's total of 459.[11]

Ervin's guiding aim was to define the mission of the department—and of the definition of homeland security—as counterterrorism.[12] At State OIG, he had followed Secretary Colin Powell's attention to IT matters and had duly established a separate IT evaluation unit within the OIG. Realizing that one of DHS's first tasks as a new department would be to coordinate, evaluate, and prune the hundreds of information systems it inherited made him designate IT as the OIG's first object of oversight. After IT, Ervin's OIG devoted much of its energies to airport security, an area that would be the focus of one of his office's most provocative sets of reviews. This choice was a direct result of the September 11 attacks, and it meant that the newly minted Transportation Security Administration (TSA) would receive well-deserved scrutiny. The reports uncovered systemic failure in airport security screening, which resulted in widely publicized statistics about TSA performance. Undercover OIG staff successfully smuggled a host of forbidden items onto flights and suggested a detection failure rate as low as in similar tests performed before September 11.[13] The project not only unearthed the failures of the moment but also condemned the department for ignoring long-standing recommendations for reform: the weak passenger screening procedures had been criticized by the IG since the late 1990s, but the recommendations remained unheeded.

Beyond the performance focus of this investigation, the airport screening tests afforded the IG the occasion to provide evidence for a partisan ideological battle over the use of the private sector in federal programs. The specific purpose of the review was to see whether the TSA's pilot program using private contractors yielded better performances. Though Bush had pushed to allow airports to hire private screeners rather than federal ones on the basis that the private sector was more efficient, the OIG's report implicitly undermined this rationale by demonstrating that the contractors were no more efficient than federal employees. However, Ervin leveled his criticism at waste rather than the ideological implications. An illegal contract with the Boeing Company to install detection machines in airports led to nearly $50 million in excess payment.[14] Though the report itself was critical of the waste, it did not directly address the broader ideological point. It did, however, provide fodder for the opposite ideological camp of the administration, and it did nothing to enhance Ervin's standing with the administration.

The long-term effect of these reviews was also limited. The TSA's efficacy in screening passengers continued to concern Congress, the GAO, and the IG over the next decade. Ervin, who had conducted the first review in 2004, testified to Congress, "The sad fact is that for all the dollars and attention that has been focused on screener performance since 9/11, study after study . . . shows that it is just as easy today to sneak these deadly weapons past screeners [as] it was on 9/11."[15] Although his original reviews did not have immediate impact on the TSA's performance, the Bush administration and Congress both based their subsequent recommendations and legislative proposals on Ervin's recommendations.[16]

Though Ervin's focus rested largely on systemic weaknesses, such as the airport screening procedures, his office also investigated a number of single instances of waste, as in a review entitled *Assessment of Expenditures*

Related to the First Annual Transportation Security Administration Awards Program and Executive Performance Awards (September 2004). Triggered by a news article, this review exposed a $461,745 event (excluding bonuses, which totaled nearly $1.5 million), with much of this money not having been secured through competitive bids.[17] The IG report judged the TSA's expenditures to be excessive (citing, among many undue costs, $1,486 for three balloon arches and $64 for each gallon of coffee) and linked them to the TSA's poor overall performance. Yet later Ervin judged his most important work to be not the single instances of fraud or waste but rather the sets of reviews that uncovered larger systemic problems.[18] Among such reviews, he counted the airport screenings and his earlier State Department OIG review of the Bush administration's potential involvement in Hugo Chávez's temporary ousting as his most consequential efforts, above and beyond the flashy, media-friendly reports of lavish agency parties.

Ervin also believed that his role as IG required him to hold the department to its legal responsibilities as specified in the Homeland Security Act of 2002. Determining what these legal responsibilities were, it turned out, was less than straightforward, and it created further friction between Ervin and the department. He identified "no fewer than six responsibilities spelled out in the Homeland Security Act for the Information Analysis unit [that] strongly implied that the DHS was to take the lead on consolidating the different federal watch lists."[19] In practice, the DHS had yielded its turf in this domain to the FBI when the White House created a Terrorist Screening Center directed primarily by the FBI. Ervin's role also thrust him into the position of interpreting ambiguous mandates. Here his background as a lawyer drove the manner in which he pushed for departmental reform. Two sources of law seemed to conflict: the Homeland Security Act, which (in Ervin's eyes) gave the DHS responsibility for consolidating federal watch lists; and the presidential directive establishing the Terrorist Screening Center and thus redirecting this task to the FBI.[20] But in his report, Ervin insisted that there was no such contradiction.

Ervin sharply criticized the DHS for its failure to insist on responsibility for the federal watch lists. The department stated in its response, "We strongly disagree with the report's premise that either DHS or IAIP [Information Analysis and Infrastructure Protection] has the lead responsibility within the federal government for consolidating terrorist watch lists. . . . Given the constraints [of starting up the Department], it was determined at the highest levels of government that DOJ was in a better position to take on the responsibility for coordinating the federal government's effort in watch list consolidation."[21] Here the limits of the IG came to bear: while Ervin pushed the scope of the IG's authorities and weighed in on the appropriate jurisdiction of the department and its agencies, his fractious relationship with Ridge and lack of credibility with Congress undermined any power of persuasion or enforcement that he may otherwise have had. Ervin's challenge to DHS policy and the scope of its responsibility pointed to the possibility of considerable departmental reform. However, he needed cooperation from within the institution, and in particular the cooperation of his direct superior. The structure of the IG Act makes a successful IG largely dependent on the department head. Despite a promising start, Ervin's relationship with DHS secretary Tom Ridge quickly deteriorated as his term went on. Ridge objected to the tone of the IG reviews, and in Ervin's view, he preferred a sugar-coated version of events. From Ridge's perspective, Ervin released the reports too quickly to the press—at times before they were shown either to Congress or to Ridge himself. Moreover, Ridge objected to Ervin's conclusions. When Ervin issued a report damning the creation of the Terrorist Threat Integration Center, which made Homeland Security's intelligence-analysis capacity redundant, Ridge protested that Ervin lacked an intimate understanding of the department's activities.[22] Unlike the monthly meetings that many IGs have with their department heads, Ervin had only two during his two-year tenure at DHS. However, Ridge refrained from preventing any of Ervin's reviews from being published.[23] But the antagonistic relationship between the two took its toll, and the Bush administration's support ultimately fell with Ridge.

Given their position straddling the barbed-wire fence, IGs find themselves torn between loyalty to Congress and loyalty to their departments (of which they are members). But further vexing the matter is the source of the IGs' position—his or her political appointment by a particular administration—which may waver in its support even of its own department head. In the case of conflict between an IG and department head (a frequent occurrence with an aggressive IG), the administration must often take sides. Dismissal of an IG occasions far less political damage than public ire at a department head.

Despite his doggedness, from the perspective of many around him, Ervin's sins mounted. Congress had shown skepticism toward him beginning with his nomination, and his tendency to privilege the media as a preferred audience alienated him further. The administration, initially his primary supporter, found that his reports did them no favors. Ervin also provoked the ire of Congress by releasing his reports to the media before showing them to Congress, though he praised "the bright light of congressional attention and the press" in making his reviews carry weight.[24] According to the staff of Senator Collins, the decision not to renew Ervin's term in 2004 "was purely a White House decision."[25]

Ervin's appointment was political—this may have contributed to the suspicion with which senators Collins and Lieberman viewed his nomination—but he ultimately remained committed to the IG mandate of nonpartisan oversight of his host department, as evident in his frequently devastating critiques of the department's programs. Despite his close ties to the Bush family and his commitment to the Republican Party, Ervin's resolutely critical stance, coupled with his failure to build a network of support, led to his own dismissal. But his truncated tenure underscored how fragile the IG's authority can be, especially when an IG is unconfirmed, and how dependent it is on the IG's relationship with the department head and with Congress. IG authority depends on leverage, persuasion, and reputation; it is a relational authority, not an absolute one, that relies on the relationships and networks forged beyond the confines of its own office.

As an IG, Ervin brought a focused political vision, and in particular a clear definition of the concept of homeland security. Ervin's strategy focused squarely on the functionality and performance of the DHS in support of his pursuit of the DHS's counterterrorism mission, and he was outspoken about being "of the school of thought that maintains that, if anything, the threat of terrorism here at home is not taken seriously enough . . . and, as a result, we are doing far less than we should be doing to combat it."[26] But because of his brief tenure and lack of confirmation, Ervin did not have the professional security to make a lasting institutional mark on the DHS OIG in the form of building suboffices or networks.

Expanding the "Homeland Security" Concept: Richard Skinner, 2004–2011

With Ervin out of the job in December 2004, the nomination fell to Richard Skinner, who had extensive experience in the IG community. He had served in various capacities in the OIG of FEMA since the early 1990s, and he became the deputy IG of DHS beginning in March 2003. He assumed the position of acting IG when Ervin left and was confirmed on 28 July 2005. Whereas Ervin's outlook had been shaped primarily by the September 11 attacks, Skinner's background at FEMA and in other parts of the IG community contributed to his adoption of a broader conception of homeland security that included natural disaster. Ervin's training in law made him attuned to the legal dimensions of DHS policy and pushed him to focus on jurisdictional matters as well as routine fraud and waste; Skinner, in contrast, brought an appreciation of administrative complexity and its effect on departmental performance. Instead of focusing primarily on counterterror capacity, Skinner reoriented the OIG's energies toward the DHS's more domestic (natural disaster management) and quotidian functions (such as the Coast Guard). But like Ervin, he interpreted the IG's mission to be one of maximizing performance. Despite the many critical reports he oversaw, Skinner's tenure would prove to be longer, more stable, and more effective than Ervin's. Skinner cultivated relationships with the department secretary and with Congress (especially the Appropriations Committee), and he tempered the OIG's relationship with the press. As much as the institutional reorganization he spearheaded, it was these relationships that contributed to the strength of his reviews.

Unlike many other OIGs, the DHS OIG was faced with a department still in the process of carving out a coherent identity for itself. Only two years old, it faced the practical challenges of integrating the myriad practices and IT systems of its component parts. Its oversight was ongoing departmental performance as well as the continuous process of departmental construction. The office that Skinner inherited was still a young one, and its difficulties reflected those of its host department. Even while acting IG, he began a reorganization of the audit division; he transferred fifty staff members from the audit division to the investigations division in 2005. Just as the DHS was composed of multiple agencies, the OIG had been formed through the merger of seven different OIGs and took staff from each of them (and not always staff members with the best credentials or records). But this posed the problem of creating a cohesive culture. Even after two years, Skinner found this problem unresolved. Moreover, the constituent parts of the OIG were not at first housed in the same building: the audit office was across town from the investigative office, and the two staffs were unacquainted with one another. However, Congress did not starve the new office of resources; on Skinner's account, and unlike the experiences of many other IGs, the Appropriations Committee responded adequately to Skinner's requests. The DHS OIG's budget as a percentage of the department's budget was never greater than 0.25 percent; the State OIG, in contrast, suffered resource deficiencies even when its budget comprised greater than 0.3 percent of its host department's budget (Figure 8.1). This indicates that the sources of departmental dysfunction and corruption are not entirely functions of a department's own

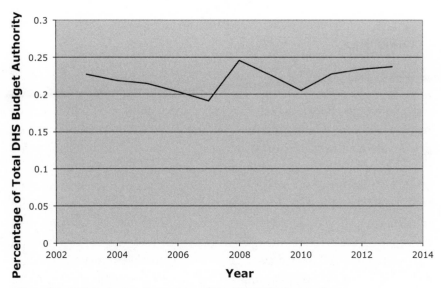

Figure 8.1. OIG Budget as Percentage of Total DHS Budget Authority

size and resources, and that the challenges of finding problems might be much greater in some departments than others.

In terms of personnel, the DHS OIG grew steadily in its first decade (Figure 8.2), but in the absence of strong leadership after 2011, even this greater capacity failed to bring about strong reviews.

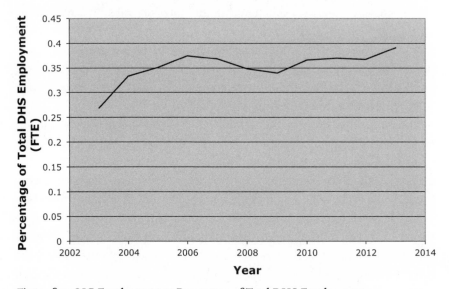

Figure 8.2. OIG Employment as Percentage of Total DHS Employment

Skinner's Innovations: Building Infrastructure for Performance

While still only acting IG, Skinner began to experiment with a set of reforms to dislodge the obstacles faced by Ervin. His first modification was to try to ameliorate the OIG's relationship with the press. Indeed, this relationship was of keen interest to Skinner's congressional interrogators during his confirmation hearing. Ervin's practice had been to notify the media of upcoming reports through e-mail and telephone, a practice that created a number of administrative burdens. (This practice was unusual among OIGs and was a source of irritation to members of Congress and the department, who felt that the reports should be released to them first.) He replaced the practice with the policy that all OIG reports be posted on the website five days after they had been sent to the relevant DHS oversight committee.[27] In so doing, Skinner shifted the OIG's primary audience and gained the trust and favor of Congress, building a crucial dimension of trust with the Hill that would serve the IG later.

Skinner pursued a three-pronged strategy for the development of the office. First, he focused on management relationships. Second, he planned to "concentrate resources on critical management control system, financial systems, and information management systems," with the aim of shoring up the integrity of DHS programs. Finally, he sought to emphasize quality control reviews.[28] His vision of the IG was firmly a post-NPR product, conceived as a proactive, collaborative, and advisory role. To that end, he arranged meetings with the DHS's chief procurement officer and chief financial officer to refine the department's procurement procedures even before the occurrence of fraud. (In his previous capacities at the Commerce and State OIGs, he had similarly promoted the IG's advisory role, especially in the development of IT security systems.)

Unlike his predecessor, Skinner enjoyed unfettered access to the Homeland Security secretary, Michael Chertoff, and even as acting IG met with him and other senior members of the department regularly.[29] Rather, the threats to his office's authority resulted from the still-ambiguous institutional setup of the OIG. The Intelligence Reform and Terrorism Prevention Act of 2004 elevated the privacy officer, authorizing it to report directly to the secretary and thus giving it overlapping jurisdiction with the IG. The privacy office was short-staffed and repeatedly tried to use the OIG's resources by mandating OIG investigations, but Skinner declined. Similarly, the civil rights office interpreted its mandate as overlapping with the OIG's. Neither of these jurisdictional overlaps was resolved formally, but through conversation and informal policy, the two offices arrived at a modus vivendi that largely preserved the OIG's standing jurisdiction.[30]

In addition to the ambiguity of the OIG's domain, Skinner felt pressure from Congress to pursue particular reviews. While some IGs react to highly political matters and some obey all congressional requests, he settled on a particular formula for obeying them: if a committee chair signed a request for an investigation or audit, he would automatically accept; if the ranking member signed the request, he would do background work but would frequently accept.[31] He also laid out very specific criteria for determining the allocation of the OIG's limited resources. These included relevant statutory and regulatory requirements; the newness or sensitivity of the program under review; dollar magnitude; management and congressional needs to be met; prior investigative attention; nature of reviews performed by other oversight bodies (e.g., the GAO); and availability of audit resources.[32] His systematized, managerial approach to case selection mirrored his performance-based conception of accountability. Skinner also struggled with a Congress increasingly inclined to include unfunded mandates for IG oversight in legislation, thus compromising the IG's ability to choose priorities. The DHS OIG was particularly affected by this trend; for instance, oversight of the 287(g) provision (immigration) and of drug controls was mandated by congressional legislation. Congress doubled the number between 2003 and 2005. By 2012, these mandates totaled more than two dozen.

Circumventing Rights

Many of Skinner's major early reviews were long-term investigations inherited from Ervin. One of the most widely publicized and controversial reviews investigated the alleged unlawful treatment of terrorist detainee Maher Arar. (Initially this investigation was the result of a congressional request by Representative John Conyers Jr. [D-MI].) A Syrian-born Canadian citizen, Arar was detained by US officials in New York on suspicion of involvement with terrorists and was soon deported to Syria. There, Arar claimed, he was tortured by the Syrian police for a year before being returned to Canada. The IG investigation set out to determine whether US officials had acted wrongly or illegally by deporting Arar. The enquiry was widely supported by human rights groups, such as Human Rights First and the ACLU, and many expressed faith that Ervin's record of critical reports boded well. The case proved to be a test of the administration's ability to uphold its stated commitment to civil rights and its capacity for self-criticism. The ACLU applauded Ervin's decision to "focus not only on the specific case of Mr. Arar, but more generally on cases involving the removal of alleged terrorist suspects to a country where they may risk being subjected to torture," and thus to pass judgment on the phenomenon of extraordinary renditions as a concept without legal status.[33]

The investigation was still underway when Ervin's tenure expired, and it was left to acting IG Skinner to take over. The switchover proved to be a source of worry for observers. A lawyer for Human Rights First, Priti Patel, voiced concern that the enquiries would be "shelved" once Ervin left.[34] This fear reflected the knowledge that IG reviews, though written by teams of lawyers and investigators, depend heavily on the direction of the IG itself. Skinner continued with the review and in 2008 released a classified report for Congress and a one-page summary for the public. It came under considerable criticism by watchdog groups, civil rights groups, and academics for the weakness of its judgments regarding government wrongdoing, the small number of recommendations, and the slowness and incompleteness of the final report released to the public. (It was released only under additional congressional pressure.) In later questioning by Congress, Skinner defended the department's refusal to provide documents in a timely fashion on the grounds that exposing such information would void the department's legal privileges in parallel litigation, but he ultimately deemed the matter resolved as a result of a memorandum of understanding.[35] However, as the Committee on Governmental Affairs was quick to point out, Skinner did not invoke the IG's statutory right to demand assistance from the secretary (under subsection 6[b][2] of the IG Act) when he was initially denied access. Though both Ervin and Skinner encountered serious external hurdles to the investigation—hurdles set by members of the administration—Ervin himself condemned the OIG investigators for failing to fight against the resistance they encountered.[36] An academic assessment of the review noted that the OIG's two recommendations neglected to establish any form of compliance monitoring and that the OIG had failed to interview many key actors in the controversy, such as the acting attorney general.[37]

Given the many rigorous reviews issued by the same IG, the weakness of the Maher Arar review was puzzling. Skinner had not shown himself to be reluctant to criticize the administration in previous investigations, so the weakness of the review could not be attributed to hierarchical or partisan deference. In part, the unorthodox and unprecedented circumstances of the review—the parallel civil litigation, the documents' security classification issued by other departments, the DHS's lack of familiarity with the protocols of the intelligence community, and a department staff unfamiliar with IG authorities—made Skinner cautious and uneasy about asserting his authorities. But the OIG's failure to evaluate the INS's morality also revealed a reluctance to criticize the administration's counterterror policy more broadly, as well as a distinctive conception of accountability that privileged performance concerns over constitutionality. The IG's potential influence here, based on a subjective framing of a problem, was considerable. A clear statement of government wrongdoing by the OIG in the Maher Arar case would have had ideological ramifications: were the administration's claims about the legality of its counterterror practices bogus, or were they legitimate and necessary components of its strategy? Skinner shied away from making this judgment. Moreover, the OIG's failure to find fault with the government's actions rested on a particular interpretation of what the government should be doing, and the IG avoided wading into nebulous legal and moral territory. Similarly, one of Skinner's more rigorous reviews, criticizing the REAL ID program of 2009, did so on administrative grounds rather than the civil rights grounds advocated by the ACLU.[38]

Skinner's vision of accountability was performance based, and he steered his efforts toward improving the DHS's efficiency and outcomes. Despite his lack of overt partisanship, the managerial democracy pursued by his OIG was thus rooted in prior partisan and even ideological commitments, but it also reflected his training and experience. Even as acting IG, he had helped to bring the office in line with the NPR-era Government Performance Results Act standards by steering and implementing the OIG's first two annual performance plans and by defining the criteria and evaluation methods for office performance.

It was not a terrorist attack but rather a natural disaster, Hurricane Katrina, that offered the DHS its first national crisis to manage. The OIG's orientation shifted to address this. Whereas Ervin had channeled the office's capacities toward counterterrorism, Skinner showed sensitivity to the need to create institutional structures directed toward the reactive nature of the department's activity and inaugurated the Office of Inspections and Special Reviews, which was "specially structured and staffed to meet exigent deadlines for the conduct of non-traditional examinations into DHS operations."[39] In theory, this suboffice provided a springboard for pursuing the urgent reviews needed in the context of DHS's management of emergency. Using a similar rationale, he set up a special oversight group in response to Katrina, the Emergency Management Unit (EMU, later the Emergency

Management Oversight Unit), as a permanent institutional response to the often unpredictable nature of emergency that is a central target of DHS operations. Beyond this innovation, the Katrina reviews offered a particular model of IG investigations, which involved ongoing reviews rather than one-off investigations. In this way, the dominant institutional features of the DHS OIG grew out of contingency and the expectation of permanent emergency.

The Gulf Coast Recovery was not the only major review the OIG undertook at this time. Beginning in 2006, the office assumed a series of audits and investigations of the Coast Guard's troubled, decade-long modernization project, the Deepwater program. The bureaucratic reorganization of the nation's defense structures through the establishment of the DHS affected and confused the missions of its constituent parts, and this proved to be a fertile territory for IG commentary and intervention. Senator Olympia Snowe (R-ME) argued that the Coast Guard's resources needed to be rethought in light of its homeland security mission: "As the Homeland Security Inspector General's recent report makes clear, the sheer scope of the Coast Guard's mission is taking a toll on their ships and aircraft and ultimately on their personnel."[40] While Coast Guard modernization had been on the military's agenda since a 1995 review of its requirements, 9/11 and Katrina expanded its missions (for instance, by adding the sea marshals program) and strained its resources. In 2002, the Coast Guard was granted $1.8 billion to overhaul and modernize its fleet, and this was used to procure assets and services from a private contractor, Integrated Coast Guard Systems.

The IG's reports on the Deepwater program served as a direct instrument of congressional oversight. They also revealed the perils of the military's reliance on contractors, both for the physical integrity of assets and for the potential for financial waste. Two reviews, the first in 2006 and the second in 2009, tracked the Coast Guard's efforts to rebuild its fleet and its disastrous choice of contractors. The IG reviews found that Integrated Coast Guard Systems failed to meet the requirements of many of the contracts, leaving much of the Coast Guard's fleet cracked and unusable. In 2009, the IG reviewed the Coast Guard's efforts to recoup their funds from the unsatisfactory earlier contracts. An article later published by the Coast Guard itself reflected, "In the end, the general consensus is that we ceded too much responsibility to the contractor, including some functions that should have been reserved for government employees."[41] The Deepwater program was finally laid to rest in 2012, much to the satisfaction of crit-

Table 8.2. Number of Media Citations for Selected DHS OIG Reviews

Review	Review Date	Media Citations	Date Range
TSA airport screening[a]	September 2004[b]	127	1 June 2004–1 June 2008
Gulf Coast recovery[c]	August 2005–December 2008	2,113	1 August 2005–31 December 2012[d]
Maher Arar[e]	March 2008	74	1 January 2003–1 January 2011[f]
Deepwater Horizon[g]	August 2006	295	1 January 2004–31 January 2010
Secure Communities[h]	April 2012	100	1 March 2010–1 March 2014

Source: Factiva database.

[a]Search terms: ("department of homeland security" OR "dhs") AND "inspector general" AND "tsa" AND "screening" AND "weapons."

[b]The two primary reviews were: *Evaluation of TSA's Contract for the Installation and Maintenance of Explosive Detection Equipment at United States Airports* (September 2004); and *An Evaluation of the Transportation Security Administration's Screener Training and Methods of Testing* (September 2004).

[c]Search terms: ("department of homeland security" OR "dhs") AND "inspector general" AND ("gulf coast recovery" OR "katrina").

[d]The date range reflected the time from the landing of the first hurricane to four years after the final report was released.

[e]Search terms: ("department of homeland security" OR "dhs") AND "inspector general" AND "maher arar."

[f]This date range was extended because the investigation was ongoing and not released until 2008, yet was discussed in the media as the investigation proceeded.

[g]Search terms: ("department of homeland security" OR "dhs") AND "inspector general" AND "deepwater" AND "coast guard."

[h]Search terms: ("department of homeland security" OR "dhs") AND "inspector general" AND "secure communities."

ics on both sides of the partisan spectrum. A later independent analysis deemed it to be the rigorous oversight, spearheaded by the DHS IG, that largely contributed to the program's demise.[42]

A Hurricane Hits the OIG: Charles K. Edwards as Acting IG, 2011–2014

Skinner's retirement on 12 January 2011 gave way to a three-year absence nominally filled by deputy (and later acting) IG Charles K. Edwards. Edwards had worked in the office as deputy IG under Skinner and before that had experience in the Post Office OIG. Though an engineer by training, he had spent his professional life in government service. The Obama administration quickly nominated Justice Department OIG member Roslyn A. Mazer to the position in July 2011, but Susan Collins, the same senator who had objected to Ervin's appointment nearly a decade earlier, blocked Mazer's confirmation.[43] After her rejection by the Senate, Obama neglected to nominate a new IG candidate until mid-2013, leaving Edwards to head the office.

Within the first few months of Edwards's leadership, the House approached the OIG with a civil rights–related project. In April 2011, Representative Zoe Lofgren (D-CA) requested that the OIG investigate the Secure Communities program, a deportation program administered by a network of federal, state and, local officials and organized by the Immigration and Customs Enforcement arm of DHS. Secure Communities proved to be controversial on a number of grounds. Critics argued that its statistics often distorted who was apprehended and that its guidelines were so vague as to lead to wide variation in its implementation. The program relied on networks of actors and databases to pool information, and it targeted criminal aliens for deportation. Secure Communities was created administratively and not by congressional mandate. For this reason, it lacked regulations and guidelines for its operation and development, and it also proved to be a source of conflict.

The program's principal defect, in the eyes of watchdog groups, was the potential for racial profiling and the possibility of unlawful detention.[44] But its administrative vagueness was precisely what Lofgren hoped the IG would target and reform. After reading the OIG reports, Lofgren commented, "The OIG found Secure Communities effective in finding and removing immigrants with criminal convictions. That wasn't the question. Does the program also ensnare victims and others with no criminal history? Is it susceptible to racial profiling? Does it ultimately undermine community policing efforts—leaving us all less safe?"[45] The OIG evaluated the program's performance while neglecting the question of rights violations, which had been the essence of the opposition to the program. The rigor of an IG's review can have as much to do with the framing of the problem as with the methodology. In this case, the first review's narrow aim—"to see if Secure Communities was effective in identifying criminal aliens and if Immigration and Customs Enforcement appropriately prioritized cases for removal action"—permitted the IG to evade the question of rights violations entirely.[46]

On the inside, in the absence of a permanent IG, the office began to stumble into trouble. An external audit at the end of 2011 found fault with a number of the OIG's policies and determined that the OIG's auditors lacked a thorough understanding of information systems controls. It also stated that OIG auditors needed a subtler analysis of testimony and needed to refrain from interfering in parallel legal proceedings when carrying out their work.[47] In Congress, complaints about the work conditions of the OIG began to surface, eventually leading the Senate Committee on Homeland Security and Government Oversight to begin an investigation into Edwards's management practices. Moreover, the turf wars within the department that Skinner had kept under control began to rear their head again, with the DHS's internal affairs office claiming the authority to conduct criminal investigations of DHS employees. Edwards insisted that while the internal affairs office should conduct preemployment investigations, the OIG had legal authority over corruption cases of department staff.[48]

It was not long before Edwards found himself at the center of just such an investigation.[49] The complaints from OIG staff to the Senate committee ranged from harsh and incompetent mismanagement to nepotism and waste. The fruits of the Senate's investigation, launched in June 2013, revealed an office with "a 'toxic, totally dysfunctional and oppressive' work environment characterized by low morale, paranoia, and fear." In addition to evidence of nepotism and improper use of agency resources, they found that "Mr. Edwards did not understand the importance of independence" and that, "unlike most IGs, [he] does not have experience conducting audits, investigations, or inspections." Amid a host of other allegations, the committee also reported that "nearly all the officials interviewed by the Subcommittee share the belief that Mr. Edwards is reading their e-mail."[50] The subcommittee found evidence to substantiate a large number (though not all) of the allegations and scheduled a hearing. The week before he was called to testify in December 2013, Edwards resigned and the hearing was canceled.

Although the subcommittee had substantiated a number of the serious allegations in their investigation, Edwards asked to be transferred to the DHS's office of science and technology. He was reassigned without repercussions. This move prompted observers of the IG community, including POGO and Congress, as well as members of the community itself to place the question of the IGs' own accountability on the legislative reform agenda.

However, even in the absence of a permanent IG, the subcomponents of the DHS OIG worked on. Rapidly evolving IT demands, especially those related to security, were a growing concern of all IGs, but especially so for the DHS, which commands multiple, unintegrated information systems with highly sensitive data.[51] The challenge, from an oversight perspective, was not only to develop expertise but also to keep up with the scale of oversight required for the security of multiple databases and IT systems. IGs Ervin and Skinner had both placed special emphasis on developing IT systems to make their oversight more comprehensive. During the Katrina recovery, the OIG used data-mining techniques to uncover unorthodox spending patterns to track the vast number of purchase card transactions (a significant source of fraud). The OIG's use of such methods would later intensify in response to the Obama administration's demands for ever-faster agency responses to cyber threats. The administration's permanent anxiety over cybersecurity led it to issue ever-more demanding metrics for reviewing and reporting on each agency's IT assets for security weaknesses. Shortly after the resignation of the disgraced Edwards, the DHS OIG chief IT security officer, Jaime Vargas, pushed for and designed a continuous monitoring program that increased the OIG's coverage from an average of 20 percent of the department's IT assets in summer 2013 to between 80 and 90 percent by summer 2014.[52]

Forging a Managerial Democracy

The managerial vision of the first two IGs regarding the proper role of the IG and the meaning of accountability—primarily as a performance-maximizing, management consultancy role—set the tenor for the office's first decade. Both Ervin and Skinner issued multiple rigorous, critical reviews, but Skinner's greater success in effecting departmental change depended on the diplomatic network he formed with the secretary and with the congressional committees capable of pressuring DHS to reform. Skinner also augmented the quality of his office's work by reorganizing the OIG to hone expertise in emergency management and to reflect the heavy investigative load the office acquired in its first few years.

By some obvious measures, the OIG was effective. The department accepted nearly all (at least 90 percent) of the OIG's recommendations during its first decade.[53] Yet numbers alone fail to convey the IG's positive and negative impacts. These figures suggest success—they are much higher than the self-determined goal of a 75 percent annual acceptance rate—but they say nothing of the rigor of the recommendations or of the recommendations' long-term effect on bureaucratic behavior. (One IG suggested that a high departmental acceptance rate is less of an indication of success than of weak recommendations.[54]) A more indicative figure—the percentage of recommendations implemented—was only statutorily required to be tracked according to 2007 legislation and was not collected by the DHS OIG until 2012; that year, 77 percent of recommendations were implemented one year after issue. As the IG's experience with FEMA reform and the recovery of hurricane relief–related funds demonstrate (which I discuss in Chapter 9), the IG's effectiveness depends crucially on the open ears of the department—and on the support of Congress and the White House in opening the department's ears, if necessary. One indication of the efficacy of the Katrina-inspired FEMA reforms lies in the agency's more competent performance after Hurricane Ike in 2008.

Quantitative measures also fail to impart the significance of building a legal and procedural framework of emergency governance to constrain the executive, a topic of tremendous import to legal scholars. Many of the DHS OIG's investigations contended with situations governed by the contingency of laws under a state of emergency. As with previous disasters, the Katrina emergency prompted lawmakers to suspend the normal safeguards in place to control spending—a suspension justified by the urgency of delivering aid to the victims of the disaster. Nor do the numbers convey the larger institutional developments spearheaded by the IGs. The Gulf Coast Recovery project was an exercise in web building, and it brought a new emphasis on network building, resource pooling, and coordination to the different branches of government and levels of vertical federalism, both within agencies and in the structure of accountability. In both its value focus and its institutional evolution, the OIG forged a managerial democracy.

Where the DHS OIG excelled in performance-based accountability, it fell short regarding questions of constitutional rights. On multiple occasions, both Congress and rights groups such as the ACLU criticized the rigor of the OIG's reports (for instance, the Maher Arar and Secure Communities reviews). As Shirin Sinnar notes, the DHS OIG completed few reviews directly addressing rights abuses as such. The Maher Arar review did evaluate DHS's behavior with respect to rights but was largely redacted on national security grounds. The Traveler Redress Inquiry Program review also dealt with rights abuses indirectly by evaluating the program's effectiveness. Sinnar assessed the Maher Arar review as being less than consequential partly on the grounds that it failed to recognize the moral and legal ambiguity of the overall phenomenon of extraordinary rendition when its authors were in a position to do so. And when confronted with a disaster recovery widely alleged to be racist, the IG team focused on the organizational and financial aspects of the project.

The nature of IG-inspired reforms also points to the role of IGs in effecting slow, gradual change. Skinner often emphasized the broader context of the problems at hand, and he tailored his analyses and recommendations accordingly. For instance, his critique of FEMA's performance, and his later insistence that FEMA remain inside DHS, were based on an acknowledgment of the tremendous changes that FEMA and the other component parts of DHS had undergone since 9/11. Given that any large-scale bureaucratic reorganization is likely to take many years, if not decades, to complete, expectations for agency performance and capacity must be realistically modest in the first years after a change. Skinner cautioned that much of the administrative dysfunction seen in the aftermath of Katrina resulted simply from significant ongoing reforms, the redefinition of FEMA's mission, and the agency's attendant reorganization, and was to be expected until the dust of the DHS's creation finally settled. Bearing this in mind, the expectation that a set of IG recommendations would quickly and completely solve deep and long-standing problems, be they FEMA's efficiency or the success of airport screenings in deterring terrorists, would be quixotic. Rather, by their very nature, IG recommendations lend themselves to slow, incremental change.

The history of the DHS OIG underscores the institutional fragility of the IG position, which can result in unheeded recommendations or inaction on the part of the OIG tout court. Congress can co-opt it by swamping the OIG with unfunded mandates, and its credibility can be undermined when Senate obstructionism prevents a permanent IG from being confirmed. The post-Skinner era demonstrated the difficulty of any OIG without a confirmed IG to provide leadership and stability.

CHAPTER NINE

A MANAGERIAL DEMOCRACY AT HOMELAND SECURITY

A Web of Accountability in the Gulf Coast Recovery Project, 2005–2009

When spiderwebs unite, they can tie up a lion.
—Ethiopian proverb

Introduction

Hurricane Katrina was one of the most destructive natural disasters in American history. The government's response was widely derided as an unparalleled failure, attracting international headlines for its inadequacy. Katrina occasioned the creation of a bureaucratic world unto itself—one that bridged federal, state, and local capacities, brought the public and private sectors into partnership, and brought together multiple federal agencies to mobilize an unprecedented disaster response. That the first major challenge to the DHS was a natural domestic disaster rather than a terrorist attack forced both the department and the OIG to modify the scope of their efforts. Whereas Clark Ervin had clearly defined the DHS's mission as one of counterterrorism, the experience of Katrina, coupled with Richard Skinner's own long-term IG and FEMA experience, forced the OIG to reconceptualize its approach to disaster management more generally. Hurricane Katrina proved to be the first significant test of DHS competence and capacity, and thus a major project for the OIG.

Below, I take the ensemble of reviews investigating various aspects of the Gulf Coast Recovery oversight effort and place them in the context of wider oversight activity by Congress and government watchdog groups. In so doing, I locate the IG's role in a quickly mobilized web of accountability while still identifying the OIG's specific contributions (institutional, legal, administrative) to the maintenance of executive accountability. The immediate and deliberate web comprised the coordinated IGs themselves—the twenty-two OIGs who pooled resources and expertise to divide the task of disaster oversight. The instrumental use of IG reviews by a greater web of external actors—the media accounts that depended on the IGs' reviews as the basis for their critique, and the congressional critics who used IG reviews as the prompts for legislation—led the IGs' work to effect accountability indirectly through monitoring and providing narratives rather than through direct sanctions.

Evidence of departmental ineptitude flooded the press within days of the hurricane's arrival, and former IG Ervin had no reluctance publicly weighing in on the department's performance: "It obviously raises very serious, troubling questions about whether the government would be prepared if this were a terrorist attack. It's a devastating indictment of this department's performance four years after 9/11."[1] The scale and speed of the disaster required that the OIG begin its investigations even before the extent of the DHS's difficulties became apparent. Rather than one single report, Katrina oversight came in dozens of small audits and inspections over the following year that focused on individual field offices and contracts. This too differed from the traditional IG approach of single indictments and exposures of bureaucratic wrongdoing. Skinner's strategy established a mode of operation that routinized the continuous monitoring of departmental activity.

Katrina also prompted the IG community as a whole to develop its collective capacity for oversight. After the Katrina relief bill reserved $15 million of the original $51.8 billion post-Katrina relief package for individual IGs for oversight purposes,[2] senators Max Baucus (D-WI) and Charles Grassley of the Senate Finance Committee addressed a separate letter to the PCIE/ECIE to ask for advice on developing an overall model of collective oversight. At least ten different proposals floated in Congress regarding the appropriate approach to Katrina recovery oversight. These varied from "creating an independent inspector general . . . to creating a stand-alone government agency modeled after New Deal programs" to appointing a chief financial officer to monitor recovery spending.[3] Adopting a weblike approach to the Katrina recovery followed from the IG community's reaction to 9/11, during which it had formed a working group and similarly pooled resources among multiple IGs in overseeing the recovery process. PCIE president Greg Friedman and ECIE president Barry Snyder asserted their commitment to using the federal IG structure but requested additional resources.[4] Friedman and Snyder's response also underscored how the concept of homeland security had been instrumental in overcoming the boundaries between individual OIGs and IG initiatives. Even before Katrina, the PCIE and ECIE had established a homeland security working group to coordinate the federal IG communi-

Table 9.1. Scale of Gulf Coast Recovery Joint OIG Resources, September 2006

Characteristic	Variable	Value	
Object of oversight	Cost of recovery	$87.75 billion	
	Number of contracts	8,408	(over $12 billion)
IG inputs	Number of IG audits or		
	reviews of contracts	835	(monitoring $8.5 billion)
	IG hotline complaints	22,647	
	IG personnel, of which:		
	Auditors/inspectors	337	
	Criminal investigators	88	
	Support personnel	55	
IG outputs	Indictments	439	
	Arrests	407	
	Convictions	225	

ty's approach to all such investigations and audits.[5] Homeland security was not merely a department; it was also a paradigm that played an increasingly important role in the IG community's self-definition.

Representatives Waxman and Pelosi, as well as other Democrats in the House, repeatedly called for a variety of oversight measures, including regular hearings, and attempted to pass legislation establishing a formal oversight framework and to create an independent commission for oversight.[6] (Waxman argued for an independent commission instead of a Republican-led commission, one modeled after the 9/11 investigation panel, citing a lack of rigor in previous Republican oversight.) Much of the congressional critique centered on the lack of preparation and the failure of the response to disburse aid in a timely and effective manner, but later, it also touched on the fraud, waste, and abuse that plagued the use of the recovery funds. Congress pointed to FEMA director Michael Brown's failure to address the IG criticisms of FEMA's preparedness months before Katrina (June 2005).[7] In this context, the IG's investigations and audits were merely one source of criticism and analysis. The focus of the IG investigation was at Skinner's discretion, and he steered the OIG's attention to the fraud surrounding the recovery funds.

Within the DHS OIG itself, on 19 September 2005, Skinner announced the creation of the Office for Hurricane Katrina Oversight. He intended the office to be proactive and preventative in its oversight, with an aim to preempting problems "through a proactive program of internal control reviews and contract audits" by safeguarding disaster assistance funds.[8] The creation of the office was in part a response to a congressional call for Katrina funding to be spent properly; in the Senate, senators Collins and Lieberman introduced a bill to create a special IG for Katrina oversight in the manner of SIGIR, and in the House, the House Government Reform Committee chairman, Representative Tom Davis, and Representative Todd Platts (R-PA) concurrently introduced a bill to create a council of IGs involved in Katrina recovery.[9]

Congress was not the only source of deliberation about the organization of Katrina IG oversight. The IG community itself met to plan its response and developed a coherent strategy to guide the audits and investigations. The Katrina strategy "focus[ed] heavily on prevention, including reviewing controls; monitoring and advising department officials on contracts, grants and purchase transactions before they are approved; and meeting with applicants, contractors and grantees to advise them of the requirements and assess their capability to account for the funds."[10] Katrina thus offered a novel opportunity: the chance for diverse OIGs to pool resources and provide a comprehensive oversight team above and beyond the contribution of each office.

Initially, a total of thirteen departmental and agency OIGs devoted resources to the oversight effort.[11] This broad institutional base enabled the oversight project to expand beyond fraud investigations and evaluate the efficacy of FEMA's disaster response and recovery strategy, and its execution in the cases of hurricanes Katrina and Rita. FEMA's programs were largely directed through grants and contracts, providing the opportunity for financial fraud, waste, and abuse. The structure of these contracts contributed to the permanence of a state of emergency as a mode of governance, and it placed the private sector as a key player in this governing arrangement: "[Government watchdogs and congressional critics] say FEMA's no-bid and limited-bid contracts are of such magnitude that they will give prime contractors an advantage that will last far beyond the initial emergency phase."[12] In the first three months of recovery alone, FEMA entered into more than $1.6 billion of contracts with private entities.[13] The IG adapted its own response to the government's reliance on the private sphere. In effect, it legitimated the use of a public accountability mechanism to investigate the private sector. Although the broader movement during the Bush administration years steered toward privatization (and the hybridization of public–private partnerships), the elevation of the IG's role meant that the mechanisms of accountability in place to check private sector behavior were not purely market mechanisms.

If the hurricanes themselves were one disaster, FEMA, "a Cold War relic," was another.[14] FEMA's transfer to DHS in 2003 had weakened its bonds with state and local governments because a number of grant programs had been scattered within the DHS and were no longer coordinated.[15] The OIG issued its Gulf Coast reports in the context of a long series of critical reviews of the DHS and FEMA's capacities that preceded Katrina by both the IG and in congressional investigations, many of which focused on FEMA's capacities and plans. Although it judged FEMA's performance in garden-variety disasters favorably, it cautioned that FEMA was ill-equipped to face a truly catastrophic event, both because it lacked sufficient resources and because it had failed to develop any of the necessary contingency plans for orchestrating a large-scale disaster recovery. Well before Katrina, Skinner (and the GAO and Congress) had already warned of FEMA's lack of preparedness. An IG report only three months before Katrina charged that FEMA lacked critical capacities, including balancing three poorly integrated information systems and maintaining no systems to track commodities and personnel; these deficiencies left the agency singularly unable to assess continuing need or monitor progress. But the problem was not just of recent vintage; an OIG report on FEMA's performance after Hurricane Andrew in 1992 produced similar criticisms.[16] The IG reports in 1992 and 2004 both failed to have an impact.

Katrina exposed FEMA's many weaknesses. The agency overrode many of its financial safeguards in awarding contracts (especially in granting sole source contracts) to meet the exigencies of the emergency, and according to GAO estimates, it wasted roughly $1 million on improper disaster aid.[17] In continuing to administer housing programs for forty-four months, it violated Stafford Act regulations that stipulate an eighteen-month maximum.[18] More broadly, FEMA was charged with poor leadership and capacity as well as insufficient communication systems.

The Oversight Context

Three main sources of oversight covered Katrina and related disasters (including hurricanes Rita and Wilma): Congress, the GAO, and a network of what would ultimately be twenty-two OIGs. Alongside these broad units, the Justice Department also steered the Hurricane Katrina Fraud Task Force, established on 8 September 2005 by Attorney General Alberto Gonzalez; the task force fielded roughly 6,000 tips regarding fraud and waste in the first year.[19] Each of these sources of accountability provided distinctive forms of oversight, with some overlap, and considerable coordination and communication, among them. The three sources varied slightly in the methodology, audience, and nature of their recommendations, as well as in their short- and long-term effects on policy and procedure.

Congress

Congress held twenty-two hearings on various aspects of the response and recovery between September 2005 and February 2006.[20] The House established the Select Bipartisan Committee to Investigate the Preparation for and Response to Hurricane Katrina, chaired by Representative Tom Davis, whose work culminated in a final report entitled *A Failure of Initiative* in February 2006.[21] This report demanded not only a revised national response plan but a national action plan that would require federal action in the event of a future emergency. In the Senate, the bipartisan committee released a comprehensive report and set of recommendations, *Hurricane Katrina: A Nation Still Unprepared*, in May 2006, and a follow-up hearing a year later monitored changes made in response to oversight.[22] The Senate report recommended consolidating the nation's emergency coordination bodies, and dissolving FEMA completely and replacing it with an independent body, the National Preparedness and Response Authority within DHS. This was a position that the DHS IG strongly opposed. Both the House and Senate reports homed in on the lack of communication and coordination among federal, state, and local actors and among different federal entities. In response to Katrina, and as part of its oversight, Congress also enacted the Post-Katrina Emergency Management Act of 2006, part of the National Emergency Management of the DHS Appropriations Act of 2007.[23] This act, one of many attempts at statutory reform of emergency governance after Katrina, called for FEMA's complete reorganization, a new mission, heightened responsibility in the department, and more autonomy.[24] Skinner's reviews from 2007 onward included observations of FEMA's success in managing this organizational transformation.

However, broadly speaking, Congress's oversight was as inadequate as the administration's. In 1992, after Hurricane Andrew, the GAO determined that the sheer number of congressional oversight committees had hindered the recovery process and issued recommendations for reform. However, with the post-9/11 incorporation of FEMA into DHS, the number of committees with emergency oversight authority increased, with nearly all committees having some say in the process.[25] The dispersed authority made effective and coordinated oversight nearly impossible.

The GAO

For some reports, the GAO used a similar methodology as the IGs, conducting interviews, performing data reliability assessments of FEMA databases, and comparing National Emergency Management Information System data with FEMA data, but it could access fewer agency internal documents than the IGs.[26] For other reviews, the GAO relied on on-site visits, interviews, informal discussions on the ground with governmental officials, the House Select Committee report, and the White House report on lessons learned.[27] Their analyses resulted in a full report presented to the Senate Homeland Security and Governmental Affairs Committee, as well as testimony in Katrina oversight hearings. In contrast to the IGs, who targeted Congress, their department heads, and the public, the GAO's primary audience was the congressional committees. The GAO issued further reports but did not have a system in place to monitor compliance with their previous recommendations.

Joint Federal OIGs

From September 2005 to January 2006, the coordinated federal IG team reported every two weeks to Congress about the state of the recovery. From February onward, they issued semiannual reports on the oversight through March 2008. The OIG oversight plan relied, first and foremost, on the work of the Office of Management and Budget and the DHS OIG, who together identified the major potential problem areas for IG review.[28] The group (originally thirteen but later expanded to twenty-two OIGs) mirrored the bureaucratic web that FEMA itself had assembled to carry out the recovery. After the hurricane, FEMA outsourced its responsibilities by delegating $7 billion through mission assignments to other departments, $6 billion alone of which went to the DOD and the Army Corps of Engineers.[29] The OIG network built on an existing IG structure, the Homeland Security Roundtable subgroup of the PCIE and ECIE, which had been formed in June 2005 with the emergency oversight demands of 9/11 in mind.[30] Less than a month after the disaster, the joint OIGs issued an overview of their oversight plans, with the intention not only of focusing on continuing audits and investigations but also of reviewing the existing controls, monitoring contracts and advising department officials on appropriate procedures before contracts were issued, and assessing and informing relief fund applicants of their responsibilities as recipients of government support.[31] It anticipated a high degree of fraud in the recovery, so it established protocols for preventing fraud rather than taking a reactive "gotcha" approach.

The three sources of oversight also used one another as sources of information and as forums for disseminating their analyses and recommendations. The IG network cooperated closely with the GAO to steer the oversight, using such novel modes of coordination as a joint forensic audit of DHS's purchase card program.[32] Moreover, the IGs appeared regularly as witnesses in more than a dozen Katrina-related congressional hearings. In designing the oversight efforts, the PCIE/ECIE stated a desire to reduce redundancy in oversight as much as possible.[33] In this way, they triangulated to form a network of accountability. The IG web stood at the helm of the overall oversight effort, with the DHS IG at the center. The web extended to other OIGs and departments; it also created links with state and local audit organizations in Louisiana, Mississippi, and Alabama.

DHS OIG Reviews

Within this broad web of oversight—unfolding alongside and in reaction to the recovery, and not always with clear lines of responsibility—the DHS OIG focused on the role carved out for it by the PCIE. Skinner appointed a special inspector general for Gulf Coast hurricane recovery, Matt Jadacki (originally the deputy IG for disaster assistance), to lead the oversight. His team's work consisted of multiple reviews that targeted recovery fund fraud, waste, and abuse, as well as FEMA's performance, especially the adequacy of the National Disaster Medical System and disaster response plan. The Gulf Coast Recovery group not only monitored the funds themselves but also the overall relief effort's coordination as well (i.e., the process by which FEMA delegated tasks and funds to other federal bodies). In the initial oversight plan, the DHS OIG was delegated responsibility for FEMA's performance; joint field office operations; public assistance projects; documentation review for mission assignments; ongoing financial control monitoring; and review of major contracts and expanded micropurchase authority.[34]

The DHS OIG issued its first major review of FEMA's performance seven months after Katrina's landfall.[35] Its analysis was scathing, and it presented FEMA with thirty-eight recommendations with which to contend. The recommendations were wide-ranging and demanding of both FEMA and DHS as a whole. A first set of recommendations suggested that FEMA set measurable, reasonable goals, determine the necessary resources to achieve them, and then allocate these resources to the appropriate subcomponents of the agency. A second set provided specific suggestions on how to implement the National Response Plan, the national emergency plan codified in December 2004. When Katrina struck, the DHS and FEMA had only partially transitioned to this new plan, which included guidelines for coordination between state, local, and federal actors. A third set focused on increasing capacities, from training opportunities to formalizing work plans. A fourth attacked FEMA's management practices, especially with regard to disaster assistance, and demanded that the agency revise its method of testing pilot programs. Having eviscerated its mission, resources, management, practices, and organization, few areas of FEMA's performance went untouched by the IG's critique.

Nearly four years after the hurricanes, Skinner still testified regularly on DHS's—and especially FEMA's—progress in implementing IG recommendations and the statutory demands of the Post-Katrina Act of 2006. His criticism continued to target FEMA's approach, its planning strategies, its mode of coordination and communication (both internally and with other actors), and the potential for innovation in its practices. The focus of his assessments encompassed much more than compliance monitoring; it bore witness to his belief in a collaborative, constructive IG, with a role akin to that of a management consultant. Most striking was his contextualization of FEMA's incompetence, which challenged the demands for better government action evident in much public outcry. Skinner distinguished legitimate criticism of FEMA's performance—of which he issued plenty—from the criticism that stemmed from unclear or unrealistic expectations on the part of state and local officials and the public about what the federal government could, or should, achieve. His overall diagnosis, while highly critical of FEMA's overall performance, cautioned that setting achievable goals and communicating its aims more clearly to state and local officials would limit future confusion. He also took Congress to task for failing to provide FEMA with adequate funds and, more important, legislative authorities with which to manage its operations.[36]

Despite the contextualization, Skinner's censure did not spare FEMA. He faulted the agency for failing, when asked by Congress, even to identify the additional authorities it would need to carry out its responsibilities. Per the requirements of the Post-Katrina Act, FEMA drafted a national disaster housing strategy. Skinner eviscerated the final product, insisting that FEMA specify precise goals, a definition of "success," and criteria by which to evaluate those goals.[37] His analyses hardly used existing regulations as the basis of critique. Instead, his testimony relied on an independent assertion of what FEMA should be doing, identifying the systemic sources of failure and offering specific recommendations to these ends. A previous DHS OIG audit in 2008 had demonstrated that many failures in FEMA's housing programs stemmed more from a lack of communication and coordination between FEMA and local authorities than from a misuse of resources.[38] By identifying the nature of the problem, Skinner called attention to the need for FEMA to focus energies on clarifying the lines of authority and responsibility and communicating expectations to other actors. Similarly, in a September 2008 review, the OIG encouraged FEMA to experiment with "innovative" solutions to its perennially plagued disaster housing program and offered a number of OIG-generated ideas as possibilities.[39] Moreover, it reviewed current FEMA pilot programs and judged their viability, suggesting, for instance, that "although FEMA's Individuals and Households Pilot Program shows promise, it is uncertain whether the program is sufficiently scalable and flexible to be effective following a catastrophic disaster."[40]

These periodic reviews not only offered specific management reform ideas but also dealt with the status of previous recommendations. A June 2009 OIG review of FEMA's reaction to Hurricane Ike compared the agency's activity favorably to its Katrina performance, indicating that in terms of sheer numbers—registering victims, inspecting houses, installing temporary housing, disbursing funds—FEMA's management reforms had improved performance.[41] However, by October 2009, the OIG's semiannual report indicated that the recommendations of twelve FEMA-related financial assistance disaster audits still remained unresolved.[42]

The oversight project's most immediate goal was to recover the funds lost through fraudulent contracts, poorly designed programs, and dishonest individuals and groups exploiting government relief programs. This was, in some ways, the easiest part of the recovery effort to quantify and evaluate, and the numbers issued by the OIG and the GAO unveiled steady fraud throughout. One GAO review of FEMA's disaster assistance funds in June 2006 estimated (with 95 percent confidence) a range of $600 million to $1.4 billion in improper or fraudulent payments between September 2005 and May 2006 alone.[43] Despite the rigor with which this oversight had taken place, its concrete consequences, in terms of recovering lost taxpayer money, remained dubious. Six years later, Skinner continued to report the government's failure to recoup much of the lost funds that could have been recovered. In 2008, partly because of the IG and GAO reviews, a federal court ordered FEMA to revamp its procedures for recovering funds. But because FEMA, three years later, had yet to finalize the process, it had not even attempted to recover $643 million in Katrina aid funds—nearly the entirety of its estimated improper payments to individuals.[44] A 2013 IG review at the Housing and Urban Development Department revealed similar patterns of fraud in housing assistance, citing $700 million in as yet unaccounted for funds, eight years after the disaster.[45] At best, much of the IGs' financial oversight resulted not in restoration of the funds but only in public awareness of governmental waste and in organizational and procedural change.

However, by continuing the oversight of the Katrina recovery, Skinner opened an ongoing dialogue with FEMA, pushing and guiding it through agencywide reforms well past the Katrina era. The IG's role also extended beyond the original compliance model to an advisory role in Congress, thus permitting the IG to weigh in on matters far wider and more consequential (in the long term) than an agency's immediate performance. In February 2009, the OIG issued a report assessing the relative merits of returning FEMA to its pre-DHS autonomy, ultimately arguing strongly in favor of keeping FEMA within the folds of the DHS.[46] On the basis of this report, Skinner was later called to make a statement in a House homeland security committee hearing on the fate of FEMA.[47] The debate over the agency's placement and autonomy had both concrete institutional and definitional consequences.[48] Ervin described the political situation thus:

> In the immediate aftermath of the [Katrina] disaster a bipartisan consensus quickly began to form around the notion that the problem was essentially structural—the Federal Emergency Management Agency (FEMA) was no longer an independent agency reporting directly to the President. If only, certain political leaders in both parties and FEMA insiders argued, the Homeland Security bureaucracy were reorganized yet again to take FEMA out of the department, all would automatically be well.[49]

Yet with his insistence on keeping FEMA within DHS, the IG—the primary institutional voice arguing against an independent FEMA—ultimately helped to win the battle. The topic was shelved until Mitt Romney, the 2012 Republican presidential candidate, questioned FEMA's very existence three years later.

Effects of the Katrina Reviews

The Katrina reviews made their mark institutionally and administratively, and helped to formalize the procedures of emergency governance, including specifying the legal scope of executive action. Institutionally, the IG pioneered an event-based, communitywide IG network of accountability that pooled resources and expertise. The IG also occasioned the establishment of the EMU (later the Emergency Management Office), a permanent unit within the DHS OIG that honed and channeled disaster management expertise. Administratively, the reviews recommended a host of procedural reforms, all of which were ultimately implemented and resolved to the IG's satisfaction by 2010. For instance, although the original draft manual for the DHS's Post-Katrina Purchase Card program had included control procedures for the management of the program, infighting over the specifics of the controls resulted in the control procedures being omitted from the final manual entirely. After the first year, the Katrina IG team insisted on the implementation of new control procedures.[50]

Unlike some Justice OIG reviews, the DHS Gulf Coast reviews did not fundamentally challenge existing law. However, they contributed to the institutionalization of emergency governance through the standardization of governing procedures in emergencies. The reviews had the effect of creating new concepts and evaluative categories as part of a comprehensive national disaster management plan: "With regard to the National Response Plan, the use of incident designations, the role of the principal Federal official, and responsibilities of emergency support coordinators were not always well understood, causing confusion on the ground, which, in turn, impeded FEMA's initial response efforts."[51] In testimony, Skinner pushed these plans for emergencies as well as guiding principles with which to restructure the relationships between different levels of government. "Both NIMS [National Incident Management System] and the National Response Plan are watershed planning concepts that restructure how Federal, State, and local emergency responders conduct disaster response and recovery activities."[52] Moreover, Skinner's recommendations pointed to a web of coordination in the management of the response plans: "DHS needs to develop operating procedures under both NIMS and the National Response Plan, and it needs to offer training on those procedures to all levels of government, including DOD. DOD participation is essential so that it may solidify its role and responsibilities under the National Response Plan to facilitate an enhanced understanding among the Federal, State, local, and non-profit organizations that participate after a disaster."[53] The recommendations also targeted emergency plans on the micro level. For instance, a review of nursing homes struck by the hurricanes showed that many homes lacked substantive emergency plans and information for coordinating with state and local services in the event of an emergency. The group recommended stricter federal certification standards.[54]

Despite its strengths, the overall Katrina oversight project also suffered from the birthing pangs of a novel approach to coordinated oversight. One participant, a longtime member of the IG community, chastened the IG audit community for its "untimely and not very effective [reaction], especially as respects fast reaction to and reporting of problems" and suggested that "the overall result was widely varying actions as respects the timeliness, results and depth of Hurricane Katrina reviews."[55] This perspective on the Katrina project was not unique within the community, but the potential shown by the web approach prompted CIGIE to refine the coordinated model in 2008 when it designed the recovery board task force in response to the economic emergency of 2008.

Creating a Web of Accountability

The Katrina reviews had noticeable influence on DHS (especially FEMA) reforms and internal improvements through dialogue between the OIG and the department, as well as through the continuous monitoring of open OIG recommendations. Yet the mere word of the IG was not enough to spur departmental action; the IG's earlier, similar criticism had fallen on deaf ears. It took the political pressure of a national disaster, coupled with a disapproving public and a watchful Congress, to encourage FEMA and the DHS to heed the recommendations of its IG. Only once the department was shamed by public failure could the IG perform its management consultancy role, thus underscoring both the power of the IG (to design and spearhead reform) and its weakness (its reliance on political actors to implement its reforms and heed its warnings). However, the IG web was less successful in pursuing material recoveries. The joint OIGs' financial monitoring proved successful in uncovering and publicizing fraud and waste, but it was far less successful in recouping funds and holding perpetrators to account.

PART III

THE DEMOCRATIC PERSPECTIVE

CHAPTER TEN

FORGING A NEW DEMOCRATIC FORM
Cometh the Hour, Cometh the Inspector

Where is the wisdom we have lost in knowledge?
Where is the knowledge we have lost in information?
—T. S. Eliot, "Choruses from 'The Rock'" (1934)

Introduction

The State, Justice, and Homeland Security OIGs each engaged in distinct but complementary modes of democratic practice, with greater or lesser consequence, and in so doing, they have together forged a new democratic form of monitory governance. These modes of practicing democracy are each directed toward particular democratic mechanisms—preserving the ethical function of bureaucratic neutrality, protecting constitutional rights, and promoting the state's capacity to govern in an emergency.

A Political Democracy at State

The State OIG reviews investigated issues of privacy, but these investigations were framed and pursued in the context of their political significance rather than for their performance or constitutional import. In his 1992 passport privacy breach review, Sherman Funk framed the incident as a single instance of a politically motivated lack of integrity. This interpretation may have been warranted, but it failed to address the procedural factors that enabled the breach to occur, and it recommended individual sanctions rather than systemic or procedural reforms. Similarly, in the 2008 instances of passport privacy breaches, the reviews did not offer clear suggestions or forceful recommendations to change the legal administrative structure or overall security framework. The OIG tested the privacy protection system, coming to the conclusion that the faults were indeed systemic, but it relied on the data provided by the department—data in which the OIG had already noted inconsistencies. The thrust of the report's recommendation was simply to review the existing framework rather than to offer concrete suggestions or strategies for developing a comprehensive procedural framework.

In each of the State OIG cases, accountability in the sense of sanctions or punishment for individuals yielded minimal discipline. In the 1992 passport case, one person was fired and another resigned; both were subsequently exonerated and offered formal apologies by an independent special investigator. Sixteen years later, two personnel were terminated and a third admonished, and the IG review provoked an ongoing criminal investigation of contractors that ultimately found nearly a dozen of them guilty of privacy breaches. Yet these prosecutions often resulted only in suspensions of a few weeks or short terms of community service. In all of the cases, the individuals charged were low-level contractors or administrators, and no one responsible for oversight or procedural reform was implicated.

The State OIG's visibility in the media spiked in 1992 and 1993 as a result of the Clinton passport files, but Funk's contribution to the visibility of government wrongdoing was an ambiguous one. The review captured attention because of the definitive blame it placed on two political appointees and because it led to the appointment of a parallel process of accountability (the IC). Thus, the fact of the IG review arguably aided the process of accountability more than the specific outcomes it recommended; the punishment it recommended was wrongfully bestowed. Fundamentally, its diagnosis was deemed to be incorrect, which led to the public sanction and dismissal of an appointee who was not directly responsible for the breach. (Both accused parties were later exonerated publicly by the government at the behest of the IC.) The special prosecutor himself showed frustration at what he perceived to be the wastefulness and redundancy of his own investigation. In other words, the IG stayed mired in the political fray rather than managing or tempering it. In theory, the OIG could have contributed to the maintenance of healthy democratic deliberation through its review, but because the 2008 review was so heavily redacted, its results did little to contribute to public knowledge about privacy security or about the specific facts of the case at hand. No new information reached citizens or the media; even a lawsuit against the State Department to release an unredacted version, filed by the Electronic Privacy Information Center, a watchdog group, failed to bring new information to light.

Although a number of State IGs attempted to evaluate the efficacy of the State Department's programs and policies—that is, to pass judgment on US foreign policy—their opinions often fell on deaf ears. In the late 1980s, Sherman Funk indicated dissatisfaction with the entire war on drugs but was informed that, for political reasons, such a position could not be maintained. Similarly, after inspecting the State Department's embassies in Southwest Asia, Harold Geisel questioned the realism of the first Obama administration's strategy in Afghanistan on the basis that its goals were unattainable with the available resources. Despite their judgments, the reviews (and the IG's voice more generally) had no real lasting consequence. Because of the weak successive strategies of individual IGs and a departmental environment hostile to IG work, the IGs' efforts failed to promote the bureaucratic neutrality necessary to legitimate the State Department's activity.

A Constitutional Democracy at Justice

Justice's war on terror reviews allowed the IG to engage in a constitutional mode of democratic practice by issuing recommendations to strengthen administrative procedure and pointing out underspecified law. These reviews also contributed to the standardization of procedures and definitions relating to the confinement of aliens, as well as to the clarification of vague policies regarding the length of detainment and the treatment of detainees. The framing implicitly addressed concerns of civil and human rights, but it did so without directly using the language of rights. This strategic choice had both advantages and disadvantages for future rights claims. On the one hand, it did not set a precedent for making purely rights-based claims, but on the other, it provided defendants with an alternative language and strategy with which to fight rights abuses. Also significant was the IG's willingness to pursue the spirit of the law rather than its letter in making a diagnosis of wrongdoing in cases where no law had been broken, and to set a precedent that the FBI and INS would be held to such a standard in the future. Finally, the reviews called attention to the need for, and for the construction of, constraints on executive emergency governance.

Despite not always affecting direct accountability, Justice's war on terror reviews contributed to a number of parallel processes of accountability, partly as a result of their high visibility (see Table 6.2). Congress held three hearings for the first set of reviews, and its conclusions were cited by at least two parallel processes of litigation. The information the NSL reviews brought to light had been unsuccessfully sought after by many public interest organizations, and once released, it was used as evidence in parallel cases.

The Justice OIG appeared to be the most willing to address rights concerns directly. The FBI forensic lab reviews (both by Bromwich in the 1990s and by Horowitz two decades later) both directly addressed the rights of defendants, provoking wider debate about the death penalty by attesting to the frequency of faulty FBI analyses and their consequences. Both the September 11 detainee and NSL reviews clearly addressed rights concerns, though without using the language of rights as such. In some ways, the lack of recourse to the language of rights strengthened the reviews' potential long-term impact: by building a precedent for arguing for rights without accruing the complex ideological baggage that can accompany rights claims, the IG reviews neutralized (and strengthened) their arguments. But in other ways, the unwillingness to invoke rights claims was symptomatic of the IGs' broader inability to address abstract principles as standards for evaluation or compliance.

In the Justice OIG, transparency proved to be one of the strongest features of the September 11 and NSL reviews, as well as many of the other reviews discussed. The information published and disseminated by the IG in these reviews was gathered from sources to which citizens and media groups did not have access, leading to significant disclosures about the workings of hitherto secret national security programs. Not only was the information on which the reviews were based unreleased, but it also consisted of complex data culled from many documents that would have been difficult for observers without extensive legal knowledge to parse. The reviews publicized information that had been denied by the FBI when unsuccessfully sued by the ACLU for the data.[1] They also reinforced standards for the equal treatment of persons regardless of their legal immigration status.

A Managerial Democracy at Homeland Security

The DHS IG took a managerial approach to building a framework for emergency governance. This involved pushing the department to formalize and elaborate on national emergency plans, including defining the scope and limits of federal action in times of emergency. In this way, the OIG shaped administrative procedure by pointing out underspecified law and regulations, not only for predictive ease and efficiency but also to guide and constrain the executive's future actions. The distinctive challenge of the DHS OIG, especially in the Katrina case, was to become the watchdog of wrongdoing when the law was suspended during emergency. For instance, in order to expedite the recovery process, the government suspended its commitment to competitive contracts in the direct aftermath of the hurricane, and in many cases, it awarded contracts on a sole-source or limited-competition basis. In the first three months of the disaster, 58.8 percent of the contracts awarded were sole-source contracts; a year later, 44.5 percent were still being awarded without competition.[2] In some ways, this pattern bolstered the government's responsiveness and allowed it to provide services to victims of the hurricane, but it also violated the established regulations for emergency action. However, the IGs' insistence that the department rewrite and specify its procedures was ultimately heeded. This enhanced the legal framework underpinning the state's emergency governance.

At DHS, after Hurricane Katrina, the administration was criticized and forced to reconsider its performance and overall emergency management structure on many fronts, through public, congressional, and even international scrutiny. By March 2008, the OIGs had cumulatively achieved 1,186 arrests, 1,362 indictments, and 874 convictions related to disaster assistance fraud.[3] Yet as was evident from the quantity of unrecovered funds eight years later, this accountability did not necessarily result in repercussions for the perpetrators or redress for victims (including the government itself). Its success in the immediate task of recouping funds was limited, in part because the host agencies failed to implement the procedures needed to recoup the vast majority of fraudulent payments.

The DHS OIG shied away from rights judgments, producing a weak review on Maher Arar, then failing to address the civil rights dimension of the Secure Communities program despite an explicit congressional request to do so. While the Katrina disaster did not necessarily lend itself to evaluation in the domain of constitutionality or rights (whether political, civil, or social), aside from some acknowledgment that the Katrina disaster disproportionately affected underprivileged populations (the poor, elderly, and disabled), the reviews made no mention of rights concerns. On the surface, the fraud and mismanagement that the IGs were tasked with monitoring did not obviously spark questions of rights as such, perhaps making the performance-oriented focus adopted by the OIGs the logical strategy. Yet the alleged racial disparities in service provision, as well as the related concerns of social and economic rights, went unaddressed in the IG reviews. Beyond the Gulf Coast reviews, though the OIG issued a number of rigorous and critical reviews of the TSA's passenger screening procedures (and continuing matter of controversy and object of public and congressional criticism), the OIG's reviews in its first decade focused squarely on the performance of the TSA rather than on oft-cited potential rights violations and sexual harassment claims by passengers.[4] (The IG did periodically investigate individual claims of harassment within TSA itself, but not rights violation as a result of the screening procedures themselves.)

However, the DHS IG reviews did contribute to healthy deliberation in the public sphere. The narratives and reports provided regular fodder for media outlets and watchdog groups, which often used and even disseminated the public IG reports. The research and government watchdog group POGO created an online compendium of Katrina-related IG and GAO reviews, tracking the overall oversight effort, with regular analysis of the IGs' findings that were then used as the basis for POGO's own testimony and lobbying on the Hill.

In the DHS, the Gulf Coast Recovery reviews analyzed the material recoveries as well as the structural and procedural vulnerabilities in the agencies performing the recovery. The question of the fair and equal distribution of resources, however, did not appear on the IG agenda. In the wider public, the Katrina recovery became the poster child for entrenched racism in America, famously leading rap artist Kanye West to proclaim, "President Bush doesn't care about Black people."[5] In fact, public debate about the disaster, both domestically and abroad, was concerned as much with the racial dimensions of the disaster as with the bureaucratic incompetence of the recovery effort. The significance of the disaster for the African American community was profound. Sociologist Darnell M. Hunt declared, "You'd have to go back to slavery, or the burning of Black towns, to find a comparable event that has affected Black people this way."[6] While monitoring institutional racism is arguably outside the purview of a single IG review, other (private) investigations of the Gulf Coast Recovery uncovered evidence of a racial disparity in service provision that could have been the focus of IG attention. For instance, one study, conducted by students at the University of Connecticut, discovered that FEMA supplied 63 percent of a predominantly white neighborhood with trailers but only covered 13 percent of a mostly African American neighborhood.[7] In contrast, the IGs couched the disaster in terms of performance and efficiency, eliminating the potential for questions about racial parity.

The DHS reviews and their recommendations were framed specifically to evaluate and promote efficient and accountable administration of government programs. But while the reviews were rigorous and critical, providing Congress with the information and proposals with which to undertake reform, the agencies themselves were at times unresponsive to the very recommendations offered to improve their performance. Where agencies did implement IG recommendations, they improved the quality of activity in the future (as with FEMA's enhanced performance at the time of Hurricane Ike), but because this was dependent on compliance with IG recommendations, the IGs' effect was limited. The IG network's wider effect, however, was to supply the narrative, data, and recommendations that were then used as the basis for legislative overhaul of the national emergency management system, as well as the continuous specification of DHS's mission.

Ultimately, the IGs' most meaningful contributions were realized only in conjunction with the efforts of a broader set of actors. Their authority was dependent on the power of persuasion associated with their narratives, the legitimacy stemming from their reputation and expertise, and their place in a broader web of accountability that included other OIGs and government bodies, Congress, the media, the courts, and groups in civil society.

CHAPTER ELEVEN

CONCLUSION

Quis Custodiet Custodem Ipsum Custodum?

In a fully developed bureaucracy there is nobody left with whom one could argue, to whom one could present grievances, on whom the pressures of power could be exerted. Bureaucracy is the form of government in which everybody is deprived of political freedom, of the power to act; for the rule by Nobody is not no-rule, and where all are equally powerless we have a tyranny without a tyrant.
—Hannah Arendt, "Reflections on Violence" (1969)

Introduction

Juvenal's classic question about the locus of power—who will watch the guardians?—returns us to the paradox of the administrative state's antidemocratic impulses. Since 1978, American federal inspectors general have served as the guardian's guard by watching the state to ensure that it conforms to the standards of integrity appropriate to the exercise of legitimate power. But who watches the IGs themselves, the guardians of the guardians? How do we assess the IGs' own effects on the state and on democracy? In the modern administrative state, these standards of integrity have acquired an economic valence measured by efficiency, at times in tension with the classic democratic values of impartiality, justice, and rights. Our assessment tools need to take into account the value judgment inherent in the quest for efficiency—efficiency to *what end?*, as Dwight Waldo often queried—and the way that these values produce democracies of different kinds. The IGs' ambiguous foundational mandate to root out fraud and abuse and to restore integrity to the executive branch has permitted these two values to play off each other through the continuous process of accountability. The IGs do not resolve the tension between administrative and democratic values, but they do walk the line between the two, and in so doing, they set the stage for the political confrontation between them. Through their continuous critique of bureaucratic behavior, the IGs have helped to make administration a site of contestation over fundamental political values.

The experiences of the three OIGs presented in this book—in the departments of State, Justice, and Homeland Security—demonstrate how this supposedly apolitical administrative setting has given birth to political battles over the meaning of accountability and over its consequences for the shape of American democracy. The three histories also suggest responses to the institutional question of how the IGs have risen to their role as an arbiter of political values, and to the theoretical question of their democratic significance.

State, Justice, and Homeland Security: Three Modes of Democratic Practice

The IGs' arrival was the momentous consequence of a political battle over the control of the executive branch. Since 1978, the fruits of that battle have spawned a bevy of inspectors general across the federal government. In terms of sheer numbers, their ranks have swelled, as have their budgets and congressional mandates. Institutionally, the coordination among them and with other political actors has grown into a web that mirrors the broader trends of horizontal governance seen in recent decades. Substantively, they have pursued distinct conceptions of accountability that have pushed their work into the realms of performance maximization, management consulting, and rights protection, amplifying the political role that they play. I address the puzzle of how this has occurred, both institutionally and discursively, by returning to the propositions laid out in Chapter 2.

The first proposition—that some IGs have transcended their structural bias toward compliance monitoring and intensified the effect they have on democratic integrity—was true of two OIGs in different ways. Successive Justice IGs regularly issued reviews that assessed government behavior using not only existing rules but also self-generated standards of integrity and appropriate government action. These reviews paid attention to the spirit of the law in addition to its letter, suggesting procedural reforms that addressed the systemic sources of breaches of integrity. When their analyses did not provoke direct or immediate accountability, the Justice reviews often prompted external actors to take up the pursuit of accountability. The longest-serving DHS IG, Richard Skinner, also chose strategies beyond compliance monitoring. His reviews not only criticized his department for its performance failures but also demanded that it generate clear and rigorous goals, accompanied by standards with which to evaluate its progress. In the absence of satisfactory existing regulations, he demanded the creation of new rules with which to comply and new institutional structures with which to buttress the reforms.

In contrast, many State Department OIG reviews effected little direct accountability, made few marks on the host department, attracted little attention, and were rarely taken up by external actors in parallel political processes. State OIG lacked a sufficient cadre of qualified staff, with many of its members deficient in auditing and investigative skills, and its budget diminished as the department's outlays grew. It also balanced expensive congressional mandates to continue its biannual consular inspections with a poorly managed bureau in Washington. It thus found its resources spread too thin to redesign the department's faulty institutional and procedural architecture. The shift away from simple compliance monitoring seen in the Justice and Homeland Security OIGs was not uniform, and moreover was not a rule across time even within single OIGs: the absence of a permanent IG in DHS after 2011 brought the office into disarray and led it to issue a number of weak reviews.

The success of the DOJ and DHS IGs in going beyond compliance monitoring was based in concrete institutional strategies and organizational innovation. In both offices, IGs created specific units designed to address particular problems—bodies that channeled expertise and overcame long-standing cultural divides between audit and investigative staff. Whereas the DHS OIG's institutional innovations were thematic and focused on emergency management, the DOJ IG's innovations were capacity and skill based (insofar as they privileged particular skills and expertise rather than a topical focus). In Justice, successive IGs built the SIRU (later the O&R) with a specific staff profile that combined mostly legal investigative expertise with audit and inspection expertise. Moreover, the narrative skills cultivated by the Justice IGs provided a counter to the periodic external criticism that IG reviews, especially semiannual reports, are excessively long and incomprehensible. The office invented the special review—a new tool to improve visibility and coordinate skills—as a vehicle for pursuing matters above and beyond compliance. The unit became the backbone of the OIG's high-profile and often consequential reviews. Similarly, the first two DHS IGs altered the OIG's initial staff ratio to develop its investigative skill base and created the EMU to house the interdisciplinary teams devoted to the immediate oversight of emergency. The DHS OIG also forged links with other OIGs to share resources and import expertise that it lacked on its own. State OIG, in contrast to the other two OIGs, failed to develop a coherent and robust skill base, instead relying on the experiential expertise of its temporary, rotating inspectors. It had no intermediary body with which to combine the interdisciplinary skills often required for complex investigations, and as a result, it struggled with internal cultural divisions among audit, investigation, and inspection sections that stymied office productivity and capacity.

Though related to its heightened institutional reach, the diversification of the IGs' value orientation, and thus of their modes of democratic practice, proceeded separately from its institutional evolution. Over its first three decades, the IG community's early focus on immediate departmental fraud, waste, and abuse migrated into the domains of performance improvement, politically and ideologically related wrongdoing, and rights monitoring. This expansion was effected both through congressional fiat (dictating that IGs act as policy-generating consultants and that they monitor compliance with civil rights and liberties) and by individual IGs' exploitation of their interpretative latitude. The discursive construction of accountability—its value orientation—differed by IG and reflected personal experience and bias, as well as the focus of the department. The three cases thus partially supported the second proposition—that personal background and professional experience affect the mode of democratic practice. The lawyers at Justice concentrated heavily on constitutional and statist concerns, and they channeled the office's resources into a unit that primarily investigated breaches of constitutional values. In contrast, the primary IG at DHS, a longtime federal manager with business and public administration training, framed his enquiries in terms of maximizing performance. Of the IGs surveyed in the cases, Richard Skinner (at DHS) was the IG perhaps most influenced by the performance themes of the Reinventing Government movement in the preceding decade. He pushed the IG model decidedly into the direction of management consulting. Given his training in both public and business management, as well as his placement in various OIGs when the Reinventing Government movement began in the early 1990s, his inclinations were not surprising.

However, not all IGs conformed to this tendency for lawyers to privilege constitutional concerns and for managers and accountants to favor efficiency. While at the State OIG (before 9/11), lawyer Clark Kent Ervin led reviews that investigated such political and ideological matters as the Bush administration's alleged involvement in the 2002 Chávez ouster in Venezuela. He deemed this review to be emblematic of the type of problem that IGs ought to be reviewing—that is, they should produce reviews ensuring the political and ideological neutrality of the state bureaucracy. Yet once at DHS, he moved his focus to the department's performance problems. Here, his personal reaction to the events of 9/11, as well as his ideological commitment to the war on terror, pushed him to change from a political orientation to an efficiency- or performance-based one. This shift, however, demonstrated not so much a commitment to the value of efficiency as an administrative virtue in itself as to a commitment to a particular political program. (This view is born out in his memoir, in which he laments the DHS's ineptitude, because of the practical and ideological import of its primary mission, to prevent a terrorist attack.)

State OIG's general orientation toward a political mode of democratic practice was not based in the professional background of any single IG. Many of its IGs, such as Funk, Geisel, and Williams-Bridgers, had management backgrounds of various sorts—some academic, some experiential. Yet their respective approaches to OIG work varied considerably. In part because of the diplomatic nature of State Department work, State IGs paid attention to politically sensitive matters, though without always addressing the underlying ideological, constitutional, or performance-based problems that underpinned them. Also relevant to the modes of democratic practice seen in many reviews was the fact that State OIG did not have the kind of intermediary body within the office to channel resources; the SIRU (O&R) in Justice and the EMU in DHS served the function not only of concentrating resources but also of focusing these resources on particular kinds of issues. This predisposed each of the OIGs to review problems related to particular democratic values or institutions.

The three cases also partially supported my third proposition: that material resources and independence condition the ability of an IG to adopt the more intense institutional strategy of building legal and institutional infrastructure. Material resources were most effective when channeled into long-standing organizational structures that focused on multidisciplinary coordination. The cases also revealed that an indirect factor in the success of IG reviews was the length of IG tenure. IGs who instituted the internal OIG reforms that underpinned their consequential reviews stood at the helm of their respective offices for a minimum of five years. In contrast, no single State Department IG even approached this length of tenure after Sherman Funk retired in 1994 at the end of a six-year term. Here, the need for coherent visions of accountability to guide an OIG and a corresponding set of institutional strategies became clear. It was this extended tenure that afforded IGs the stability and time to build the crucial internal structures and external networks that magnified their existing capacities and resources.

IG independence varied on two dimensions: the subjective and the objective. To produce consequential reviews, IGs needed both objective independence (having sufficient resources and a cooperative, responsive department head) and subjective independence (being free of personal political ties). The State Department OIG's inadequate performance and compromised reviews in the mid-2000s were duly criticized by the GAO, Congress, and POGO. However, during that time, the OIG had suffered deep budget and personnel cuts that left it to struggle to fulfill its congressional mandates and perform its routine consular inspections, let alone investigate further instances of departmental dysfunction. Subjective independence also mattered. Clark Kent Ervin, who supervised many strong and critical reviews at both State and Homeland Security, was criticized for conducting a methodologically weak review that exonerated the Bush administration for its alleged role in the 2002 attempted Venezuelan coup d'état. Critics argued that his political ties to the Bush family compromised his subjective independence for this particular review and undermined its potential effects.

Though difficult to measure aside from subjective accounts, the constructive or mutually respectful relationship between each IG and its department head played an important role in enabling the IGs to conduct rigorous reviews. According to a number of IGs, the most consequential reviews were those that were highly critical of the department, and even challenged by department heads, but that were nonetheless permitted to be released to Congress without significant amendment. Both of the war on terror reviews conducted by Glenn Fine were challenged publicly by the respective attorneys general at the time, but in both cases, the attorney general ultimately refrained from interfering with the IG's work and willingly engaged in long-term conversation with the IG over the implementation of his recommendations. In contrast, at the State Department, Secretary of State Madeleine Albright often dismissed IG Williams-Bridgers's acerbic reviews and ignored her recommendations for departmental reforms or individual accountability.

The typology of modes of democratic practice laid out in Chapter 2 also underscores the far-reaching and diverse effects that accountability work can have on democratic integrity. Affecting far more than material recoveries and even public trust, the work of the IGs in the three very different modes of democratic practice demonstrated that modern administration has taken on functions that transcend the administrative–democratic dichotomy. Each OIG had the potential to promote the democratic values of political neutrality, constitutionality, and responsiveness, all the while being attentive to the bureaucratic demands of efficiency. Ultimately the two values were not ipso facto incompatible, although their resolution was not always successful; this development has posed new challenges to the practice of democracy.

The success of each OIG in marking democracy above and beyond its host department depended not only on its mode of democratic practice and institutional strategy but also on its ability to make reviews relevant to external actors and to publicize its conclusions. It was in the framing of the problems and their diagnoses that IGs attracted the attention of external observers. It was here that the import of the web of accountability came to light. The IGs struggled to bring direct accountability consistently on their own, and their inability to require host departments to implement recommendations left them without the formal authority to take the lead in spearheading reform or accountability. However, their work was crucial in sparking parallel processes of accountability—and indeed in providing those processes with a legitimizing narrative and interpretation of the evidence available only from within the executive. The value of the IG thus lay in its enabling function for a broader web of accountability, rather than its position as the sole source of absolute and direct accountability.

Navigating Challenges to Democracy

These institutional developments form part of the story of the IGs. The three cases intimate when and how IGs can issue specific reviews with immediate consequences for accountability and bureaucratic efficiency. The IGs' frequent failures suggest that they may also at times simply perpetuate the bureaupathology they were designed to eliminate. But the institutional dimension of the cases alone does not fully convey the import of the IG phenomenon for the workings of American democracy.

At first blush, it might seem that IGs undermine representative democracy by taking on an accountability-holding function held in previous generations by representatives, the courts, and the citizenry. With their focus on management reform and procedural solutions, the IGs pose the threat of fostering a weak managerial conception of democracy (especially after their post–Reinventing Government turn), which could weaken civic responsibility, political engagement, and political equality.[1] "Agonist" democratic theorists, such as Sheldon Wolin and Bonnie Honig, might object to the IGs as an institution on the grounds that the "corrective" to executive wrongdoing that they provide relies too heavily "on rules and procedures to the virtual exclusion of the art of politics" (a charge Wolin leveled at constitutionalism more generally).[2] Bonnie Honig similarly faults liberal and democratic theorists for resorting to "proceduralism"—a dependence on procedural checks to safeguard democracy—in place of political engagement.[3] If IGs attempt to correct administrative wrongdoing through law and procedure, then they dislocate the site of struggle away from citizen politics. These concerns also echo the specific criticisms of legal theorists Eric Posner and Adrian Vermeule, who describe the IGs as having "created a large apparatus of compliance monitoring and bureaucratic reporting, and . . . [having] used a great deal of paper," but having effected little accountability.[4] (Unfortunately, they fail to provide any evidence for their claims.) Their opposition to liberal legalism (a form of proceduralism) stems from the same objection voiced by Wolin and Honig: that procedural or legal infrastructure is not sufficient to curtail the abuse of power in any form, and may even facilitate its perpetuation. If the IGs' work merely falls under the banner of proceduralism, then their direct work arguably does little to enhance democratic practices in the administrative state.

Paradoxically, given their roots in statute and their commitment to procedural reform, IGs may contribute less to the legal constraints on the executive than to the political constraints. They access, interpret, and disseminate information to the media, to Congress, and to the public, and in their strongest reviews, they create legitimate counternarratives that can be used by other political actors. In the modern world, political checks on state power depend crucially on the media and groups within civil society. In a reflection on the rapidly changing environment of the news media, historian and sociologist Michael Schudson details the increasing reliance of the media on "political observatories," of which the IGs are a chief example: journalists now need assistance penetrating thick government apparatuses for data, much of which is protected by law.[5] Such observatories, which also include think tanks, research organizations, and government bodies such as the GAO, began to multiply and flourish in the 1970s, and they have since emerged as a prominent feature in the contemporary media landscape, crucial for informed journalism. The traditional oversight function of civil society is, moreover, challenged by the intensifying claims of national security and emergency politics seen in the past century, as well as the technological developments, such as the use of databases, that complicate the process of information interpretation. In such cases, IGs may provide the primary, or even only, informational conduit between the executive and the media, or the citizenry as a whole. Through their work, IGs render complex legal and technical information intelligible and present it to be judged by the public. If, as political theorist Russell Hardin argues, "the central epistemological concern of representative democracy is what the typical citizen knows about the actions of public officials," then the IGs' narrative function responds to the heart of the legitimation crisis of the administrative and emergency states.[6]

A New Democratic Legitimacy

The new bodies to which Schudson refers not only furnish the media with the information it needs to enter into the process of public accountability but also provide the foundations of a new democratic legitimacy. Political philosopher Pierre Rosanvallon locates contemporary democratic legitimacy in precisely such independent authorities and extragovernmental watchdog organizations, which he notes have similarly expanded rapidly in many Western democracies. These bodies are not elected, nor are they "delegates in any legal or practical sense," nor are they "incarnations of the community in a sociological or cultural sense," and thus they are in no traditional understanding democratic.[7] Yet by Rosanvallon's account, such forms of governance provide alternative forms of representation through their impartiality, which serves to "represent," albeit indirectly, the perspectives of all groups by incorporating the views of all. The bodies thus protect the values of impartiality and reflexivity and deserve a place in contemporary theories of democracy and democratic legitimacy. John Keane's concept of monitory democracy similarly captures the stakes of this widespread institutional development in democracies.[8] In such a democracy, "power-scrutinizing mechanisms" such as oversight bodies, public integrity committees, judicial activism, think tanks, and transnational regulatory bodies all serve to shift the locus of power from the core of the state to parallel processes that bridge across state and society as well as across national borders, all centered on the continuous process of accountability. In Waldron's vision, the ritual self-justification of public accountability has become the duty of the state rather than that of the citizenry, and the state's legitimacy depends crucially on it.

What is clear from these accounts of the rise of extraparliamentary oversight mechanisms is that self-justification through continuous, overlapping processes of accountability is a prominent feature of the contemporary democratic state and is integral to its legitimacy. As the three cases demonstrate, the IGs' direct impact on government accountability, whether in the form of individual sanctions or improved performance, does not always include the immediate consequences hoped for by their champions. But in their role as narrators or account givers, the IGs increasingly enter into the process of shoring up state legitimacy by providing an authoritative source of information and forcing the state to provide regular accounts of its actions. The IG is both a primary example of and contributor to the construction of the new legitimacy, thus marking a durable shift in the locus of governing authority.

The Future of the IG and the Future of IG Research

What of the future of the IGs? Congressional debates over the IGs, from the 1970s through the proposed Inspector General Empowerment Act of 2014, have focused on the extent of IGs' power. Will they serve the government better with more or less authority? While some observers suggest making IG recommendations legally binding, this would create the danger of diminishing the role of public participation and agitation in the political sphere.[9] On the one hand, as Representative Darrell Issa and others in Congress have argued, this would bring many important or much-needed structural changes to the bureaucracy and would most likely save the government a great deal of money; Issa's support of building the IG bureaucracy is notable given his staunchly conservative, antigovernment agenda. On the other hand, giving the IGs the power of force would diminish their narrative role and its implicit power of persuasion. Without binding recommendations, it is up to representatives, the public, and civil society to battle over the proper response to governmental abuse of power or over the proper way to structure government policies. By refraining from giving IGs the authority to require agency action, Congress keeps the activity of democracy out of the hands of yet another set of unelected bureaucrats, instead relocating this responsibility to the realm of politics.

It is also up to the IGs to determine the reach of their authority. A philosophy of narrative restraint in service of the political process was implicitly adopted by successive Justice IGs, who limited their own role to providing narratives and leaving the use of those narratives to the political branches of government and to the public. The case of the Justice OIG demonstrates that one of the supposed weaknesses of the IGs—their nonjudicial capacity and unwillingness to make judgments as a prosecutor would—is also their one of their strengths. In maintaining political neutrality, their narratives gain legitimacy, but more important, they preserve political judgment for political actors rather than unelected bureaucrats. Such a strategy, when adopted, leads IGs to provide a resource for political actors rather than to usurp the authority of legislative or judicial bodies.

Other questions loom about the IGs' prospects for defending democratic values. In their organization and purpose, the IGs were partly molded by the NPM-inspired reforms of the 1990s, but they have also begun to counter some of the antidemocratic effects of these reforms. The drive toward privatization, in particular contracting out public services to private companies, has nullified much of Congress's oversight capacity by removing Congress's ability to monitor performance and shifting government activity to spheres outside the remit of FOIA laws.[10] Yet IGs have increasingly demanded the inclusion of information extraction clauses in contracts with private service providers.[11] If the IGs are to retain their narrative-giving function, the authorities granted to them by Congress to gather data must be regularly adapted to the shifting sands of privatization, executive privilege, and national security exemptions.

There is also a downside to the IGs' growing capacity and coordination. As members of the law enforcement community with wide access to information and the authority with which to disseminate it, IGs constitute a risk of heightening the state's surveillance apparatus and becoming part of it. Recognizing the advantages of the IGs' access to information, other officials, such as the FBI, have started to use IGs instrumentally as an entry point for task forces and for the sharing of data between agencies and state and local law enforcement units. This trend could lead to the IGs' envelopment by a greater "police state" turned toward citizens rather than toward the state. The potential for abuse has not been lost on Congress; even staunch defenders of the IGs, such as Representative Elijah Cummings (D-MD), have cautioned that expanding the IGs' law enforcement powers "would give to the IGs powers that even the FBI does not have, and the use of that authority could, in some circumstances, impede criminal investigations and raise significant civil liberties concerns."[12] The IGs surely represent a case of American state building, but to what kind of state do they contribute: a democratic state or a police state? The perennial political question of balance in apportioning governing authority continues to vex the IGs' institutional development.

The chameleon-like character of the IGs—at times overseers, law enforcement officials, innovators, policy makers, judges, and management consultants—has been both championed and lamented, but the overwhelming trend has been for Congress to push the IGs further in these various directions. To better understand the differential mutations in their role across the state, the variations in their effects, and the possibilities for their future development, future research needs to link the material specifics—budgets, staff, and organizational shape—to the substantive outcomes of IG work. These outcomes include not only concrete procedural reforms, material recoveries, and criminal prosecutions but also the political dynamics set in motion by IGs' work. As many observers of the IGs, and as the IGs themselves, claim, the numerical data does not suffice to intimate the extent of their effects on the political process. More qualitative and narrative studies could illuminate the political pressures that condition IG strategies, OIG capacity, and the reception and use of IG reviews. Given that IG recommendations are not legally binding and rely on external actors to achieve an effect, further research that emphasizes the IGs as political, rather than as bureaucratic, actors promises to shed much light on the broad effects of IG work.

IGs embody a host of paradoxes: they are bureaucrats who act with discretion but who exist to limit the discretionary excesses of administration. Their existence adds a layer of bureaucracy in an effort to streamline an already unwieldy bureaucratic machine. They exist to check and limit government power, yet they introduce a panopticon into the state's own governing arsenal. Just as they straddle the barbed-wire fence of the executive and legislative branches, they also straddle administrative and democratic values. But like many paradoxes, these have proven to be generative. As one crucial node in a broader web of accountability, IGs have exploited these ambiguities to adapt to the exigencies of democracy in an age of administration and perpetual emergency. In so doing, they have played a role in the emergence of a new democratic legitimacy.

INTERVIEWS

I performed twenty-six elite interviews, primarily with current and former IGs, staff of OIGs, congressmen, and journalists with IG expertise. The interviews were semistructured, selected through snowball sampling using multiple points of entry. Because I used the interviews to glean specific details to build a historical narrative, only a few of the questions were common to all interviewees; the majority of questions were specific to the experience of the individual being interviewed. Some general questions were also used to elicit broad commentary about IGs. In addition to the individual interviews, I also conducted two group interviews with coordinating members of CIGIE. This type of interview has the advantage of gauging the attitudes and perspective of an organization as a whole.

Interviews have significant limitations. Actors can omit details that present them in an unfavorable light; they might misremember events (or forget details entirely); they may amend their perspective to avoid offence or retaliation. They might also be influenced by their perception of the interviewer's expectations or biases and tailor their responses accordingly ("demand characteristics").[1] In some cases, interviewees' willingness to be quoted diminishes the reliability of their accounts because it creates incentives for them to pander to certain perceived audiences and to exaggerate their own role in events. However, despite charges that they lack reliability (because actors overstate their importance or misrepresent past events), interviews remain a crucial way to gather contextual data unavailable elsewhere[2] and to "ferret out secret understandings."[3] I attempt to overcome the limitations by being explicit, when using data from interviews, about the fact that the information represents only the perspective of one actor. The biases inherent in interviews can also serve as a type of evidence when the bias itself is evidence of one side of a conflict (rather than proof of a neutral, accurate account of an event). In many of the narrative case study chapters, the explicit juxtaposition of the perspectives revealed in interviews provides evidence of the conflicts that marked the events in question. I also made use of a set of lengthy narrative interviews from the Foreign Affairs Oral History Collection of the Association for Diplomatic Studies and Training. These transcribed interviews, conducted between 1992 and 2012 and available in the public domain, proved invaluable because some key actors are no longer living or available for new interviews.

Interviews

Michael Bromwich, Former Inspector General, Department of Justice, 2 January 2013.

Tom Caulfield, Executive Director, CIGIE Training Institute, 4 January 2013 and 24 July 2014.

Charles S. Clark, Journalist, 3 July 2014.

Tom Davis, Representative, US House of Representatives (Republican, Virginia 11th District), 18 January 2013.

Clark Kent Ervin, Former Inspector General, Departments of State and Homeland Security, 2 July 2014.

Glenn Fine, Former Inspector General, Department of Justice, 3 January 2013.

Phyllis Fong, Inspector General, US Department of Agriculture and CIGIE Chair, 24 July 2014.

David Gross, Chief Strategic Planning and External Affairs, Office of the Inspector General, Department of Defense, 28 July 2014.

Crystal Hamling, Instructional Program Manager, CIGIE, 4 January 2013.

Richard Hankinson, Former Inspector General, Department of Justice, 16 January 2013.

Henry B. Hogue, Analyst in American National Government, Congressional Research Service, 17 July 2012.

Michael Horowitz, Inspector General, Department of Justice, 26 January 2013.

Charles Johnson, CIGIE Training Institute, 4 January 2013.

Mark Jones, Executive Director, CIGIE, 24 July 2014.

Lynne McFarland, Inspector General, Federal Elections Commission, and CIGIE Vice Chair, 24 July 2014.

Carol Ochoa, Assistant Inspector General, Department of Justice, 26 January 2013.

Shawn Reese, Congressional Research Service, 5 July 2012.

Harold Relyea, Analyst in American Government, Congressional Research Service, 17 July 2012.

Gary Schmitt, Resident Scholar, American Enterprise Institute, 26 July 2012.

Calvin Scovel III, Inspector General, Department of Transportation, 17 January 2013.

Richard Skinner, Former Department of Homeland Security Inspector General, 11 January 2013.

Sheryl Steckler, Inspector General, Palm Beach County, Florida, 4 January 2013.

Bennie Thompson, Representative, US House of Representatives (Democrat, Mississippi 2nd District), 28 June 2012.

Doug Welty, Public Affairs Officer, Office of Inspector General, Department of State, 15 July 2014.

David C. Williams, Inspector General, US Post Office, 14 January 2013.

Michael Yoder, Former Inspector (Foreign Service Officer), Office of Inspector General, Department of State, 23 June 2014.

NOTES

CHAPTER I. INTRODUCTION: *QUIS CUSTODIET IPSOS CUSTODIES*?

1. Dwight Waldo, "Development of Theory of Democratic Administration," *American Political Science Review* 46, no. 1 (1952): 81–103; Herbert A. Simon, Peter F. Drucker, and Dwight Waldo, "Development of Theory of Democratic Administration," *American Political Science Review* 46, no. 2 (1952): 494–503.

2. Dwight Waldo, *The Administrative State: A Study of the Political Theory of American Public Administration* (New York: Holmes & Meier, 1984).

3. Woodrow Wilson, "The Study of Administration," *Political Science Quarterly* 2, no. 2 (1887): 197–222; Max Weber, "Politics as a Vocation," in *From Max Weber: Essays in Sociology* (1919; repr., Abingdon: Routledge, 1991), 77–128.

4. Mark Thatcher and Alec Stone Sweet, "Theory and Practice of Delegation to Non-Majoritarian Institutions," *West European Politics* 25, no. 1 (2002): 1–22.

5. B. Guy Peters and Jon Pierre, *The Handbook of Public Administration* (London: Sage, 2003).

6. John Stuart Mill, *Considerations on Representative Government* (1861; repr., Auckland: Floating Press, 2009), 143.

7. David Rosenbloom, "The Politics–Administration Dichotomy in Historical Context," in "Junior–Senior Exchange: The Legacy of Dwight Waldo and *The Administrative State*," *Public Administration Review*, January–February 2008, 57–60.

8. Desmond King and Robert Lieberman, "Ironies of the American State," *World Politics* 61 (2009), 547–588.

9. Ibid.

10. Mark E. Warren, "Accountability and Democracy," in *The Oxford Handbook of Public Accountability*, ed. Mark Bovens, Robert E. Goodin, and Thomas Schillemans (Oxford: Oxford University Press, 2014), 43.

11. Jeremy Waldron, "Separation of Powers or Division of Power?," NYU School of Law, Public Law Research Paper 12-20 (2012), 2–3.

12. James Madison, Alexander Hamilton, and John Jay, *The Federalist Papers*, ed. Isaac Kramnick (London: Penguin, 1987), 304.

13. Ibid., 319.

14. Madison and Hamilton aimed to construct a republic rather than a direct democracy, distrusting the latter for its potential to devolve into tyranny. I do not mean to suggest here that their structure was designed to promote a pure democracy but rather that it established a system of political accountability that should, in theory, check what I call the antidemocratic tendencies of administration (i.e., among other things, taking policy-making authority out of the hands of elected officials).

15. David Truman, *The Governmental Process: Political Interests and Public Opinion* (New York: Alfred A. Knopf, 1951).

16. Robert Dahl, *A Preface to Democratic Theory* (Chicago: University of Chicago Press, 1956), 146; Douglas Yates, *Bureaucratic Democracy: The Search for Democracy and Efficiency in American Government* (Cambridge, MA: Harvard University Press, 1982), 5–6.

17. Though Dahl's early work implicitly affirmed the status quo, his later work questions the health of American democracy, though without addressing administration directly. He imputes the failure of the United States to achieve true procedural democracy to corporate capitalism, the welfare state, and the United States' position as an international power. Robert A. Dahl, "On Removing Certain Impediments to Democracy in the United States" and "Procedural Democracy," in *Democracy, Liberty and Equality* (Oxford: Oxford University Press, 1977).

18. William Scheuerman, "Emergency Powers and the Rule of Law after 9/11," *Journal of Political Philosophy* 14, no. 1 (2006): 61–84.

19. Posner and Vermeule provide an overview of the "liberal legalist" argument for executive constraints. They point to David Dyzenhaus, Bruce Ackerman, and Richard Epstein as exemplars of this camp. Eric Posner and Adrian Vermeule, *The Executive Unbound: After the Madisonian Republic* (Oxford: Oxford University Press, 2010).

20. *Inspector General Act of 1978*, Public Law 95-452, 12 October 1978, 92 Stat. 1101.

21. "Reflexive" refers to the fact that the state's capacity to effect change is turned back on its own apparatus rather than projected onto the citizenry.

22. Cf. William Galston, "Realism in Political Theory," *European Journal of Political Theory* 9, no. 4 (2010): 385–411. Galston gives an overview of this emerging field, its analytic concerns, and its primary contributors, among whom he counts Bernard Williams, John Dunn, Raymond Geuss, Bonnie Honig, Chantal Mouffe, Mark Philp, and Jeremy Waldron.

23. Melvin J. Dubnick, "The Ontological Challenge," in Bovens, Goodin, and Schillemans, *Oxford Handbook*, 649–654.

24. Ibid., 650.

25. John Dunn, "Situating Democratic Accountability," in *Democracy, Accountability, and Representation*, ed. Adam Przeworski, Susan C. Stokes, and Bernard Manin (Cambridge: Cambridge University Press, 1999), 330–331.

26. Jeremy Waldron, "Accountability: Fundamental to Democracy," Public Law and Legal Theory Research Paper Series, Working Paper 14-13 (April 2014), 19.

27. See J. S. Maloy, *The Colonial American Origins of Modern Democratic Thought* (Cambridge: Cambridge University Press, 2010), for a discussion of this tendency.

28. Melvin J. Dubnick, "Accountability as a Cultural Keyword," in Bovens, Goodin, and Schillemans, *Oxford Handbook*, 23–28, provides statistical evidence of a dramatic increase in the use of the word "accountability" in English-language texts beginning in the 1970s. It is noteworthy that many key modern political philosophers who deal with this concept at least implicitly—John Locke, John Stuart Mill, James Madison, and Alexander Hamilton—use the term "accountability" (and its variants) sparingly, if at all.

29. See Richard Mulgan, "Accountability: An Ever Expanding Concept?," *Public Administration* 78, no. 3 (2000): 555–573.

30. Robert Behn, *Rethinking Democratic Accountability* (Washington, DC: Brookings, 2001); Mark Philp, "Delimiting Political Accountability," *Political Studies* 57 (2009): 28–53. See Behn, chap. 1, for an extended discussion of the myriad and competing definitions of accountability in contemporary scholarship.

31. Although it discusses other forms of accountability, Przeworski, Stokes, and Manin, *Democracy, Accountability, and Representation*, devotes over half of its essays to electoral accountability. Indeed, the basic definition outlined in the introduction emphasises the ability to retain public officials in office through elections.

32. Edward Rubin, "The Myth of Accountability and the Anti-administrative Impulse," *Michigan Law Review* 103 (2005): 2075.

33. John Keane, "Monitory Democracy?," paper prepared for the ESRC seminar series Emergent Publics, The Open University, Milton Keynes, 13–14 March 2008, 3.

34. Craig Borowiak, *Accountability and Democracy: The Pitfalls and Promise of Popular Control* (Oxford: Oxford University Press, 2011).

35. Philp, "Delimiting Political Accountability."

36. Warren, "Accountability and Democracy," 42.

37. Waldron, "Accountability."

38. In addition to Philp, Waldron, and Rubin, Mansbridge offers a similar call to base the concept of accountability in account giving. Jane Mansbridge, "A Contingency Theory of Accountability," in Bovens, Goodin, and Schillemans, *Oxford Handbook*, 55–68.

39. Dunn, "Situating Democratic Accountability," 334.

40. Mansbridge, "Contingency Theory."

41. Christopher Pollitt, "Performance Blight and the Tyranny of Light: Accountability in Advanced Performance Measurement Regimes," in *Accountable Governance: Problems and Promises*, ed. Melvin J. Dubnick and H. G. Frederickson (New York: M. E. Sharpe, 2011).

42. Christopher Hood and B. Guy Peters, "The Middle Ageing of New Public Management: Into the Age of Paradox?," *Journal of Public Administration Research and Theory* 14, no. 3 (2004): 267–282.

43. Christopher Hood, *The Blame Game* (Princeton, NJ: Princeton University Press, 2010).

44. Barbara S. Romzek and Melvin J. Dubnick, "Accountability in the Public Sector: Lessons from the *Challenger* Tragedy," *Public Administration Review* 47, no. 3 (1987): 227–238.

45. Dubnick and Frederickson, *Accountable Governance*; Jonathan Koppell, "Pathologies of Accountability: ICANN and the Challenge of 'Multiple Accountabilities Disorder,'" *Public Administration Review* 65, no. 1 (2005): 94–108; Edward J. Giblin, "Bureaupathology: The Denigration of Competence," *Human Resource Management* 20, no. 4 (1981): 22–25.

46. Paul C. Light, *Monitoring Government: Inspectors General and the Search for Accountability* (Washington, DC: Brookings Institute, 1993), 223.

47. Frank Anechiarico and James Jacobs, *The Pursuit of Absolute Integrity: How Corruption Control Makes Government Ineffective* (Chicago: University of Chicago Press, 1996); Frank Anechiarico and Lydia Segal, "Public Integrity Networks," *Public Integrity* 12 (2010): 325–344; Light, *Monitoring Government*; A. Markert, "Government Oversight: A Study of the Development of Offices of Inspector General for the State of New York" (PhD diss., City University of New York, 2003).

48. Policy feedback is the looplike process by which "policies produce politics"—politics that in turn influence the shape of future policies. Policies, once enacted, can have numerous types of interrelated effects: on state building (bureaucratic development); on interest group formation and behavior; on the viability of future policies through lock-in effects; and on political participation. (That is, the mechanism by which a decision at time T1 limits the array of possible decisions at time T2, in effect locking in the previous decision; this is the mechanism that gives rise to path dependence.) See also Daniel Beland, "Reconsidering Policy Feedback: How Policies Affect Politics," *Administration and Society* 42 (2010): 568. Such feedback can come in both positive and negative varieties, with positive feedback leading to the path-dependent entrenchment of a policy or institution and negative feedback (or the recognition of failure) leading to pressures for institutional change. As a means of checking the excesses of bureaucratic behaviour, oversight mechanisms can in practice make the bureaucracy larger, less capable, and a hindrance to innovation.

49. Hood, *Blame Game*.

50. Warren, "Accountability and Democracy," 50.

51. See Christopher Hood, Oliver James, B. Guy Peters, and Colin Scott, *Controlling Modern Government: Variety, Commonality and Change* (Cheltenham: Edward Elgar, 2004), for a full explanation of this categorisation of instruments of accountability.

52. Light, *Monitoring Government*.

53. See, e.g., Mark H. Moore and Margaret Jane Gates, *Inspectors General: Junkyard Dogs or Man's Best Friend?* (New York: Russell Sage Foundation, 1986).

54. Anechiarico and Jacobs, *Pursuit of Absolute Integrity*; Albert Gore, *From Red Tape to Results: Creating a Government that Works Better and Costs Less—Report of the National Performance Review* (Washington, DC: Government Printing Office, 1993); Paul C. Light, "The Inspector General at Middle Age," *Government Accountants Journal* 47, no. 3 (1998): 40–49; Ronald Moe, "The Reinventing Government Exercise: Misinterpreting the Problem, Misjudging the Consequences," *Public Administration Review* 54 (1994): 111–122; Kathryn E. Newcomer, "The Changing Nature of Accountability: The Role of the Inspector General in Federal Agencies," *Public Administration Review* 58, no. 2 (1998): 129–136.

55. Matthew Harris, "Inspectors General: Exploring Lived Experiences, Impediments to Success, and Possibilities for Improvement" (PhD diss., Northcentral University, 2012).

56. Charles S. Clark, "Into the Limelight," *Government Executive*, March 2011, 24.

57. Ibid., quote from Danielle Brian, executive director of POGO.

58. Markert, "Government Oversight"; Patricia Salkin, "Ensuring the Pub-

lic Trust at the Municipal Level: Inspectors General Enter the Mix," *Albany Law Review* 75, no. 1 (2011): 95–132.

59. Carmen Apaza, *Integrity and Accountability in Government: Homeland Security and the Inspector General* (Farnham, UK: Ashgate, 2011).

60. Paul C. Light, "Strengthening the Inspectors General," *Washington Post*, 2 December 2010; Kathryn Newcomer, "Federal Offices of the Inspector General: Thriving on Chaos?," *American Review of Public Administration* 34, no. 3 (2004): 235–251.

61. "Inspectors General: Many Lack Essential Tools for Independence," *POGO*, 26 February 2008, http://www.pogo.org/; Salkin, "Ensuring the Public Trust"; Lydia Segal, "Independence from Political Influence—A Shaky Shield: A Study of Ten Inspectors General," *Public Integrity* 12 (2010): 297–314; Betty Vega, "Inspectors General: Evaluating Independence and Creating Capacity," *Government Law and Policy Journal* 13, no. 2 (2011): 48–54.

62. Harris, "Inspectors General."

63. Light, *Monitoring Government*, 3–4.

64. Behn, *Rethinking Democratic Accountability*, 13.

65. Gore, *From Red Tape to Results*, chap. 1, pt. 2.

66. Ibid., appx. B and C.

67. POGO, "Inspectors General: Many Lack Essential Tools for Independence"; "Inspectors General: Accountability Is a Balancing Act," *POGO*, 20 March 2009, http://www.pogo.org/.

68. Anechiarico and Jacobs, *Pursuit of Absolute Integrity*; Sean Gailmard, "Multiple Principals and Oversight of Bureaucratic Policy-making," *Journal of Theoretical Politics* 21 (2009): 161–186; James Ives, "Inspectors General: Prioritizing Accountability," *Journal of Public Inquiry*, Fall/Winter 2009–2010, 25–31.

CHAPTER 2. "ONCE YOU'VE MET ONE IG, YOU'VE MET ONE IG":
MODES OF MONITORY DEMOCRATIC PRACTICE

1. One IG reported that POGO attempted to develop a metric with which to compare federal IGs but abandoned the project as a result of the variation in IG activity. POGO staff were unavailable to verify this claim.

2. IG Act of 1978, § 2.

3. IG Act of 1978, § 4(a).

4. This body was so named in 2008, a consolidation of two separate entities, the President's Council on Integrity and Efficiency (PCIE) for departmental IGs and the Executive Council on Integrity and Efficiency (ECIE) for IGs in designated federal entities (DFEs). As is the custom within the IG community, I often use the terms "agency" and "department" interchangeably to refer to the entire host unit, regardless of whether the IG is PAS or DFE.

5. Special IGs are assigned to temporary projects such as Iraq Reconstruction (SIGIR), Afghanistan Reconstruction (SIGAR), and the Troubled Asset Relief Program (SIGTARP). Vanessa K. Burrows, *Statutory Offices of Inspectors General (IGs): Methods of Appointment and Legislative Proposals*, CRS Report R40675 (Washington, DC: Congressional Research Service, 2009), 1.

6. Independence is the degree to which an IG can pursue an issue without regard to the preferences of Congress, the agency head, or any other members of the agency; in this sense, it is closely related to the concept of bureaucratic autonomy, defined by Carpenter as a combination of "preference irreducibility and operational and discretionary latitude." Daniel Carpenter, *The Forging of Bureaucratic Autonomy* (Princeton, NJ: Princeton University Press, 2001), 25. Increasing the IGs' level of independence to increase their effectiveness has been a primary focus of congressional legislation.

7. It is outside of the remit of this study, but there remains much research to be done on the IG concept internationally. The only American-style IG outside the United States now operates in Iraq and was an American creation, partly designed and organized by PCIE/CIGIE. Data are from personal interviews with CIGIE executive staff. Multiple semistructured interviews were conducted for this book, and all interviewees were asked permission for the direct attribution of quotes. In the footnotes accompanying statements of fact or opinion in the text, I cite the interviewee's name and the date of the interview. Appendix A provides a full list of interviews, with name of interviewee, professional position, and date of interview.

8. Light, *Monitoring Government;* Moore and Gates, *Inspectors General.* It is worth noting that despite its widespread use in descriptions of IG work, including in CIGIE's reports, the term "waste" is not mentioned in the original 1978 act.

9. Light, *Monitoring Government,* 56–57.

10. Keane, "Monitory Democracy?," 1. See also Keane's *The Life and Death of Democracy* (London: Simon & Schuster, 2009); and Michael Schudson, *The Good Citizen: A History of American Public Life* (Cambridge, MA: Harvard University Press, 1999).

11. As John Dunn has observed, the term "democracy," and the uses to which it has been put, have varied widely, and its instantiations exhibit remarkable dissimilarity across history and cultures. John Dunn, *Setting the People Free* (London: Atlantic Books, 2005). Given this malleability and imprecision, measuring democracy, or disaggregating its most salient features, becomes an analytic minefield, with the danger of stripping democratic practices of their contextual specificity. A vast body of literature, both qualitative and quantitative, attempts to define and measure democracy. See in particular Michael Coppedge and John Gerring, with David Altman et al., "Conceptualising and Measuring Democracy: A New Approach," *Perspectives on Politics* 9, no. 2 (2011): 253; Gerardo Munck and Jay Verkuilen, "Conceptualizing and Measuring Democracy: Evaluating Alternative Indices," *Comparative Political Studies* 35, no. 1 (2002): 5–34; Larry Diamond and Leonardo Morlino, eds., *Assessing the Quality of Democracy* (Baltimore: Johns Hopkins University Press, 2005). My implicit argument here is that because defining the form and content of democracy is as much a task for the citizens and state officials as it is for observers, we can describe types of democracies only in cultural and historical contexts.

12. I use the terms "democratic form" and "mode of democratic practice" interchangeably because I envision democracy to be fundamentally a practice rather than a static concept.

13. By "second-order political actor," I mean an actor whose contribution to democratic politics is indirect but nonetheless crucial. In suggesting this, I reject a simplistically Schmittian conception of the political as based on the friend/enemy distinction, and in which (along with Weber) administration and law are categorically nonpolitical. I also reject the opposite view, in which the distinction between the two domains is obscured. Instead, I argue for a middle path in which the decisions of actors not directly operating in the agora of democratic politics are nonetheless understood in light of their political significance. In short, they are political of a second order.

14. Johan P. Olsen, "The Ups and Downs of Bureaucratic Reorganisation," *Annual Review of Political Science* 11 (2008): 20.

15. For a full exposition of the concept of political agonism, or agonistic pluralism as a model of democracy that challenges both Rawlsian and Habermasian consensus-based models, see, among others, Chantal Mouffe, *The Democratic Paradox* (London: Verso Press, 2000); and Bonnie Honig, *Political Theory and the Displacement of Politics* (Ithaca, NY: Cornell University Press, 1993). I use the term not to advocate Mouffe's philosophy wholesale or to imply that conflict is, ipso facto, a good in itself, but rather to suggest that the maintenance of a forum in which inevitable social and political conflict can be channeled is a democratic value in itself. It is this value that might be reinforced directly and indirectly by an IG's work.

16. See Hoggett for a neo-Weberian position that, contra Alasdair McIntyre, opposes the view that bureaucratic rationality is instrumental. Rather, it plays an important role in the substantive resolution of fundamental value conflicts that have been passed on by legislators. Paul Hoggett, "A Service to the Public," in *The Values of Bureaucracy*, ed. Paul du Gay (Oxford: Oxford University Press, 2005).

17. David Rosenbloom, "The Separation of Powers," in *Revisiting Waldo's Administrative State: Constancy and Change in Public Administration*, ed. David H. Rosenbloom and Howard E. McCurdy (Washington, DC: Georgetown University Press, 2006), 94.

18. Paul du Gay, *In Praise of Bureaucracy: Weber, Organization, Ethics* (London: Sage, 2000), 118.

19. Christopher Pollitt, Sandra Van Thiel, and Vincent Homburg, *The New Public Management in Europe: Adaptations and Alternatives* (Houndmills, UK: Palgrave Macmillan, 2007).

20. Christopher Hood, "A Public Management for All Seasons?," *Public Administration* 69 (1991): 4–5.

21. Olsen, "Ups and Downs."

22. I describe layering in greater detail below as a process of institutional change.

23. In a personal interview, one IG suggested that he overrode his own professional background (law) and allocated more resources to the audit function than the investigative component of his office when he realized that the primary challenge to his department was financial waste. Another IG similarly suggested that an IG should "let the department's problems dictate the focus of [an IG's] work" rather than the other way around.

24. Indeed, the virtues of self-limitation were a common theme among IGs in interviews.

25. *Strengthening the Unique Role of the Nation's Inspectors General*, hearing before the Senate Committee on Homeland Security and Governmental Affairs, Senate, 110th Cong. 1 (2007) (testimony of Glenn Fine).

26. Kathleen Thelen and James Mahoney, *Explaining Institutional Change* (Cambridge: Cambridge University Press, 2010), 16.

27. Vivien Schmidt, "Discursive Institutionalism: The Explanatory Power of Ideas and Discourse," *Annual Review of Political Science* 11 (2008): 303–326.

28. See Romzek and Dubnick's classic paper, "Accountability in the Public Sector," on the consequences of multiple, overlapping systems of accountability in single bureaucratic settings; see also Johan P. Olsen, "Accountability and Ambiguity," in Bovens, Goodin, and Schillemans, *Oxford Handbook*, 106–123, for a discussion of the ways that ambiguity and accountability can both conflict with and complement each other.

29. John Gerring, *Social Science Methodology: A Criterial Framework* (Cambridge: Cambridge University Press, 2001), 28.

30. John Gerring, "Single Outcome Studies: A Methodological Primer," *International Sociology* 21, no. 5 (2006): 707–734.

31. The "universe" of cases was thus limited to Homeland Security, Justice, State, Defense, and Treasury (for its role in economic emergency).

32. In their classic work on qualitative methodology, King, Keohane, and Verba present the problem of selection bias (i.e., selecting cases on the basis of the dependent variable). However, their solution to this problem is not random selection but rather carefully planned selection that preserves variation among outcomes. This is open to the charge of "selecting on the dependent variable," but because of the research-oriented approach, this risk is diminished. Gary King, Robert Keohane, and Sidney Verba, *Designing Social Inquiry* (Princeton, NJ: Princeton University Press, 1994), 128.

33. Michael Bromwich, personal interview, 2 January 2013.

34. Press accounts provide a political context for decisions and can give an indication of both official and public reactions to specific events. Attention to press accounts can also allow a limited treatment of cases that were not investigated, or were poorly investigated, by the IGs. Tracking press accounts also served as evidence of the IGs' salience. As an indicator of visibility, I used a simple form of content analysis to gather statistics about the number of media citations from the Factiva database for certain IG-related concepts and to provide an initial indication of the visibility of specific reviews. Unless otherwise stated, I used a time frame of four years in which to count media citations of particular reviews, and I include the search terms in footnotes, at times with an explanation of the choice of the terms with regards to Type I (overly inclusive) and Type II (overly exclusive) statistical errors.

CHAPTER 3. AN INSPECTOR CALLS (WITH APOLOGIES TO J. B. PRIESTLEY):
THE INSPECTOR GENERAL CATEGORY

1. Interpretations of *The Prince* often claim that Machiavelli views the prince's primary duty as being the preservation of the state, but as Ryan notes, nowhere in the text is this assertion to be found directly. Although Machiavelli places a high importance on this duty, for him it should be subordinated to the higher moral value of bringing glory to himself and therefore to his people. Alan Ryan, *On Machiavelli: The Search for Glory* (New York: Liverlight Publishing, 2014). However, the maintenance of the state is nonetheless crucial in the Florentine's treatise, and in making this observation, I suggest that it trumps other political values.

2. CIGIE, *Progress Report to the President: Fiscal Year 2014*, https://www.ignet.gov/.

3. Ibid.

4. Paul C. Light, "Fact Sheet on the Continued Thickening of Government," *Brookings*, 23 July 2004, http://www.brookings.edu/.

5. Ryan Check and Afsheen John Radsan, "One Lantern in the Darkest Night— The CIA's Inspector General," *Journal of National Security Law and Policy* 4 (2010): 249.

6. Light, *Monitoring Government*, 27. In the first part of this historical overview (from roughly 1962–93), I rely heavily, but not exclusively, on this seminal work on IGs.

7. Ibid., 29.

8. GAO, *Inspectors General: Enhancing Federal Accountability* (GAO-04-117T) (Washington, DC: US Government Accountability Office, 2003), 18.

9. Check and Radsan, "One Lantern," 253.

10. Richard Moberly, "Whistleblowers and the Obama Presidency: The National Security Dilemma," *Employee Rights and Employment Policy Journal* 16 (2012): 141.

11. Thomas Newcomb, "In From the Cold: The Intelligence Community Whistleblower Protection Act of 1998," *Administrative Law Review* 53 (2001): 1258–1259.

12. *Twenty-Fifth Anniversary of the IG Act of 1978*, hearing before the Subcommittee on Government Efficiency and Financial Management, Committee on Government Reform, House of Representatives, 107th Cong., 2 (2002) (testimony of Gaston L. Gianni Jr.).

13. In addition to the IG-HEW of 1976 and the IG-Energy in 1977, these were Agriculture, Commerce, Housing and Urban Development, Interior, Labor, Transportation, Community Services Administration, Environmental Protection Agency, General Services Administration, National Aeronautics and Space Administration, Small Business Administration, and Veterans Administration.

14. IG Act of 1978, § 3(b).

15. Light, *Monitoring Government*, 23–24.

16. Sherman Funk, "Dual Reporting: Straddling the Barbed Wire Fence," *Journal of Public Inquiry*, Fall 1996, 13.

17. Sherman Funk, interviewed by Charles Stuart Kennedy, 14 July 1994, Foreign Affairs Oral History Project, Association for Diplomatic Studies and Training, 15.

18. Light, *Monitoring Government*, 102–103.

19. Gianni testimony.

20. Light, *Monitoring Government*, 107.

21. Ibid., 102–104.

22. HR Rep. No. 100-771, Inspector General Act Amendments of 1988, at 2, 13 July 1988.

23. Newcomer, "Changing Nature of Accountability," 135.

24. Gore, *From Red Tape to Results*, 33.

25. Newcomer, "Changing Nature of Accountability," 130.

26. *Oversight of Investigative Practices of Inspectors General*, hearing before the Subcommittee on Government Management, Information, and Technology, Committee on Government Reform and Oversight, US House of Representatives, 105th Cong., 1 (1997) (testimony of Eleanor Hill).

27. Moe, "Reinventing Government Exercise," 113–114.

28. Ibid., 118–119.

29. Per Lægreid, "Accountability and New Public Management," in Bovens, Goodin, and Schillemans, *Oxford Handbook*, 324–338.

30. Ibid., 331.

31. Patricia Ingraham, "Who Rules?," in Rosenbloom and McCurdy, *Revisiting Waldo's Administrative State*, 78–79.

32. Hood and Peters, "Middle Ageing."

33. PCIE/ECIE, *Annual Performance Report: Fiscal Year 1995*, https://www.ignet.gov/.

34. Newcomer, "Changing Nature of Accountability," 131.

35. Public Law 105-272, title VII, § 701(a).

36. Newcomb, "In From the Cold,"1266–1267.

37. Elizabeth Newell Jochum, "Debate Erupts over Whistleblower Rights for Intelligence Workers," *Government Executive*, 14 May 2009.

38. Public Law 106-531.

39. "Uniting and Strengthening America by Providing Appropriate Tools Required to Intercept and Obstruct Terrorism" (USA Patriot Act of 2001), § 1001, Public Law 107-56, 115 Stat. 272.

40. IG Act of 1978, § 6 (e).

41. *Legislative Proposals and Issues Relevant to the Operations of Inspectors General*, hearing before the Committee on Homeland Security and Governmental Affairs, Senate, 106th Cong., 2 (2000) (testimony of Nicholas Gess, Associate Deputy Justice IG).

42. PCIE/ECIE, *Annual Report to the President: Fiscal Year 1995*, https://www.ignet.gov/.

43. PCIE/ECIE, *Annual Report to the President: Fiscal Year 2000*, 38, https://www.ignet.gov/.

44. PCIE/ECIE, *Annual Report to the President: Fiscal Year 2004*, 38, https://www.ignet.gov/.

45. Perri 6, "Joined-up Government in the Western World in Comparative Perspective: A Preliminary Literature Review and Exploration," *Journal of Public Administration Research and Theory* 14, no. 1 (2004): 103.

46. Mark C. Miller, "The View of the Courts from the Hill: Governance as Dialogue," *Political Science and Politics* 40, no. 1 (2007): 179.

47. Personal interview with David Gross, 28 July 2014.

48. "Bush Signs Legislation Giving More Autonomy to Government Watchdogs," *Associated Press Newswires*, 14 October 2008.

49. Beverly Lumpkin, "At Long Last, Congress Passes IG Reform Bill," *POGO Blog*, 29 September 2008, http://www.pogo.org/blog/.

50. Ibid.

51. Gianni testimony.

52. Inspector General Act of 2008, Public Law 110-409, HR 928, 14 October 2008.

53. Personal interview with Tom Caulfield, 4 January 2013.

54. Vanessa K. Burrows, *Statutory Offices of Inspectors General (IGs): Methods of Appointment and Legislative Proposals* (CRS report R40675) (Washington, DC: Congressional Research Service, 2009), 5.

55. Inspector General Act of 2008.

56. Senators Charles Grassley and Claire McCaskill on the presidential signing statement on the Inspector General Reform Act, 30 October 2008.

57. Ibid.

58. Public Law 111-203, HR 4173.

59. GAO, *Inspectors General: Reporting on Independence, Effectiveness, and Expertise* (GAO-11-770) (Washington, DC: US Government Accountability Office, 2011).

60. IG Act of 1978, § 8(e)(a)(1)

61. IG Act of 1978, § 3A

62. See, e.g., *Inspector General Act Oversight*, hearing before the Subcommittee on Government Management, Information, and Technology, House of Representatives Committee on Government Reform and Oversight, 104th Cong. 1 (1995).

63. Ed O'Keefe, "Lawmakers Question Obama's Dismissal of AmeriCorps IG," *Washington Post*, 16 June 2009, http://voices.washingtonpost.com/.

64. Funk was the Commerce IG from 1981 to 1986, and State IG from 1987 to 1994.

65. Funk interview, 15.

66. Shirin Sinnar, "Protecting Rights from Within? Inspectors General and National Security Oversight," *Stanford Law Review* 65 (2013): 55.

67. US House of Representatives, Committee on Government Reform—Minority Staff, Special Investigations Division, "The Politicization of Inspectors General," report prepared for Rep. Henry A. Waxman, rev. 7 January 2005, abstract, http://www.yuricareport.com/Corruption/PoliticizationOfInspectors General.pdf.

68. Jane Mayer, *Dark Side* (New York: Doubleday, 2008), 288–289.

69. Check and Radsan, "One Lantern," 252–254.

70. Mayer, *Dark Side*, 288.

71. Ibid.

72. Sen. Dianne Feinstein, *Statement on Intel Committee's CIA Detention, Interrogation Report*, 113th Cong., 2 (11 March 2014), http://www.feinstein.senate.gov/.

73. Smintheus, "Those FISA IG Reports," *Daily Kos*, 8 July 2008, http://www.dailykos.com/.

74. Sen. Patrick Leahy, "Senate Judiciary Committee Approves Leahy-Authored Substitute Amendment to Reauthorization of FISA Amendments Act," press release, *Patrick Leahy*, 19 July 2012, https://www.leahy.senate.gov/; Angela Canterbury, "Electronic Surveillance Law 101," *POGO Blog*, 26 June 2013, http://www.pogo.org/blog/.

75. David M. Walker, "GAO Answers the Question: What's in a Name?" *Roll Call*, 19 July 2004.

76. Public Law 108-271, 118 Stat. 811.

77. Clark, "Into the Limelight," 22.

78. See Morton Rosenberg, *Investigative Oversight: An Introduction to the Law, Practice, and Procedure of Congressional Inquiry*, CRS Report 95-464 (Washington, DC: Congressional Research Service, 1995), for a detailed overview of the parameters of congressional investigations.

79. Personal interviews with Richard Skinner (former Department of Homeland Security IG), 11 January 2012, and Calvin Scovel III (Department of Transportation IG), 17 January 2013.

80. Ken Gormley, "Monica Lewinsky, Impeachment, and the Demise of the Independent Counsel Law: What Congress Can Salvage from the Wreckage—A Minimalist View," *Maryland Law Review* 60, no. 1 (2001): 97–148.

81. Clark, "Into the Limelight," 24.

82. Ibid.

83. Eric Katz, "Whistleblowers Will Have a New Friend at Justice," *Government Executive*, 10 August 2012.

84. Clark, "Into the Limelight," 24.

85. Danielle Brian and Jana Persky, "Watching the Watchdogs: The Good, the Bad, and What We Need from the Inspectors General," *POGO*, 14 January 2014, http://www.pogo.org/.

86. Personal interviews with Glenn Fine, 3 January 2012; Richard Skinner, 11 January 2012; and David C. Williams, 14 January 2013.

87. "Where Are All the Watchdogs?," *POGO*, http://www.pogo.org/.

88. Letter from Sen. Grassley to Kevin L. Perkins, chair, CIGIE Integrity Committee, regarding "Whistleblower allegations involving Operation Fast and Furious," 8 March 2011.

89. *Open and Unimplemented IG Recommendations Could Save Taxpayers $67 Billion*, Committee on Oversight and Government Reform, US House of Representatives, Staff Report of Darrell Issa, 5 March 2013.

90. "POGO Letter to OMB's Clay Johnson Regarding Integrity of Inspector General System," *POGO*, 17 August 2007, http://www.pogo.org/.

91. Light, *Monitoring Government*, 211–13.

92. Association of Government Accountants (AGA) and Kearney & Company, *AGA's Inspector General Survey: Effective Oversight in a Changing Environment*, September 2013, https://www.agacgfm.org/.

93. Letter of US Federal Inspectors General to the Chairmen and Ranking

Members of the Committee on Oversight and Government Reform, US House of Representatives, and Committee on Homeland Security and Governmental Affairs, US Senate, 5 August 2014.

94. Tom Caulfield, Phyllis Fong, Mark Jones, and Lynne McFarland, personal interviews, 24 July 2014.

CHAPTER 4. BUNGLING BUREAUCRATS: SEARCHING FOR INDEPENDENCE AT STATE

1. GAO, *State Department Inspector General: Actions to Address Independence and Effectiveness Concerns Are Under Way* (GAO-11-382T) (Washington, DC: US Government Accountability Office, 2011).

2. GAO, *State Department's Office of Inspector General, Foreign Service, Needs to Improve Its Internal Evaluation Process* (ID-78-19) (Washington, DC: US Government Accountability Office, 1978); GAO, *Actions to Address Independence;* Public Law 96-465, 94 Stat. 2080, 17 October 1980.

3. Section 150 of Public Law 99-93; GAO, *State Department's Office of Inspector General Should Be More Independent and Effective* (AFMD-83–56) (Washington, DC: US Government Accountability Office, 1983).

4. Omnibus Diplomatic Security and Antiterrorism Act of 1986, section 4861.

5. Gordon Adams, "Running Hills: Why Senators Shouldn't Head the Pentagon or Foggy Bottom," *Foreign Affairs*, 20 December 2012.

6. Brian Friel, "The Powell Leadership Doctrine," *Government Executive*, 1 June 2001.

7. Funk interview, 36–38. The narrative in this chapter (and the following chapter) relies heavily on a set of interviews conducted between roughly 1992 and 2011 by Charles Stuart Kennedy. Because many of the main actors from State OIG's early history are deceased or unavailable for interview, this archive provided a wealth of commentary and contextual data on the relevant events, for which archival documents are limited. However, like all interviews, they must be taken as the views of single individuals who had personal stakes in the events described. When using such data, I attempt to be explicit that they represent only the perspective of the interviewee.

8. Funk interview, 47, 52.

9. Adams, "Running Hills."

10. Ibid.

11. Friel, "Powell Leadership Doctrine."

12. GAO, *Activities of the Department of State's Office of the Inspector General* (GAO-07-138) (Washington, DC: US Government Accountability Office, 2007), 1.

13. Funk interview, 26.

14. Michael Yoder, personal interview, 23 June 2014.

15. Funk interview, 27.

16. GAO, *Records Management: Retrieval of State Department's Political Appointee Files* (NSIAD-94-187) (Washington, DC: US Government Accountability Office, 1994).

17. GAO, *Actions to Address Independence.*

18. Doug Welty, personal interview, 15 July 2014.

19. GAO, *Actions to Address Independence.*

20. NASA/OIG, *Peer Review of Department of State Office of Inspector General* (Report IG-11-002), October 2010.

21. "POGO Questions the Independence of the State Department's Inspector General" (letter to President Barack Obama), *POGO*, 18 November 2010, http://www.pogo.org/.

22. Ibid.; *Watching the Watchers: The Need for Systemic Reforms and Independence of the State Department Inspector General*, hearing of the Committee of Foreign Affairs, US House of Representatives, 112th Cong. 1 (2011).

23. Funk interview, 26–27.

24. Robert S. Steven, interviewed by Charles Stuart Kennedy, 3 August 2001, Foreign Affairs Oral History Project, Association for Diplomatic Studies and Training.

25. Quote of Charles Stuart Kennedy, 3 August 2001, Foreign Affairs Oral History Project, Association for Diplomatic Studies and Training.

26. Michael Yoder, personal interview, 23 June 2014.

27. William Harrop, interviewed by Charles Stuart Kennedy, 24 August 1993, Foreign Affairs Oral History Project, Association for Diplomatic Studies and Training, 80.

28. Steven interview, 122.

29. Robert Sayre, interviewed by Charles Stuart Kennedy, 31 October 1995, Foreign Affairs Oral History Project, Association for Diplomatic Studies and Training, 40–42.

30. Harrop interview, 77.

31. Ibid.

32. Steven interview, 147.

33. Funk interview, 61.

34. Ibid., 6.

35. Light, *Monitoring Government,*177.

36. Quote of Charles Stuart Kennedy, 15 March 2000, Foreign Affairs Oral History Project, Association for Diplomatic Studies and Training.

37. Sarah Horsey-Barr, interviewed by Charles Stuart Kennedy, 15 March 2000, Foreign Affairs Oral History Project, Association for Diplomatic Studies and Training.

38. Steven interview, 156.

39. Ibid., 162.

40. Funk interview, 22–23.

41. George Gedda, "CIA Program Draws Fire from Odd Senate Alliance," *Associated Press*, 17 December 1992.

42. Funk interview, 30.

43. Stephen A. Holmes, "Man in the News; An Inspector with No Shortage of Enemies: Sherman Maxwell Funk," *New York Times*, 20 November 1992.

44. Carol Giacomo, "Israel Arms Transfer Row Far from Over," *Reuters News*, 3 April 1992.

45. "US Investigators Clear Israel of Missile Transfer to China," *St. Louis Post-Dispatch*, 3 April 1992.

46. Edward T. Pound, "US Aides Said to Have Been Hindered In Monitoring Israel's Arms Transfers," *Wall Street Journal*, 5 April 1992.

47. DOS/OIG, *Report of Audit: International Narcotics Control Programs in Peru and Bolivia*, March 1989, 1–5, 33.

48. Funk interview, 66.

49. Ibid.

50. Ibid., 66–67.

51. Ibid., 68.

52. Harold Geisel, interviewed by Charles Stuart Kennedy, 30 June 2006, Foreign Affairs Oral History Project, Association for Diplomatic Studies and Training, 106.

53. Wesley Egan, interviewed by Charles Stuart Kennedy, 28 October 2003, Foreign Affairs Oral History Project, Association for Diplomatic Studies and Training, 131.

54. Steven interview, 164

55. DOS/OIG, *Program Performance Report: Fiscal Year 2003*, https://oig.state.gov/system/files/32072.pdf.

56. Steven interview, 163–164.

57. *Oversight of Investigative Practices.*

58. Bromwich interview.

59. *Oversight of Investigative Practices.*

60. Ibid., 25.

61. Raymond Bonner, "Investigation Suggests Envoy Lied to House," *New York Times*, 18 March 1999.

62. Thomas W. Lippman, "Envoy Jean Kennedy Smith Cited for Targeting Staffers," *Washington Post*, 7 March 1996.

63. Phelim McAleer and Liam Clarke, "US Embassy Kept Secrets from Smith," *Sunday Times*, 25 January 1998.

64. Carol Giacomo, "US Diplomat Holbrooke's Nomination to UN on Hold," *Reuters News*, 11 September 1998.

65. Egan interview, 136.

66. Steven, 164.

67. Marshall Adair, interviewed by Charles Stuart Kennedy, 1 September 2011, Foreign Affairs Oral History Project, Association for Diplomatic Studies and Training, 207.

68. Steven interview, 164.

69. "US to Review Diplomacy in Chávez Crisis," *New York Times*, 14 May 2002.

70. Clark Kent Ervin, personal interview, 2 July 2014.

71. "Examining the Venezuela Coup— Gingerly," *Nation*, 2 September 2002.

72. DOS/OIG, *A Review of US Policy toward Venezuela*, November 2001, redacted for public release April 2002, 3.

73. "US Denies Backing Venezuela Coup," *Agence France-Presse*, 16 April 2002.

74. Jim Mannion, "Pentagon Gathering Facts on US Military in Venezuela,

Finds No Coup Support," *Agence France-Presse*, 23 April 2002; Jared Kotler, "Venezuelan Businessman Now a Villain," *AP Online*, 2 May 2002.

75. Juan Forero, "Documents Show CIA Knew of a Coup Plot in Venezuela," *New York Times*, 3 December 2004.

76. Clark Kent Ervin, personal interview, 14 July 2014.

77. "US Suspends Funding for Major Iraqi Opposition Group," *Dow Jones Business News*, 5 January 2002.

78. Kasie Hunt, "Are US Arabic Programs Being Heard?," *National Journal*, 16 July 2005.

79. *Assessing Whistle Blower Allegations against the State Department Inspector General, Committee on Oversight and Government Reform, House of Representatives*, 110th Congress (2007) (testimony of Howard Krongard).

80. Gordon Adams, on Iraq reconstruction funds oversight, *Minnesota Public Radio: Marketplace*, 22 June 2004.

81. A survey conducted by Representative Henry Waxman (D-CA) found that "over 60 percent of the IGs appointed by President Bush had prior political experience, such as service in a Republican White House or on a Republican congressional staff, while fewer than 20 percent had prior audit experience. In contrast, over 60 percent of the IGs appointed by President Clinton had prior audit experience, while fewer than 25 percent had prior political experience." "Politicization of Inspectors General."

82. Glenn Kessler, "House GOP Report Defends State Dept. Official," *Washington Post*, 14 November 2007.

83. Krongard testimony, 2007, 4.

84. "Inspector General Allegedly Blocked Probe," *NPR: Day to Day*, 19 September 2007.

85. Damien McElroy, "US Investigates Forced Labour Claims at Baghdad Embassy," *Calgary Herald*, 9 June 2007.

86. "Whistleblowers in State IG Investigation Report Threats of Retaliation," *US Fed News*, 28 September 2007.

87. Minutes of the CIGIE Integrity Committee Meeting, 16 January 2008.

88. "Rep. Davis Blasts Tactics in Probe of Watchdog," *Technology Daily AM*, 1 November 2007.

89. Howard J. Krongard to President George W. Bush regarding his resignation, 7 December 2007.

90. GAO, *Activities of the Department of State's Office of the Inspector General* (GAO-07-138) (Washington, DC: US Government Accountability Office, 2007).

91. Yochi J. Dreazen, "Iraq Fund Fight Brews in US—Lawmakers Battle over Who Will Oversee Cash for Rebuilding," *Wall Street Journal Europe*, 10 May 2006.

92. Ibid.

93. Reps. Ed Royce and Eliot Engel to Sen. John Kerry, 4 February 2013.

94. "State Dept. Inspector General Position Vacant for More than 3 Years," *All-Gov*, 1 June 2011, http://www.allgov.com/.

95. Dan Friedman, "State Dept. Taps Foreign Service Veteran to Be Acting IG," *Congress Daily/AM*, 3 June 2008.

96. DOS/OIG, *Report of Inspection: Embassy Kabul*, February 2010, 1.

97. Ibid., 3.

98. Matthew Nasuti, "Gold-Plated State Department Budget Wastes Billions," *Kabul Press*, 21 February 2011, http://kabulpress.org/.

99. Quoted in *Watching the Watchers* (POGO statement questioning the independence of the State Department's IG).

100. GAO, *Reporting on Independence*.

101. Welty interview.

102. Statement of Harold Geisel, *Watching the Watchers*.

103. Phyllis Fong, *CNN Q&A*, 22 September 2013.

104. "POGO Questions the Independence of the State Department's Inspector General" (letter to President Barack Obama).

105. Reps. Darryl Issa and Elijah Cummings to President Barack Obama, 24 January 2013.

106. Welty interview.

107. "Rep. Pelosi, Leading Democrats to State Dept: Use of Faulty Terrorism Data Must Be Investigated," *US Fed News*, 27 April 2005.

108. Steven interview, 119–120.

CHAPTER 5. A POLITICAL DEMOCRACY AT STATE: PROTECTING PASSPORT PRIVACY, 1992–2008

1. "Inquiry Is Ordered into US Handling of Files on Clinton," Reuters News Service, *St. Louis Post-Dispatch*, 20 October 1992.

2. Robert Pear, "Passport Inquiry Seeks Ties to Bush," *New York Times*, 12 November 1992.

3. Funk interview, 56–57.

4. Barry Schweid, "An Assistant Secretary of State Directed at Embassies Searched Files for Clinton Material," *Associated Press*, 14 October 1992.

5. Funk interview, 55.

6. Elizabeth Ann Swift, interviewed by Charles Stuart Kennedy, 16 December 1992, Foreign Affairs Oral History Project, Association for Diplomatic Studies and Training, 82.

7. Michael Newlin (29 September 2006) and Harry Coburn (22 July 2002), interviewed by Charles Stuart Kennedy, Foreign Affairs Oral History Project, Association for Diplomatic Studies and Training.

8. "The 1992 Campaign; FBI Closes Inquiry on Clinton's Passport," *New York Times*, 10 October 1992.

9. *Berry v. Funk*, [1998] 146 F.3d 1003.

10. Ibid.

11. Robert Pear, "State Dept. Official Who Searched Clinton's Passport Files Resigns," *New York Times*, 18 November 1992.

12. "Inquiry Is Ordered."

13. Robert S. Greenberger, "No Bush Link Found in Case over Passport," *Wall Street Journal*, 19 November 1992.

14. Walter Pincus, "Probe of Clinton Passport File Search Expanded," *Washington Post*, 25 November 1992.

15. Statement of Joseph diGenova, quoted in Ronald J. Ostrow, "Clinton Passport Probe Clears Bush Aides," *Los Angeles Times*, 1 December 1995.

16. David Johnston, "File Search in 1992 Race Wasn't Illegal," *New York Times*, 1 December 1995.

17. David Johnston, "No Charges to Be Filed for Search of Clinton Files," *New York Times*, 3 December 1994.

18. "Bush Team's Search for Clinton Passport 'Dumb,' Not Criminal," *Seattle Times News Services*, 1 December 1995.

19. Pincus, "Probe of Clinton."

20. Sharon LaFraniere and Michael Isikoff, "Special Counsel Probes Clinton Passport Case; diGenova Secretly Appointed to Investigate Possible Coverup by White House Aides," *Washington Post*, 18 December 1992.

21. GAO, *Records Management: Inadequate Controls over Various Agencies' Political Appointee Files* (NSIAD-94-155) (Washington, DC: US Government Accountability Office, 1994).; and GAO, *Records Management: Retrieval of State Department's Political Appointee Files* (NSIAD-94-187) (Washington, DC: US Government Accountability Office, 1994).

22. GAO, *Retrieval*, 15.

23. Michael Isikoff and Walter Pincus, "State Dept. Challenges Employee's Court Testimony on Clinton Passport Search," *Washington Post*, 2 February 1993.

24. David Alistair Yalof, *Prosecution Among Friends: Presidents, Attorneys General and Executive Branch Wrongdoing* (Austin: Texas A&M University Press, 2012), 134–135.

25. Isikoff and Pincus, "State Dept. Challenges."

26. *Berry v. Funk*, [1998] 146 F.3d 1003.

27. *Passport Files: Privacy Protection Needed for All Americans*, hearing of the Senate Judiciary Committee, Senate, 110th Cong., 2 (2008) (statement of Patrick Leahy).

28. Ibid., testimony of Marc Rotenberg.

29. Ibid.

30. Ibid.

31. DOS/OIG, *Reviews of Controls and Notification for Access to Passport Records in the Department of State's Passport Electronic Records System (PIERS)—AUD/IP-08-29*, July 2008, 29.

32. GAO, *Inspectors General: Activities of the Department of State Office of Inspector General* (GAO-07-138) (Washington, DC: US Government Accountability Office, 2007).

33. "POGO Questions the Independence of the State Department's Inspector General" (letter to President Barack Obama).

34. Biography of Harold Geisel, Department of State website archives, http://2001-2009.state.gov/.

35. "POGO Questions the Independence of the State Department's Inspector General" (letter to President Barack Obama).

36. *Passport Files*, testimony of Mark Duda.

37. DOS/OIG, *PIERS*, 45.

38. *Passport Files*, statement of Patrick Leahy.

39. Ibid., testimony of Alan Raul.

40. Glenn Kessler, "Celebrity Passport Records Popular; State Dept. Audit Finds Snooping Was Frequent," *Washington Post*, 4 July 2008.

41. "Sen. Feinstein: Americans Need Notice When Private Data Exposed," *US Fed News*, 20 April 2008.

42. DOS/OIG, *PIERS*, 17, 95.

43. DOS/OIG, *Semiannual Report to Congress*, 1 April 2010–30 September 2010.

44. GAO, *Information Security: Federal Agencies Need to Enhance Responses to Data Breaches* (GAO-14-487T) (Washington, DC: US Government Accountability Office, 2014).

45. Senators Patrick Leahy and Arlen Specter to Attorney General Michael Mukasey regarding privacy violations at State Department, 25 March 2008.

46. Dan Friedman, "Most Hill Panels Refrain From Launching Passport Probes," *Congress Daily/PM*, 26 March 2008.

47. GAO, *Alternatives Exist for Enhancing Protection of Personally Identifiable Information* (GAO-08-536) (Washington, DC: US Government Accountability Office, 2008).

48. John A. Verdi, director, EPIC Open Government Project, to Zipora Bullard, FOIA Office, US Department of State, 10 July 2008.

49. DOS/OIG, *PIERS*, 2.

50. DOS/OIG, *Reviews of Controls and Notification for Access*, 1.

51. *Passport Files*.

CHAPTER 6. LAWYERS OUT OF COURT: GUARDING THE GUARDIANS AT JUSTICE

1. Light, *Monitoring Government*, 63; Bromwich interview.

2. Section 8D(a), 1978 Inspector General Act.

3. The slowness of the IG confirmation process is a pattern seen across all OIGs and has been reported in multiple personal interviews. See also Paul C. Light, "Our Tottering Confirmation Process," *Public Interest*, 1 April 2002; *Nomination of Richard J. Hankinson To Be Inspector General of the Department of Justice*, George Bush Presidential Papers, Public Papers, 26 January 1990.

4. In interviews, a number of IGs commented on the informal link between the secret service community and the IG community (Richard Hankinson, David C. Williams, and Richard Skinner, personal interviews). Hankinson suggested that the personal connection with the president, the familiarity with detail, and the law enforcement experience that came with secret service work all lent themselves to a bridge between the two communities.

5. Richard Hankinson, personal interview, 16 January 2013.

6. *Confirmation Hearing of Federal Appointments*, hearing Before the Committee on the Judiciary, Senate, 103rd Cong., 2 (25 March 1994).

7. Michael Hedges, "Justice IG Nominee Chastised When Serving Walsh Team," *Washington Times*, 14 February 1994.

8. Bromwich interview.

9. Letter, Henry Wray, senior associate general counsel, to Representative Jack Brooks, 15 April 1994, http://www.gao.gov/assets/400/390452.pdf.

10. Deputy Attorney General Philip Heymann to Michael Shaheen, memorandum regarding the disclosure of the results of investigation of alleged professional misconduct by department attorneys, 13 December 1993.

11. James Rowley, "Head of Justice Watchdog Unit Resigns," *Associated Press Newswires*, 24 November 1997.

12. Bromwich interview.

13. *Confirmation Hearing of Federal Appointments*.

14. "Justice and the IG," editorial, *New York Times*, 2 February 2011; Dan Eggen, "FBI Cites More than 100 Possible Eavesdropping Violations," *Washington Post*, 9 March 2006.

15. This conflict of interest manifested itself in 2008 when the OPM was initially given the responsibility of investigating a set of politicized firings of US attorneys within the Justice Department. However, because the case straddled the two bodies' jurisdictions, the OIG fought successfully to share responsibility for it and ultimately spearheaded the investigation using OIG processes (Glenn Fine, personal communication).

16. Despite repeated attempts to close this institutional separation, it has been consistently rejected, most recently in a last-minute move by Sen. John Kyl (R-AZ) during the negotiations over the 2008 IG Act.

17. Michael R. Bromwich and Glenn Fine, "Investigating Major Scandals: Part II: Nuts and Bolts," *Journal of Public Inquiry*, Winter 1997, 1.

18. Bromwich interview.

19. Michael R. Bromwich, "Climate the Leads to IG Handling," *Journal of Public Inquiry*, Spring 1997, 4.

20. This is based on an analysis of the executive summaries, introductions, and recommendations of all special reviews, 1995–2013, conducted by the author. Each review was coded as either addressing a performance- or efficiency-based issue, or a constitutional/rights-based issue.

21. Andrea Shalal-Esa, "US Justice Department Launches CIA-Cocaine Probe," *Reuters News*, 21 September 1996.

22. John Diamond, "CIA Clears Itself of Role in Crack Cocaine," *Associated Press Newswires*, 18 December 1997.

23. "Reno Withholds Report on CIA, Rebels, Drugs," *Las Vegas Review-Journal*, 24 January 1998.

24. "FBI Chief," *Las Vegas Review-Journal*, 18 March 1997.

25. Toni Locy, "Judge Rejects Release of Draft Report on FBI Lab; Inspector General's Probe Has Uncovered Possible Problems in Many Criminal Cases," *Washington Post*, 18 March 1997.

26. Michael J. Sniffen, "Inspector General Finds Progress, Lingering Problems in FBI Lab," *Associated Press Newswires*, 4 June 1998.

27. Richard A. Serran and Ronald J. Ostrow, "How Fair Was Justice's FBI Crime LabProbe?," *Los Angeles Times*, 20 August 2000.

28. For instance, multiple statements in the *Legislative Proposals and Issues Rel-*

evant to the Operations of Inspectors General, 19 July 2000, suggest that the good reputation of the IG community was not at stake and that any congressional legislation should reinforce their independence. On the twenty-fifth anniversary of the IG Act in 2003, Congress issued a joint resolution commending the work of the inspectors general (SJ Res. 18-2).

29. DOJ/OIG Special Report, *The FBI Laboratory: An Investigation into Laboratory Practices and Alleged Misconduct in Explosives-Related and Other Cases*, April 1997.

30. Michael J. Sniffen, "Senator Seeks Criminal Investigation of FBI Lab Figures," *Associated Press Newswires*, 12 June 1997.

31. Bromwich interview.

32. William Safire, "Some Big Blob," *New York Times*, 3 December 1997.

33. Bromwich interview.

34. Gary Fields, "Independent Watchdog Urged for FBI Probes," *USA Today*, 19 May 1997.

35. DOJ/OIG, *Semiannual Report to Congress*, 1 April 2001–30 September 2001.

36. Michael J. Sniffen, "Wider FBI Lab Probe Sought, Whistle-Blowers Get New Protections," *Associated Press Newswires*, 17 April 1997.

37. Vernon Loeb and David A. Vise, "Security Violations at Justice Dept. Cited," *Washington Post*, 21 September 2000.

38. *Association of Inspectors General Newsletter* 4, no. 4 (Winter 2008).

39. *Strengthening the Unique Role of the Nation's Inspectors General.*

40. Michael Horowitz and Carol Ochoa, personal interview, 26 January 2013.

41. Ibid.

42. Ibid.

43. Glenn Fine, personal interview, 3 January 2013.

44. "Feds' Ranks Grow, but Not Probes of Conduct," *Arizona Daily Star*, 17 August 2001.

45. Jerry Seper, "Justice Sees Top Threat as Terrorism," *Washington Times*, 18 November 2003.

46. Mary Dudziak, "A Sword and a Shield: The Uses of Law in the Bush Administration," in *The Presidency of George W. Bush*, ed. Julian Zelizer (Princeton, NJ: Princeton University Press, 2010), 39–40.

47. This section requires the OIG to investigate potential abuses of rights and liberties not only associated with the Patriot Act but also more generally.

48. Report of the House Committee on the Judiciary on the Patriot Act of 2001, 11 October 2001.

49. Tom Davis, personal interview, 18 January 2013.

50. "Terror Bill Civil Rights Watchdog Is Now in Place," *St. Louis Post-Dispatch*, 10 January 2002.

51. "Justice Report Finds No Complaints," *New York Times Abstracts*, 16 August 2005.

52. Susan Schmidt, "Ashcroft Wants Stronger Patriot Act," *Washington Post*, 6 June 2003.

53. *Strengthening the Unique Role of the Nation's Inspectors General.*

54. Fine interview.

55. *Strengthening the Unique Role of the Nation's Inspectors General.*

56. DOJ/OIG, *Top Management and Performance Challenges in the Department of Justice—2006*, https://oig.justice.gov/.

57. Carrie Johnson, "Justice Watchdog Looks Back on Ten Years in Post," *National Public Radio*, 28 January 2011.

58. "Backward at the FBI: Overreaching New Rules for Surveillance Threaten Americans' Basic Rights," *New York Times*, 19 June 2011.

59. David Ingram, "Horowitz Cruising toward DOJ IG Post," *National Law Journal*, 24 October 2011.

60. Evan Perez, "Sides Dig In Over Gun Documents," *Wall Street Journal*, 20 June 2012.

61. *IG Report: The Department of Justice's Office of the Inspector General Examines the Failures of Operation Fast and Furious*, hearing before the House of Representatives Committee on Oversight and Government Reform, 112th Cong., 2 (2012), 50–51.

62. DOJ/OIG, *A Review of ATF's Operation Fast and Furious and Related Matters*, September 2012, 428–429.

63. "Justice Department Watchdog Creates Whistleblower Post," *Dow Jones News Service*, 8 August 2012.

64. Terry Frieden, "Justice Inspector General Promises an Ear for Whistleblowers," *CNN Wire*, 8 August 2012.

65. "FBI Malfeasance Undercuts Death Penalty," *Charlotte Observer*, 22 July 2014.

66. Spencer S. Hsu, "Report: 'Irreversible Harm' When FBI Didn't Reveal Flawed Lab Work in Death-Row Cases," *Washington Post*, 16 July 2014.

67. Michael R. Bromwich, "Running Special Investigations: The Inspector General Model," *Georgetown Law Review* 86 (1998): 2037, 2043.

68. *Lessons Learned—The Inspector General's Report on the 9/11 Detainees*, hearing before the Senate Committee on the Judiciary, Senate, 108th Cong. 8, 12 (2003) (testimony of Glenn Fine), 15.

69. *Failures of Operation Fast and Furious*, 49.

70. Sinnar, "Protecting Rights from Within?," 43–45.

71. Bromwich, "Climate the Leads."

CHAPTER 7. A CONSTITUTIONAL DEMOCRACY AT JUSTICE: FORGING DEMOCRATIC NORMS IN THE WAR ON TERROR, 2002–2010

1. The two reviews under analysis in this chapter have also been discussed in Sinnar, "Protecting Rights from Within?" I chose to focus on these two reviews, with the risk of some redundancy, because they are two of relatively few DOJ OIG reviews that address rights concerns directly and explicitly, and they are illustrative of the potential for an IG to provide an effective check on the executive in a period of emergency governance. I rely heavily on her legal analysis in my exposition of these reviews.

2. Steve Fainaru, "Justice Department to Examine Treatment of Detainees at 2 Jails," *Washington Post*, 3 April 2002.

3. Marcia Coyle, "Walking a Fine Line," *National Law Journal*, 24 January 2011.

4. See also Sinnar, "Protecting Rights from Within?," 1066.

5. Quoted in Christopher Smith, "Hatch OKs Hearing on Detentions," *Salt Lake Tribune*, 4 June 2003.

6. DOJ/OIG, *The September 11 Detainees: A Review of the Treatment of Aliens Held on Immigration Charges in Connection with the Investigation of the September 11 Attacks*, June 2003.

7. Eric Lichtblau, "Report on Detainees Shines a Brighter Spotlight on an Inspector General," *New York Times*, 5 July 2003.

8. Eric Lichtblau, "Ashcroft Seeks More Power to Pursue Terror Suspects," *New York Times*, 6 June 2003; Lichtblau, "Report on Detainees."

9. DOJ/OIG, *Analysis of Department of Justice and Department of Homeland Security Responses to the September 11 Detainees Report*, September 2003.

10. Ibid.

11. Ibid.

12. DOJ/OIG, *Top Management and Performance Challenges*.

13. DOJ/OIG, *Analysis of the Response by the Federal Bureau of Prisons to Recommendations in the OIG's December 2003 Report on the Abuse of September 11 Detainees at the Metropolitan Detention Center in Brooklyn, New York*, March 2004.

14. Testimony of Glenn Fine, *Lessons Learned*.

15. DOJ/OIG, *Analysis of the Second Response by the Department of Justice to Recommendations in the Office of the Inspector General's June 2003 Report on the Treatment of September 11 Detainees*, January 2004, 6.

16. Ibid., 24.

17. DOJ/OIG, *September 11 Detainees: A Review*, chap. 10.

18. DOJ/OIG, *Analysis of the Second Response*, recommendation 12.

19. See Sinnar, "Protecting Rights from Within?," for a discussion of this point.

20. DOJ/OIG, *Analysis of the Response by the Federal Bureau of Prisons*, recommendation 4; see also Sinnar, "Protecting Rights from Within?," 1071.

21. Testimony of Glenn Fine, *Lessons Learned*.

22. DOJ/OIG, *September 11 Detainees: A Review*, chap. 6, emphasis added.

23. US Department of Justice, Hearing before the House Committee on the Judiciary, 108th Congress, 5 June 2003; *Lessons Learned; Oversight Hearing: Law Enforcement and Terrorism*, hearing before the Senate Judiciary Committee, 108th Congress, 23 July 2005.

24. Sen. Orrin Hatch (R-UT), *Lessons Learned*.

25. Congress also referred to the IG narratives when drafting the Civil Liberties Restoration Act bill, which ultimately died. HR 4591 (108th).

26. *Turkmen v. Ashcroft*, 02-civ-2307 (E.D.N.Y. filed 17 April 2002).

27. Center for Constitutional Rights Cases, *Turkmen v. Ashcroft*, http://ccrjustice.org/.

28. *Analysis of the Second Response*, recommendation 6.

29. Sinnar, "Protecting Rights from Within?," 1077–78.

30. US Senate, "NSL Inspector General Report," *Congressional Record*, 28 March 2007.

31. Barton Gellman, "The FBI's Secret Scrutiny; In Hunt for Terrorists, Bureau Examines Records of Ordinary Americans," *Washington Post*, 6 November 2005.

32. US Senate, "NSL Inspector General Report."

33. Gellman, "FBI's Secret Scrutiny."

34. "Senators Question Terrorism Inquiries," *Washington Post*, 7 November 2005.

35. "Checking FBI Spying," editorial, *Washington Post*, 10 November 2005.

36. "Tailor the Patriot Act," editorial, *Washington Post*, 19 November 2005.

37. "Senators Question Terrorism Inquiries."

38. DOJ/OIG, *A Review of the Federal Bureau of Investigation's Use of National Security Letters*, March 2007, xxxiii.

39. Ibid., xxxiii.

40. *Misuse of Patriot Act Powers: The Inspector General's Findings of Improper Use of the National Security Letters by the FBI*, hearing before the Senate Committee on the Judiciary, Senate, 110th Cong., 1 (2007).

41. DOJ/OIG, *Review of the Federal Bureau of Investigation's Use of National Security Letters*, xxxviii.

42. Ibid., xlix.

43. DOJ, "Actions on FBI Use of National Security Letters," press release, Department of Justice Documents, 9 March 2007; DOJ/OIG, *Federal Bureau of Investigation's Integrity and Compliance Program*, November 2011.

44. DOJ, "Corrective Actions on the FBI's Use of National Security Letters," press release, Department of Justice Documents, 20 March 2007.

45. In addition to the aforementioned hearings, see also *Responding to the IG's Findings of Improper use of NSLs by the FBI*, Subcommittee on Constitution, Senate Judiciary Committee, 110th Cong., 1 (2007).

46. *National Security Letters: The Need for Greater Accountability and Oversight*, hearing of the Committee on the Judiciary, Senate, 110th Cong., 2 (2008).

47. *Misuse of Patriot Act Powers*, statement of Glenn Fine.

48. Ibid.

49. Ibid.

50. Ibid.

51. *The Report by the Office of the Inspector General of the Department of Justice on the FBI's Use of Exigent Letters and Other Informal Requests for Telephone Records*, hearing before the Subcommittee on the Constitution, Civil Rights, and Civil Liberties, Committee on the Judiciary, House of Representatives, 111th Cong. 2 (2010), 274, 276.

52. *Misuse of Patriot Act Powers*.

53. Statement of Sen. Russell Feingold to the president, "NSL Inspector General Report," *Congressional Record*, 28 March 2007.

54. DOJ/OIG, *A Review of the FBI's Use of National Security Letters: Assessment of Corrective Actions and Examination of NSL Usage in 2006*, March 2008, 3–4.

55. *FBI's Use of Exigent Letters Hearing*, testimony of Glenn Fine.

56. Ibid.

57. Sinnar, "Protecting Rights from Within?," 1064–1065.

58. *FBI's Use of Exigent Letters Hearing*.

59. DOJ/OIG, *FBI's Use of Exigent Letters Review*, 214.

60. DOJ/OIG, *FBI's Use of National Security Letters*, 157.

61. American Civil Liberties Union v. Department of Justice, 265 F. Supp. 2d20 (D.D.C. 2003).

62. "National Security Letter Gag Order FOIA," press release, American Civil Liberties Union, 9 May 2012.

63. DOJ/OIG, *FBI's Use of Exigent Letters Review*, 256.

64. Ibid., 276.

65. DOJ/OIG, *A Review of the FBI's Use of National Security Letters: Assessment of Progress in Implementing Recommendations and Examination of Use in 2007 through 2009*, August 2014.

66. Ibid., summary of findings, 2.

67. DOJ/OIG, *FBI's Use of Exigent Letters Review*, 275.

68. DOJ/OIG, *NSL Review 2008*, 149.

69. DOJ/OIG, *FBI's Use of Exigent Letters Review*, 284.

70. Ibid., 282–286.

71. Ibid., 288–289.

72. DOJ/OIG, *FBI's Use of Exigent Letters*, 288.

73. Ibid., 287.

74. Ibid., 262–264.

75. Sinnar, "Protecting Rights from Within?," 1069.

76. DOJ/OIG, *FBI's Use of Exigent Letters Review*, 263–64; see also Sinnar, "Protecting Rights from Within?," 1071–1072.

77. DOJ/OIG, *FBI's Use of Exigent Letters Review*, 288.

78. Ibid., 268.

79. *Doe v. Mukasey*, 549 F.3d 861 (2d Cir. 2008).

80. Matt Zimmerman, "In Depth: The Court's Remarkable Order Striking Down the NSL Statute," *Electronic Frontier Foundation*, 18 March 2013, https://www.eff.org/.

81. Order Granting Motion to Set Aside NSL Letter, US District Court for Northern California, No. C 11-02173 SI, 14 March 2013.

82. *FBI's Use of Exigent Letters Hearing*, testimony of Glenn Fine.

83. DOJ/OIG, *FBI's Use of Exigent Letters Review*, 263–268.

84. David H. Rosenbloom, "The Separation of Powers," in Rosenbloom and McCurdy, *Revisiting Waldo's Administrative State*, 99–100.

CHAPTER 8. FROM TERROR TO HURRICANES: CRAFTING EMERGENCY GOVERNANCE AT HOMELAND SECURITY

1. Clark Kent Ervin, "State of Emergency: Interview with Thad Allen," *CNN Late Edition with Wolf Blitzer*, transcript at *CNN.com*, 18 September 2005, http://edition.cnn.com/.

2. *Protecting the Homeland: The President's Proposal for Reorganizing Our Homeland Defense Infrastructure*, hearing before the Senate Committee on the Judiciary, 107th Cong. 2 (2002) (statement of Sen. Patrick Leahy).

3. Statement of Senator Daniel Akaka, *Congressional Record* 148, pt. 16 (12–14 November 2002).

4. The establishment of the OIG was based on the following authorities: IG Act 1978; Homeland Security Act 2002, Title 6, USC Section 103.

5. Homeland Security Act of 2002, Public Law 107-296.

6. *Nomination Hearing of Richard L. Skinner and Brian D. Miller*, hearing before the Committee on Homeland Security and Governmental Affairs, Senate, 109th Cong., 1 (18 July 2005), prehearing questionnaire for Richard Skinner, 23–61.

7. Ibid., 39.

8. Mathew D. McCubbins and Thomas Schwartz, "Congressional Oversight Overlooked: Police Patrols versus Fire Alarms," *American Journal of Political Science* 28, no. 1 (1984): 165–179.

9. See Clark Kent Ervin's memoir, *Open Target: Where America Is Vulnerable to Attack* (New York: Palgrave Macmillan, 2006).

10. "Kerry–Edwards 2004 Releases Fact Sheet on Bush–Cheney Ad," *US Newswire*, 11 August 2004.

11. Ervin, *Open Target*, 8. These inherited staff did not all arrive until FY2004; the OIG operated with only 390 personnel in its first year.

12. "ABC News Exclusive: The Inspector," *ABC News: World News Tonight*, 9 December 2004.

13. DHS/OIG, *Transportation Security Administration Review of the TSA Passenger and Baggage Screening Pilot Program*, September 2004.

14. "ABC News Exclusive: The Inspector."

15. *Cover Blown: Did TSA Tip Off Airport Screeners about Covert Testing?*, Hearing before the Committee on Homeland Security, House of Representatives, 110th Cong. 1 (2007) (statement of Clark Kent Ervin), quoted in Bart Elias, *Airport Passenger Screening: Background and Issues for Congress* (CRS Report R40543) (Washington, DC: Congressional Research Service, 2009).

16. Elias, *Airport Passenger Screening*.

17. DHS/OIG, *Assessment of Expenditures Related to the First Annual Transportation Security Administration Awards Program and Executive Performance Awards*, September 2004.

18. Clark Kent Ervin, personal interview, 2 July 2014.

19. Ervin, *Open Target*, 165.

20. DHS, *Integration and Use of Screening Information* (Homeland Security Presidential Directive 6) (Washington, DC: Presidential Directive, 16 September 2003).

21. Ervin, *Open Target*, 165–166.

22. Robert Block, "Homeland Security Watchdog Makes Politically Risky Moves," *Asian Wall Street Journal*, 16 November 2004.

23. Robert Draper, "Truth, Justice and the (Un)American Way," *Texas Monthly*, April 2005.

24. Block, "Homeland Security Watchdog."

25. Michael Scherer, "Not Mild-Mannered Enough," *Mother Jones*, March/April 2005.

26. Clark Kent Ervin, "I'd Rather Err on the Side of the Believers," *Cato Unbound*, 12 September 2006.

27. *Nomination Hearing of Richard L. Skinner and Brian D. Miller*, prehearing questionnaire for Richard Skinner, 26.

28. Ibid., 28.

29. Ibid., 8.

30. Richard Skinner, personal interview, 11 January 2013.

31. Ibid.

32. *Nomination Hearing of Richard L. Skinner and Brian D. Miller*, prehearing questionnaire for Richard Skinner, 31.

33. American Civil Liberties Union, "Coalition Sign-On Letter to Clark Kent Ervin at the Department of Homeland Security Expressing Concerns about the Case of Maher Arar," 16 July 2004.

34. Jim Bronskill, "Departure of US Watchdog Raises Concerns about Future of Arar Review," *Canadian Press*, 16 December 2004.

35. *Nomination Hearing of Richard L. Skinner and Brian D. Miller*, prehearing questionnaire for Richard Skinner, 45.

36. Clark Kent Ervin to Representative John Conyers Jr., 14 July 2004, reprinted in *Maher Arar Report*, DHS/OIG, *The Removal of a Canadian Citizen to Syria*, March 2010.

37. Shirin Sinnar, "Protecting Rights from Within?," 1052.

38. DHS/OIG, *Potentially High Costs and Insufficient Grant Funds Pose a Challenge to REAL ID Implementation*, March 2009, https://www.oig.dhs.gov/.

39. *Nomination Hearing of Richard L. Skinner and Brian D. Miller*, prehearing questionnaire for Richard Skinner, 25.

40. "Homeland Security Inspector General Report Reaffirms Sen. Snowe's Call for Accelerated Deepwater Program," *US Fed News*, 13 October 2004.

41. Jake Korn, "Deepwater RIP—A Leadership Perspective," *Servicelines*, US Coast Guard, 8 December 2011.

42. Trevor L. Brown, Matthew Potoski, and David M. Van Slyke, *Complex Contracting: Government Purchasing in the Wake of the US Coast Guard's Deepwater Program* (Cambridge: Cambridge University Press, 2013).

43. Jake Weins, "All Along the Watchtower: One Year Anniversary of DHS Inspector General Vacancy," *POGO Blog*, 27 February 2012, http://www.pogo.org /blog/.

44. American Civil Liberties Union, "ACLU Statement on Secure Communities," *ACLU*, 10 November 2010, https://www.aclu.org/.

45. Michele Waslin, "DHS Inspector General Issues Disappointing Reports on ICE's Secure Communities," *Immigration Impact*, American Immigration Council, 9 April 2012, http://immigrationimpact.com/.

46. DHS/OIG, *Operations of United States Immigration and Customs Enforcement's Secure Communities*, April 2012, 1, https://www.oig.dhs.gov/.

47. USPS/OIG, *External Peer Review of DHS OIG—System Review Report for the Fiscal Year Ended September 30, 2011*, 28 June 2012, https://www.oig.dhs.gov/.

48. Joe Davidson, "Drug Cartels Corrupting US Law Enforcement," *Washington Post*, 9 June 2011.

49. *Unresolved Internal Investigations at DHS: Oversight of Investigation Management in the Office of the DHS IG*, hearing before Committee on Oversight and Government Reform, House of Representatives, 112th Cong. 2 (2012).

50. *Investigation into Allegations of Misconduct by the Former Acting and Deputy Inspector General of the Department of Homeland Security*, Subcommittee on Financial and Contracting Oversight, Committee on Homeland Security and Government Oversight, Senate, Staff Report, 113th Cong., 2 (2014).

51. AGA and Kearney & Company, *AGA's Inspector General Survey*.

52. Nicole Blake Johnson, "DHS Inspector General Embraces Continuous Monitoring," *FedTech Magazine*, 10 July 2014.

53. DHS/OIG, *Annual Performance Plan*, FY 2004–2013.

54. POGO, "Inspectors General: Accountability Is a Balancing Act."

CHAPTER 9. A MANAGERIAL DEMOCRACY AT HOMELAND SECURITY:
A WEB OF ACCOUNTABILITY IN THE GULF COAST RECOVERY PROJECT,
2005–2009

1. "Secretary Chertoff Awol as Katrina Strikes," *Fed News*, 19 September 2005.

2. Humberto Sanchez, "Hurricane Relief: Bush Signs $51.8B Emergency Funding Bill," *Bond Buyer*, 12 September 2005.

3. "Grassley Releases Recommendations on Accounting for Katrina Dollars," US Senate Committee on Finance, 4 October 2005, http://www.finance.senate.gov/.

4. Barry Snyder, ECIE chair, and Gregory Friedman, PCIE chair, to Sen. Charles Grassley, chairman, Senate Committee on Finance, 29 September 2005.

5. This included the Department of Homeland Security, Department of Defense, Department of Transportation, Environmental Protection Agency, Department of Health and Human Services, General Services Administration, Department of Justice, Department of Agriculture, United States Postal Service, Department of Housing and Urban Development, Department of Commerce, and the Department of the Interior.

6. Rep. Henry Waxman to Rep. Tom Davis regarding hearings about Katrina-related contracting waste, 20 March 2006; Reps. Nancy Pelosi and Henry Waxman, *Hurricane Katrina Accountability and Clean Contracting Bill* (HR 3838); Statement of Rep. Henry Waxman on the Hurricane Katrina Accountability and Clean Contracting Bill, 20 September 2005.

7. "DHS IG Found FEMA Systems for Deploying Personnel and Supplies to Disaster Zones Inadequate," Fact Sheet of Minority Staff, Committee on Government Reform, House of Representatives, 109th Cong., 1 (2005).

8. "DHS Inspector General Initiates Special Office for Hurricane Katrina Oversight," press release, Department of Homeland Security Documents, 19 September 2005.

9. Paul Hoversten, "DHS Creates Special Oversight Office to Monitor Post-Katrina Contracts, Grants," *Homeland Security and Defense*, 21 September 2005.

10. DHS/OIG, *Overview of OIG Plans for Hurricane Katrina Oversight*, Department of Homeland Security Documents, 21 September 2005.

11. In addition to DHS, these included the Department of Commerce, Department of Defense, Department of Energy, Department of Interior, Department of Justice, Department of Labor, Department of Transportation, Department of Health and Human Services, Department of Housing and Urban Development, Environmental Protection Agency, General Services Administration, and NASA.

12. Charlie Cray, "Disaster Profiteering: The Flood of Crony Contracting following Hurricane Katrina," *Multinational Monitor*, 1 September 2005.

13. PCIE, *Compendium of Hurricane Oversight in the Gulf States*, Homeland Security Roundtable, 12 December 2005, 3.

14. Testimony of Barbara A. Mikulski (D-MD), *Hurricane Katrina: Recommendations for Reform*, hearing, Senate Committee on Homeland Security and Governmental Affairs, 8 March 2006.

15. *Hurricane Katrina: A Nation Still Unprepared—Special Report of the Senate Committee on Homeland Security and Governmental Affairs*, 109th Cong. 2 (S. Report 109-322) (2006).

16. FEMA/OIG, *FEMA's Disaster Management Program: A Performance Audit after Hurricane Andrew*, 14 January 1993.

17. "Katrina Fraud Swamps System, Water Mark: Tracking Recovery on the Gulf Coast," *USA Today*, 7 June 2007.

18. Hearing of the Committee on Homeland Security, House of Representatives, 111th Cong. 1 (8 July 2009) (testimony of Richard Skinner).

19. PCIE/ECIE Oversight Report (October 2006), 4.

20. The American Geosciences Institute provides a list of twenty related hearings (http://www.agiweb.org/gap/legis109/katrina_hearings.html).

21. *A Failure of Initiative: The Final Report of the Select Bipartisan Committee to Investigate the Preparation for and Response to Hurricane Katrina, House of Representatives* (H. Report 109-377), 109th Cong., 2 (2006).

22. *One Year Later: Are We Prepared?*, hearing before the Committee on Government Affairs and Homeland Security, Senate, 109th Cong. 2 (2006).

23. Title VI of Public Law 109-295 (HR 5441).

24. Keith Bea, "Federal Emergency Management Policy Changes after Hurricane Katrina: A Summary of Statutory Provisions," Congressional Research Service, 6 March 2007.

25. Jason Mycoff, "Congress and Katrina: A Failure of Oversight," *State and Local Government Review* 39, no. 1 (2007): 27.

26. GAO, *Hurricanes Katrina and Rita Disaster Relief: Continued Findings of Fraud, Waste, and Abuse*, 6 December 2006.

27. *Hurricane Katrina: GAO's Preliminary Observations Regarding Preparedness, Response, and Recovery*, hearing before the Senate Homeland Security and Governmental Affairs Committee, 109th Cong., 2 (2006) (testimony of GAO), 2–3.

28. PCIE/ECIE, *Oversight of Gulf Coast Hurricane Recovery: A 90-Day Report to Congress*, 30 December 2005, 7.

29. DHS/OIG, *Overview of OIG Plans for Hurricane Katrina Oversight*.

30. Mission statement of the PCIE/ECIE Homeland Security Roundtable, 2005.

31. DHS/OIG, *Overview of OIG Plans for Hurricane Katrina Oversight*.

32. This program, which issued purchase cards with a limit of up to $250,000 for both micropurchases and payment of other purchases relating to recovery, was instituted to provide immediate relief for victim; see PCIE/ECIE, *Oversight of Gulf Coast Hurricane Recovery*, 9.

33. Ibid., 8.

34. PCIE, *Compendium*, 9.

35. DHS/OIG, *A Performance Review of FEMA's Disaster Management Activities in Response to Hurricane Katrina*, 31 March 2006.

36. Skinner testimony, 8 July 2009.

37. Ibid.

38. DHS/OIG, *FEMA's Preparedness for the Next Catastrophic Disaster*, March 2008.

39. DHS/OIG, *FEMA's Sheltering and Transitional Housing Activities after Hurricane Katrina*, September 2008.

40. Skinner testimony, 8 July 2009.

41. DHS/OIG, *Management Advisory Report: FEMA's Response to Hurricane Ike*, June 2009.

42. DHS/OIG, *Semiannual Report to Congress*, 1 April–30 September 2009.

43. GAO, *Hurricanes Katrina and Rita Disaster Relief: Improper and Potentially Fraudulent Individual Assistance Payments Estimated to Be Between $600 Million and $1.4 Billion*, 14 June 2006.

44. Mike M. Ahlers, "Inspector: Millions in Improper Katrina, Rita Aid Not Yet Recovered," *CNN US Edition*, 4 January 2011.

45. Jeff Zeleny, "$700 Million in Katrina Relief Missing, Report Shows," *ABC News*, 3 April 2013.

46. DHS/OIG, *FEMA: In or Out?*, February 2009.

47. Hearing before the Subcommittee on Emergency Communications, Preparedness and Response, Committee on Homeland Security, US House of Representatives, 111th Cong. 1 (2009) (statement of Richard Skinner).

48. DHS/OIG, *FEMA: In or Out?*

49. Ervin, *Open Target*, 179.

50. PCIE/ECIE, *Semiannual Report*, October 2006, 4.

51. Skinner testimony, 8 March 2006.

52. Ibid.

53. Ibid.

54. PCIE/ECIE, *Semiannual Report*, October 2006, 4.

55. Statement of Hubert Sparks, quoted in POGO, "Inspectors General: Accountability Is a Balancing Act."

CHAPTER 10. FORGING A NEW DEMOCRATIC FORM:
COMETH THE HOUR, COMETH THE INSPECTOR

1. Sinnar, "Protecting Rights from Within?," 38.

2. DHS/OIG, *Semiannual Report to Congress*, October 2006, 10.

3. PCIE/ECIE, *Semiannual Report to Congress*, March 2008.

4. See, e.g., Bart Elias, "Airport Passenger Screening: Background and Issues for Congress," Congressional Research Service, 23 April 2009, https://www.fas.org/sgp/crs/homesec/R40543.pdf.

5. David A. Love, "Pardon Me Bush, but Kanye Never Called You Racist," *Grio*, 10 November 2010, http://thegrio.com/.

6. Quoted in Kristen Henkel, John Dovidio, and Samuel Gaertner, "Institutional Discrimination, Individual Racism, and Hurricane Katrina," *Analyses of Social Issues and Public Policy* 6, no. 1 (2006): 99–124.

7. Thomas Craemer, "Investigating Racial Inequalities in Hurricane Katrina Relief by Counting FEMA Trailers," United States Federal Emergency Management Agency, 1 January 2008.

CHAPTER 11. CONCLUSION: *QUIS CUSTODIET CUSTODEM IPSUM CUSTODUM?*

1. Tom Christensen and Per Lægreid, "New Public Management: Puzzles of Democracy and the Influence of Citizens," *Journal of Political Philosophy* 10, no. 3 (2002): 267–296.

2. Sheldon Wolin, *Politics and Vision: Continuity and Innovation in Western Political Thought* (Princeton, NJ: Princeton University Press, 2004), 349.

3. Bonnie Honig, *Emergency Politics: Paradox, Law and Democracy* (Princeton, NJ: Princeton University Press, 2009).

4. Posner and Vermeule, *Executive Unbound*, 87.

5. Michael Schudson, "Political Observatories, Databases and News in the Emerging Ecology of Public Information," *Daedalus* 139, no. 2 (2010): 100–109.

6. Russell Hardin, "Democratic Epistemology and Accountability," in *Democracy*, ed. Ellen Frankel Paul, Fred Miller, and Jeffrey Paul (Cambridge: Cambridge University Press, 2000), 111.

7. Pierre Rosanvallon, *Democratic Legitimacy: Impartiality, Reflexivity, Proximity*, trans. Art Goldhammer (Princeton, NJ: Princeton University Press, 2011), 88.

8. Keane, *Life and Death of Democracy*.

9. Rep. Darrell Issa (R-CA) and POGO, among others, have championed this position.

10. David H. Rosenbloom, "The Separation of Powers," in Rosenbloom and McCurdy, *Revisiting Waldo's Administrative State*, 100.

11. David Gross, personal interview, 28 July 2014.

12. Charles S. Clark, "Agency Watchdogs Could Get More Freedom to Roam," *Government Executive*, 16 January 2014.

APPENDIX: INTERVIEWS

1. Roger Gomm, *Social Research Methodology: A Critical Introduction* (London: Palgrave Macmillan, 2004).

2. Han Dorussen, Hartmut Lenz, and Spyros Blavoukos, "Assessing the Reliability and Validity of Expert Interviews," *European Union Politics* 6, no. 3 (2005): 315–337.

3. Richard Ned Lebow, "Social Science and History: Ranchers versus Farmers," in *Bridges and Boundaries*, ed. Colin Elman and Miriam Elman (Cambridge, MA: Harvard University Press, 2001), 133.

INDEX

liberties abuse monitoring, 27, 53, 60, 134, 136, 138–139. *See also* rights monitoring

Lieberman, Joseph, 58, 87, 169, 173, 190

Lieberman, Robert, 4

Light, Paul C., 16, 18

Linick, Steve, 62 (table), 84 (table), 102

Lofgren, Zoe, 182

Machak, Frank M., 110

Machiavelli, Niccolò, 43

Madison, James, 5–6

management reforms, State Department OIG and, 89–91

managerial democracy
Department of Homeland Security OIG and, 41, 184–186, 187–189, 206–209
Gulf Coast Recovery reviews and, 187–199
inspectors general as a threat to, 216–217
overview and description of, 28–29

managerial paradox, 16

Mann, Carleton, 168 (table)

Mansbridge, Jane, 16

Maor, Moshe, 16

Mazer, Roslyn A., 182

McCaskill, Claire, 58

McCullough, I. Charles, III, 62 (table)

media
relationship of the Department of Homeland Security OIG with, 176
reliance on inspectors general as "political observatories," 217

mediated accountability, 14

Meyer, Jane, 60

Mill, John Stuart, 4

misconduct, by inspectors general, problems of, 68

modes of democratic practice
overview and description of, 25–29
by the three study OIGs, 41, 215–216
See also constitutional democracy; managerial democracy; political democracy

Moheban, Steven M., 107

Monitoring Government (Light), 18

monitory democracy, 13, 218

Moscato, Anthony C., 126 (table)

"multiple-accountabilities disorder," 16

Mutual Security Act amendments of 1959, 47

narrative-building, Michael Bromwich and, 133, 141

NASA Inspector General, 68, 79, 101, 112

Nation (magazine), 111

National Emergency Management Information System, 193

national emergency management system, 150

National Incident Management System, 198

National Performance Review (NPR) of 1993, 18, 20, 50–52. *See also* Reinventing Government Act of 1993

National Reconnaissance Office Inspector General, 61

National Response Plan, 195, 198

national security
inspectors general and monitoring of, 52–53
role of inspectors general in the national security state, 61–63
sensitive information and exceptions to the authority of inspectors general, 59

National Security Agency Inspector General, 61

National Security in the 21st Century (Hart-Rudman Commission report), 76

National Security Letter Reform bill of 2007, 156

National Security Letters reviews
contributions to administrative procedures, 159–160
contributions to standards, 159
Department of Justice OIG investigations, 135 (table), 136, 154–158
effects of the reviews, 148–159
legal effects, 160–161
limits to, 161–162
rights concerns and, 206